Introduction to

REAL ESTATE LAW

Second Edition

Charles S. Coit

REAL ESTATE EDUCATION COMPANY
a division of Longman Financial Services Publishing, Inc.

© 1985, 1981 by Longman Group USA Inc.

Published by Real Estate Education Company/Chicago, a Longman Group USA company

Printed in the United States of America.

86 87   10 9   8   7   6   5   4   3

Sponsoring editor: Bobbye Middendorf
Project editor: David Walker
Copyeditor: Chris Benton
Cover design: Constance Meyer, Agnes McGregor

Library of Congress Cataloging in Publication Data

Coit, Charles S.
  Introduction to real estate law.

  Includes index.
    1.   Real property—United States. 2. Vendors and purchasers—United States. 3. Real estate business—Law and legislation—United States. I. University of Southern Maine. Center for Real Estate Education.
II. Title.
KF570.C55 1985   346.7304'3   85-2054
ISBN 0-88462-508-7   347.30643

Contents

Preface

This textbook was developed for students preparing for a real estate broker's or salesperson's licensing exam, as well as for people just interested in real estate law. Most topics addressed here were identified as relevant topical content for a real estate law course by an extensive survey of real estate professionals done by James R. Brown, Jr., assistant professor of Real Estate and Land Use Economics, University of Nebraska at Omaha.

These topics are presented in a manner that will enable students to understand more easily the application of real estate law to the practice of real estate brokerage. Each chapter begins with an introduction to establish the professional context and relevance of the information that follows. Abundant examples illustrate the laws in action and the broker's role therein. Each chapter concludes with a series of multiple choice questions and discussion problems which the student may use to test comprehension of the material.

I am pleased to credit John Kortecamp, Phd., currently Vice President of Education for the National Association of Realtors® for his suggestions, and to Meridith Small for her many insights and contributions to the professional context.

Much credit goes to Gretchten Bath, Michael Cantara, Julie Dothuit, Jeanne Gardiner, Fred Fenton, Rick Murphy, T. David Plourde and Robert Veasley, former students at the University of Maine Law School for their contributions to researching and drafting materials for the first edition, the raw stone from which this second edition has been carved.

Many people have been involved in the ultimate production of this text, including reviewers of the first edition: Lennard Steinberg, Esq.; F. Wayne Jarvis, Esq.; Rick Sellars, Esq.; and Henry Olivieri, Esq. The second edition was reviewed by John D. Ballou, Attorney at Law; Larry D. Rickard, Broker/Owner, Realty School of Kansas; Dennis Schulz, Secretary/Treasurer of North Dakota Real Estate Commission; Nancy Daggett White, Mississippi County Community College; Jerry Scott, Judge, Tennessee Court of Criminal Appeals; Durwood Ruegger, Assistant Professor, University of Southern Mississippi; Billy J. York, Bill York and Associates, Inc.

Finishing this second edition has been somewhat like finishing a marathon running race: the first half isn't really too bad, but those last few miles get longer and longer. It is at this point that the crowd along the way, with its cheers and advice, "chin up", "just a few more yards", "Lookin' good"...really makes the difference. How fortunate I have been in the crowd at Real Estate Education Company...Libby McGreevy, Anita Constant, and Bobbye Middendorf with their encouragements, and David Walker who oversaw the editing with a hawk's eye for excess words. Thank you all for the contributions you so graciously made.

With this book I have come to believe that behind a successful man stands a generous and supportive woman...Diane Coit, thank you.

Charles S. Coit, Esq.

1

Ownership of Real Property

────────────── KEY TERMS ──────────────

bundle of sticks   metes and bounds
constructive attachment   ownership
emblement   personal property
encroachment   physical property
fixture   real estate
fructus industriales   rectangular survey
fructus naturales   system
legal description   trade fixture

It's happening every day. From the state of Washington to Florida, from Maine to California, in Hawaii and Alaska, people are buying and selling, renting, leasing, and exchanging *real estate* for residential, recreational, commercial, and investment purposes. The sheer number of transfers each year would lead to the conclusion that real estate transactions are routine occurrences. Real estate transactions are, in fact, routine, but in the same way that appendectomies are routine—a great deal of thought and professional expertise lies behind each sale, lease, or exchange. In transactions put together by a licensed real estate agent, it is his or her knowledge of all the pieces involved and expertise in tapping the appropriate related professionals—including lawyers, accountants, surveyors, bankers, insurance brokers, etc.—that enable these sales to be consummated routinely.

Three special characteristics of real estate dictate specialized knowledge and skills for a successful real estate broker: land is indestructible, and immobile, and each parcel is absolutely unique on the face of the earth.

Consider for a moment that land is indestructible. It is an economic asset that is essential to the health and well-being of mankind, either in the production of food, as a place to build shelter, or as an income-producing asset in the form of commercial property. It has value to today's owner, to tomorrow's owner, and to all future owners. The fact that land lasts forever and is a valuable resource for all future generations has led to the creation of state and federal land use and environmental protection laws, as well as town and city zoning regulations that govern the permitted use of land. All real estate brokers, in their listing and selling of land, must understand the implications of these laws for each parcel they handle. For example, if land is zoned residential, it would clearly be illegal to sell it for commercial purposes.

Consider, too, how the immobility of land affects its use in commerce. A bank will lend a homebuyer literally thousands of dollars to purchase a home because it knows that, if the new homeowner loses his or her job or health, and thus the ability to repay the loan, it can, by foreclosing its mortgage, sell the real estate and recoup its money. Although a jobless homeowner may skip town to find employment elsewhere, the home and its lot will be left behind for the bank. Furthermore, the immobility of land has led to the evolution of public record-keeping systems of land ownership so that lenders and other creditors, as well as owners of real estate, can protect their interests in land by recording in a public registry their ownership or security interest in it. Practicing real estate brokers understand and know how to use the public registries of deeds as resources for information about their listings.

Last, each parcel of land is unique. Each parcel occupies a unique place on the face of the earth and thus is considered to have a special value that cannot be replaced by a substitute parcel of land. Although two parcels in a housing development may be substantially similar, a buyer may prefer one because of its particular slope or orientation to the sun, or its distance from a busy highway. Like a masterpiece of original art, the Mona Lisa for example, there is no duplicate, no substitute, no copy of the one parcel of land that will be exactly identical to it or any other parcel.

It is important for real estate licensees to understand how real estate law recognizes the uniqueness of each parcel of land. When a buyer and seller have signed a purchase and sale contract and the seller then refuses to sign a deed to the property, what is the buyer to do? Must he or she look for another property, or is there some way to force the seller to sign a deed? Because the law recognizes each parcel of land as unique, a court will order a reluctant seller to convey the property. The reasoning is that the buyer bargained for a unique property for which there is no adequate substitute. Since the seller agreed to sell it, a court will compel the seller to have his contract.

Real estate: immobile; indestructible; the basis of wealth for individuals, businesses, and communities; legally and physically unique. Clearly, much expertise is required to handle real estate transactions as matters of routine. The following chapters introduce and explain principles of real estate law that have developed from the special characteristics of land, including a definition of real estate, proper legal descriptions, ownership rights in land, public and private limitations on use of real estate, special considerations of the agency relationship of the broker to the seller, general principles of contract law, and their application to real estate contracts. The text concludes with a brief consideration of tax law and other federal regulations real estate brokers must understand if their transactions are to close smoothly and routinely.

To begin, consider the following story, which raises several legal issues real estate agents will need to master.

Phillip and Elizabeth were married in 1920 on a high knoll at Eagles' Nest, the Rhode Island farm that had been in Elizabeth's family since the original grant to her ancestors by the king of England. As a wedding gift, her parents gave Phillip and his blushing bride 200 acres, including pastureland, woods, and the farmstead surrounding the wedding knoll. In 1920, Eagles' Nest was 30 miles from East Overshoe, a sleepy college town on the shores of the Atlantic Ocean. Today, East Overshoe is a thriving metropolitan city whose suburbs are poised to engulf the family's land holdings. The value of the land as food-producing farmland is minuscule compared to its value as house lots for the influx of families attracted by employment at the high-tech industries around the university.

In their many years on the property, Phillip and Elizabeth have built a large house, a barn with stalls for horses, and fences in the fields. They have planted several acres of apple trees and corn and have dedicated 100 acres of pine to be groomed as a tree farm. Around the house they have added a tennis court, an above-ground swimming pool, and elaborate landscaping, including a stand of birch trees, rose gardens, and an arboretum.

The 1830 farmhouse is furnished with antiques, including a valuable glass chandelier installed in the dining room, which came from England with the family's ancestors; it is an antique of exceptional value. On the front door is a simple brass door knocker, a "treasure" Phillip and Elizabeth found at a flea market on their honeymoon; it is worth only $50 but has much sentimental value to them. In their 60 years at Eagles' Nest, they have installed a modern kitchen, though only the microwave oven is built-in. Other appliances include a stove and refrigerator; all are ten years old. The house has central air conditioning and heating.

The property borders on Alewife Stream, where the family has fished for years; several companies upstream now rent canoes to summer tourists who paddle by their boundary. The stream empties into Merrymeeting Bay, a tidal estuary on which Eagles' Nest also enjoys 1,000 feet of frontage. On the southeastern corner of the property is a gravel pit that is currently being excavated by Sam's Sand and Gravel Company.

Phillip and Elizabeth, both in their 80s, have decided that the property is too much to manage; the taxes are too high, and their five children are not interested in farming the property. Though it breaks their hearts, they have decided to sell and have asked a real estate agent to help them.

The agent's first task is called *taking the listing;* that is, adding this property to the list of other properties for sale in the agent's office. The agent's responsibility during the listing process is to determine exactly what it is that Phillip and Elizabeth have to sell so he or she will be able to describe to others what it is they are purchasing. The agent's questions to the sellers during the listing interview will focus on:

    a. the legal description of the land; i.e., its boundaries;

    b. the physical property; i.e., the real estate to be sold versus the personal property they wish to keep;

    c. *fixtures:* personal property like the door knocker, which, although attached to the real estate, is not to be sold;

    d. intangible rights to the property, i.e., what parts of the property can be developed or are subject to easements or to interests of other people.

The gathering of descriptive information about the property should be orderly and methodical. Conveniently, virtually all of the real estate for sale will fall within certain boundaries that can be found in the seller's deed. Although obtaining a copy of the deed may not be the first step in taking a listing, it is handy to begin here with the legal description of the property, which defines the boundaries of what the agent will be selling.

LEGAL DESCRIPTION

Thus, the first step in preparing a listing is to get an adequate *legal description* of the property. This is defined as one by which a competent surveyor could locate the boundaries of the property. A description that merely says "the Jones's property at 21 Main Street..." is satisfactory for the postman but not for real estate transactions. The broker wants a good description of the boundaries of the property which states where the owner's interests end and where the neighbor's begin. This description enables the broker to show the prospective purchaser exactly what is to be sold.

In the United States, there are four generally recognized forms of legal description: metes and bounds, rectangular survey, reference to a plan, reference to a prior deed. Each of the four methods is described below.

Metes and Bounds

In most of the eastern states where land transactions took place
before the federal government came into being, land was and is
today often described by *metes and bounds*.

Example ────────────────────────────────────

Beginning at the stone monument on the northwest corner of the
land of Smith and thence running 687 feet in a southwesterly direction to the stone wall of Jones, thence southeasterly 521 feet to
Indian River, then northeasterly 1,200 feet along the bank of said
Indian River to the road from Portland to Windham, thence 700
feet along said road back to the point of beginning.

A metes and bounds description has a point of beginning and
runs from that point to other monuments or landmarks and
back to the point of beginning. The distance between points is
generally given in feet and the direction in degrees of the com-
pass. A metes and bounds description must close to be legally
adequate; it must leave no gaps.

Rectangular Survey System

The second method of legal description is more common in western states. In the late 1780s, the then new federal government
passed a law creating the *rectangular survey system*, which
placed a grid over the undeveloped western two-thirds of the
nation. Certain lines running north and south were deemed principal meridians, which were crossed by base lines running east
and west. The meridians and base lines can be located exactly
with reference to degrees of latitude and longitude. The grid is
made up of perpendicular lines, six miles square. Townships are
further subdivided into 36 sections of one square mile each,
which are again subdivided into the base unit of land measure-
ment, the acre.

Each principal meridian has a name, and each township is identified with reference to a named meridian—for example, Township 7 North, Range 2 East of the Indian Meridian.

A metes and bounds description may be used with the rectangular survey system to describe a lot that does not conform to lot lines.

Reference to a Plan

A third method of describing real estate is by reference to a plan. When a land developer wants to convert open land to a residential subdivision, a survey will be made and a plan prepared on which individual lots will be drawn. A proper legal description then would be: "Lot 14 on a plan of land in Newton belonging to Jones, by R.E. Engineering Company, recorded in the Middletown County Registry of Deeds."

Reference to a Prior Deed

A fourth method of describing real estate is by reference to a prior recorded deed. If an older deed contains a proper description by one of the previously explained methods of description, a deed of land by reference to an earlier deed is adequate.

Example ————————————————————————

I grant to Mary all my property in Middletown, more particularly described in a deed to me by Smith dated September 1, 1981, and recorded in the Oxford County Registry of Deeds in book 14,697 [at] page 368.

Water Boundaries

Occasionally, one property boundary may be a stream or navigable waterway. Where the boundary is a nonnavigable brook, the owners on either side are deemed to own to the middle of the stream. Where the waterway is navigable, the boundary line of the adjacent property runs to the low-water mark of the stream. If the boundary of the property is lake frontage or tidal ocean frontage, the boundary is deemed to be the normal high-water mark.

In gathering information for the listing of Eagles' Nest, the agent will need to consider how Alewife Stream affects the boundary of the property. Although the stream carries canoeists in the spring, its flow is inadequate in the summer and fall to support any navigation at all. Part of the agent's job will be to find out if such a watercourse is deemed navigable or nonnavigable and how, under the law of the state, this affects title to the bed of the stream. Brokers will not be expected to know the answers to all questions about the property; their job is to be aware of these questions and to provide the answers to prospective buyers.

Inadequate Descriptions

Adequacy of legal descriptions is an important issue for real estate brokers who want their transactions to be closed professionally, without a hitch. Only lawyers make money in cases of inadequate descriptions of real estate that have to be resolved in litigation. Consider how the following descriptions might be inadequate to define property boundaries:

- "The Old Merchant Farm";
- "all the land owned by the grantor" in a particular town;
- "the property at 21 Main Street";
- "the southeast half" of a certain parcel;
- "my home and lot."

Although it is lawyer's work to draft deeds and make judgments on whether the descriptions are legally sufficient, a good broker should know whether the description of the property is legally precise and whether the boundaries can be adequately identified. In urban and suburban areas, where virtually all land has been subdivided and developed, an adequate legal description is usually readily available.

Difficulties arise more often in rural areas, where land value may not justify the services of a surveyor, or where, many years ago, the seller and his or her neighbor walked the property to set their own boundaries, establishing one property marker at the corner of a field and a tree stump at another. Today, 75 years later, when the stump is gone and the field is overgrown, the old boundaries cannot be located and must be established by litigation. One way or the other, it is the broker's responsibility to see that the principals to the transaction know the boundaries of what is being purchased and sold.

Occasionally, however, a situation arises in which the legal description is deficient. It concerns land sold at a fixed price per acre.

Example ————————————————————————

A purchaser buys Blackacre for $89,000—$1,000 per acre—and accepts a deed with a proper metes and bounds description that includes the statement "containing 89.239 acres, more or less." Actually, the parcel contains 82 acres. The purchaser sues for $7,000, arguing that he overpaid for the land because the actual acreage is less than he bargained for.

The law in these cases is that, if the error in acreage is minor and the purchase price is for the overall parcel, no relief will be granted to the purchaser. However, if the purchase and sale agreement specified that the land was sold for $1,000 per acre and the buyer got fewer acres than he bargained for, he will be given relief.

PHYSICAL PROPERTY

Assume that the agent has a copy of the deed to Eagles' Nest, that he or she has walked the boundaries and determined that Alewife Stream is nonnavigable, and thus that Phillip and Elizabeth own to the middle of the stream. Secure in the knowledge of the property's boundaries, the agent now turns to gather information on what, within the boundaries, is real estate for sale. The real estate within these boundaries is defined, in *The Language of Real Estate,* as "the physical land at, above, and below the earth's surface with all appurtenances, including structures."

Ownership of the real estate includes the land, including most obviously the surface—the fields, roads, etc.—and all the earth below the surface area down to the very center of the earth.

While ownership to the core of the earth may seem unimportant for most residential lots, consider that ownership to the earth's core includes ownership of minerals, oil, gravel, water, etc.; it includes the right to dig wells for water and otherwise use the subsurface resources of the property as the owner sees fit. Indeed, it is these rights to subsurface resources that enable Phillip and Elizabeth to sell the rights to excavate the gravel from the southern corner of their property to Sam's Sand and Gravel.

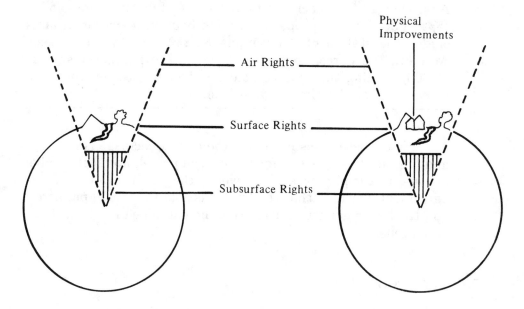

Graphic representation of air, surface, and subsurface rights. Ownership of land extends from the core of the earth to the highest of heavens.

In listing the property, the agent will need to know what rights Sam has to the gravel pit; i.e., whether Sam has the right to excavate for ten years or until all the gravel is gone. This will be discussed further later in the chapter.

In addition to owning subsurface rights, Phil and Elizabeth own all the air rights above their land "to the highest of heavens." Their ownership of air rights above the property gives them the right to build buildings, erect flagpoles, grow crops, including the 100-acre tree farm, etc. In a theoretical sense, every airplane that flies over their property is a trespasser; in more realistic terms, their air rights extend as far as reasonably necessary for them to enjoy the benefits of their ownership of the land.

On a more down-to-earth level, the branches of a neighbor's apple tree that extend across a boundary line are an *encroachment*. An encroachment is a *trespass* if it involves the land, and a *nuisance* if it violates the property owner's airspace. If Phil likes apples, they are his for the picking; if, however, in the autumn the unpicked fruit rots and falls into his swimming pool, he has the right to trim the offending branches. Prior consultation with the owner is suggested, however. Figure shown is a graphic representation of real estate ownership—of air, surface, and subsurface rights.

Phillip and Elizabeth's real estate includes all the land from the "core of the earth to the highest of heavens" that lies within those boundaries set out in their deed. However, they own more than just "all the land" inside those boundaries; they also own the buildings, tennis courts, animals, tree farm, landscaping, kitchen appliances, garden tools, chandelier, and door knocker. If they are selling Eagles' Nest, are they selling *all* these items as well?

The answer depends on whether the tennis court, swimming pool, chandelier, door knocker, etc., are characterized as real estate or as *personal property*, sometimes called *personalty*.

Personal property includes all items of property that are movable, kitchen appliances, garden tools, household furnishings, animals in the barn, etc. When a broker takes a listing of real estate, he or she distinguishes between real estate and personal property. The listing applies only to the real estate, everything within the legal boundaries that is part of the real estate. The personal property is treated separately from the purchase and sale of the real estate. The sellers may agree to sell personal property such as the garden tools, kitchen appliances, or animals to the buyers of the real estate, but generally do so in a separate bill of sale.

Real estate, then, means all the land from the core of the earth to the highest of heavens that lies within the described boundaries and includes all property that is permanently attached to it. For example, the nails, lumber, bricks, mortar and paint used in the construction of the building were once items of personal property, they were quite movable. However, when they were used in the construction of the barn and home, they became attached to and permanently part of the real estate and therefore are sold as real estate. In the same way, the furnace, the plumbing, the shrubs used in landscaping, and the *built-in* kitchen appliances were once personal property but have now become attached to the real estate and are sold as part of the real estate as well.

The sellers have an option as to whether some special items, such as the door knocker and chandelier—which, like the furnace and built-in microwave oven, are part of the real estate—will be sold with the real estate. Standing alone, these items are considered personalty, but because they are affixed to the real estate the law classifies them as fixtures, and fixtures are considered real estate.

Suppose the sellers, because of their special feelings for some of these fixtures, do not want to sell them with the property. Are they compelled to do so? The answer is no; they may specify in the purchase and sale agreement those fixtures not to be included in the sale of the real estate. It is the responsibility of the real estate agent to ask the sellers which items, if any, are not to be sold with the real estate.

When taking a listing, the agent must be aware of those items the seller may consider personal and thus intend to take with them following the sale. If the buyers move into a home for which they have just paid their lives' savings, they will be understandably upset if there are holes in the front door and dining room ceiling where the sellers have removed the door knocker and chandelier, items the law characterizes as fixtures. Often, the sellers will have moved "to California," leaving the broker to face irate buyers who want the door knocker and chandelier reinstalled. The problem can be prevented by the astute agent who provides in the listing agreement and in all the promotional brochures a list of the items *not* included in the sale. For these reasons it is important for a real estate agent to understand the law of fixtures.

THE LAW OF FIXTURES

The law of fixtures provides answers to the question: What articles of personal property have now become a part of the land so as to pass by a conveyance without being mentioned in the deed? The controlling test today in determining whether personal property has become a fixture is the *intention* with which it was attached to the real estate. *Intention* is the objective or manifest intention as evidenced by all the surrounding facts and circumstances.

Indicators of Intent

To determine intent, the law considers:

1. the manner in which the article is attached;
2. the adaptability of the article to the real estate;
3. the annexing person's relationship to the real estate;
4. the relationship of the parties.

Method of Annexation of Attachment

One way of determining the intent of the annexor is to focus on the way in which the personal property has been incorporated into the real estate. If the personal property is attached in such a way as to lead a reasonable person to believe that it is part of the real estate, then it will usually be considered a fixture.

In determining whether an item was intended to be a fixture, and thus part of the real estate, it may help to ask: Will detaching the item cause material damage either to the thing itself or to the realty? If significant damage is likely to occur, then the item is presumed to be a fixture, part of the real estate. For example, a built-in sprinkler with pipes running inside plaster walls will be viewed as a fixture.

By this test the brass door knocker would clearly be a fixture. A reasonable person seeing the large bolt through the door would conclude that it was intended to be permanent; detaching it would leave holes in the door. A reasonable person would come to the same conclusions about the chandelier. Thus, to take fixtures from the real estate, the sellers must specifically exclude them from the sale in the listing with the broker and again in the purchase and sale agreement with the buyers.

But what would a reasonable person conclude about the built-in microwave oven or an above-ground swimming pool or curtain rods? Are these items fixtures permanently attached to the real estate? In considering curtain rods, would it make any difference whether the rods were custom-made for an unusual window or were the common variety available in any hardware store? What would a reasonable person think? More importantly, what do the buyers and sellers think?

Real estate licensees should understand that personal property need not be physically attached to the realty at all times to be a fixture. It is possible to have *constructive attachment* as well as actual attachment. Examples of personal property constructively attached or annexed to real estate are storm windows, storm doors, shutters, etc.—items that are removed for the summer but are intended to be used with the real estate. If the article is essential to the use of the real estate, but is not always attached to it, it is nonetheless considered part of the real estate. Again, the key is intention: Was the intention to make the item a permanent addition to the real estate?

Unless otherwise stated, a seller of real estate ordinarily intends whatever is necessary for the use and enjoyment of the property to pass with it at the time of sale.

Adaptability to the Realty

If the personal property is necessary or convenient to the use of the real estate to which it is attached, then it is usually regarded as part of the realty and will therefore be considered a fixture. The application of this test may bring about different results in different times and places. What one generation may regard as luxury may be seen as an essential item by the next—

for example, bathtubs—and what may be thought of as a necessary part of every building in one locality may not be considered essential in another. For instance, storm windows are usually regarded as necessary to a building in cold climates, but certainly not in warm climates.

The type of both the real estate and the personal property can be of great importance in deciding whether personalty is "necessary or convenient" for the use of the real estate. For example, a pipe organ would be considered essential to a church, but not to an ordinary house. Although ordinary chairs in a house are without doubt personal property, the pews in a church are part of the real estate. In determining whether personal property is a fixture, consideration must always be given to the nature and the use to which it has been put, as well as to the intent of the owner to make a permanent annexation to the real estate.

Relationship of the Parties

The previous sections dealt with situations in which, at the time of annexation, the same person owned both the personal property and the real estate. For other situations, in which the owner of the personal property has attached it to land owned by another, the question is whether or not by its annexation an article becomes the property of the landowner. To help answer this question, the courts will consider, in addition to the tests mentioned above, the relationship of the parties.

The relationship of the parties is important because the general and most important test is *the apparent intention to permanently improve the land.* Whether or not personal property is a fixture could rest upon whether the relationship of the parties is that of landlord-tenant, mortgagor-mortgagee, or vendor-vendee.

Landlord-tenant: trade fixtures. When a tenant, for the purpose of benefiting his or her business or trade, attaches an item to the property of the landlord, the item is called a *trade fixture.* One of the aspects of a trade fixture is that the person who attached it to the real estate has the right to remove the item when he or she moves.

It is presumably the intent of the tenant who attaches articles to the leased property not to improve the landlord's property permanently, but only for his or her benefit. The right of a tenant to remove those things that he or she has attached for personal use is based on the reasoning that it would be unfair for improvements made at the tenant's expense to benefit the landlord, who has paid nothing for them.

Examples

A nationally franchised convenience store leases a corner lot and building. The tenant installs coolers for its dairy products, display cases for its general merchandise, and tanks and pumps to dispense gasoline. Each of these items—coolers, display cases, tanks, and pumps—is a trade fixture, and the tenant may remove them the end of the lease.

A barber opens an old-fashioned shop and installs a traditional barber pole, a sink, and a hydraulic chair. At the end of the lease, the barber may remove these trade fixtures.

A tenant may remove trade fixtures any time before the end of the lease. If the lease term is uncertain, the tenant is usually given a reasonable time after termination of the lease to remove the fixtures. If the tenant does not remove them within a reasonable time, they become the property of the landlord.

Again, if a fixture is so attached to the real estate that its removal will cause extensive damage to the property, then the fixture may not be a removable trade fixture, but will become realty that belongs to the landlord. This is particularly true if the fixture generally benefitted the property; for example, when a tenant installs a sprinkler system or central air conditioning. Where serious damage to the property is threatened by the removal of a fixture that contributes to the property's general usage, a tenant may be prevented from removing the fixture.

Mortgagor-mortgagee. Another application of the law of fixtures, whereby personal property attached to real estate becomes part of the real estate, occurs between mortgagor and mortgagee. Consider a property owner (mortgagor) who borrows money and gives a mortgage to the lender (mortgagee). The mortgage is an agreement that gives the lender the right to take over the property if the borrower does not repay the loan. If the property owner installs central air conditioning, or any other personal property that is so attached as to become a fixture, the lender's mortgage covers those items in addition to the property originally covered.

Vendor-vendee. A third situation concerning the law of fixtures that a broker should understand occurs between the property owner, as purchaser of personalty to be attached to the property, and the vendor of the item soon to become a fixture. Suppose the purchaser buys an expensive humidifier or heat exchanger on an installment basis from the vendor. The installment sale agreement provides that the purchaser will pay for the merchandise to be attached to the real estate in 60 monthly installments and that the vendor will keep title to the goods until the final monthly payment is made. The vendor can protect his or her title to the humidifier by having the seller sign a security agreement, which the vendor will file with the town clerk where the property is located. Some states require an additional filing with the secretary of state's office and/or the registry of deeds. This filing of the security agreement in a public place gives notice to any other interested person that the vendor has a special interest in the personalty now attached to the real estate. Consequently, should the purchaser of the humidifier fail to make his or her payments, the seller may repossess the item in spite of the fact that it is a fixture.

Fixture Agreements

Even though personal property may be so attached to the realty as to become part of it, the parties to a sale may agree that an item shall not be considered a fixture but shall remain personal property. Such special agreements are binding only upon the contracting parties and upon those who have knowledge of the agreement. Those who have no knowledge of the special agreement are not bound by it. Thus, Phillip and Elizabeth can take their door knocker and chandelier if they want to, but the broker must be very careful to explain to the buyers that these fixtures are not included in the sale; this must be spelled out in the purchase and sale contract, which the buyers will sign.

Property That Grows on the Land

In selling real estate, the agent will also need to consider the disposition of trees and crops.

Trees

Trees are considered part of the land and thus pass by conveyance with the land. Generally, trees lying on land at the time of conveyance are real estate and pass by the deed; but downed trees that are cut into wood, logs, or other lumber are personal property. Thus, a century-old oak standing in the yard would be considered real property, but once felled and cut into firewood, it would become personal property. Therefore, the 100-acre tree farm is real estate that will be conveyed by Phillip and Elizabeth with their deed, unless special arrangements are made.

Crops

The major question involving growing crops is whether they are to be treated as realty or personal property. To answer this question, the law recognizes two categories of crops: those that are the result of the care and work of people are called *fructus industriales* or *emblements*; those that come from the bounty of nature are called *fructus naturales*. Cultivated crops are viewed as personalty, while produce that grows wild is generally considered part of the real estate. Crops, however, whether fructus naturales or fructus industriales, growing at the time of a conveyance of the land and in the absence of a valid reservation by the seller or grantor, usually pass as part of the land to the purchaser. If the land is sold and the seller is to remain in possession of the land, ownership of the crops should be spelled out in the purchase and sale contract. The privilege of a tenant to harvest and keep a crop depends upon when the crop was sown and when the tenancy expires. For instance, if a year-to-year tenant plants crops before receiving notice of the lease termination, the tenant probably will be allowed to return and harvest the crop. But a tenant who plants with knowledge that harvesttime will occur after the tenancy has expired probably cannot reenter to harvest the crops. Of course, parties may agree to allow reentry for the purpose of harvesting crops, even when harvest would occur after the cultivator or tenant's term had expired.

In many localities, especially in sales involving timberland, two contracts are made—one concerning the real property, the other covering the personal property—to assure complete understanding between the parties. Phillip and Elizabeth's tree farm presents an interesting issue. Growing trees are normally considered part of the real estate and would pass by deed at the time of conveyance. But cultivated crops are viewed as personalty that does not normally pass with a deed to real estate. Although a cultivated crop, the trees would pass with the deed in the absence of a reservation by the grantor. The broker would be wise to see that the purchase and sale agreement specifies who gets the trees in the tree farm.

INTANGIBLE RIGHTS OF OWNERSHIP

Transferred along with the deed to every tangible parcel of real estate is a collection of rights often referred to as the *bundle of sticks*, with each stick representing a different right of ownership. These rights include the right to occupy and use the land; to drill for water, oil, or gas; to mine for coal, gravel, or other minerals; to raise crops; to build buildings; to rent office, residential, or farmland space. The bundle of rights also includes the right to collect rents; to sell, subdivide, and develop; to give easements; to put restrictions on the land; to leave it to heirs in a will. These numerous rights fall into three general categories: the right to occupy the land, the right to use the land, and the right to convey the land.

The most complete collection of rights would allow an owner and the owner's heirs to occupy a parcel of real estate forever, to use it in any manner desired, and to convey it to anyone at any time. Owning this comprehensive bundle of rights is referred to as owning the *fee* interest, short for *fee simple* or *fee simple absolute,* in the property, which will be discussed further in the next chapter. At this point, the licensee should understand that most owners encountered will have the fee interest, the broadest collection of ownership rights in connection with the real estate, which includes the rights to occupy, use, and convey.

Right to Occupy

The right of an owner to occupy a parcel of real estate depends upon the type of estate that he or she owns. The most common type of estate is the fee simple absolute, which allows the owner and his or her heirs to occupy the land forever.

Example

A deed reads: "I, John, convey Blackacre to Mary Smith and her heirs and assignees forever . . . ."

A qualified fee will convey an estate that can be ended upon the occurrence or nonoccurrence of an event or events, at which time the buyer's ownership and, thus, right to occupy is ended, with the property reverting to the seller.

Example

A deed reads: "I, John, convey Blackacre to Mary Smith so long as alcoholic beverages are never sold on the premises."

A life estate will convey ownership only as long as the lifetime of a specified person, usually that of the recipient of the life estate.

Example

A deed reads: "I, John, convey Blackacre to Mary Smith for life, and on Mary Smith's death, to Susan Smith."

Right to Use

The owner of the fee has the broadest range of possible uses of the property, the largest bundle of sticks. There are, however, private and public limitations on the fee owner's right to use land.

Private restrictions generally take the form of easements and restrictive easements. An easement generally allows one person to use another's land for a particular purpose—e.g. to drive over a portion of it—and prevents the burdened owner from using the land in a way that will interfere with that person's easement, such as building a fence across the easement road. Restrictive easements are contractual arrangements made by an owner promising not to do something upon his or her land—e.g. not to erect a fence higher than ten feet.

Public restrictions on land use usually take the form of either zoning ordinances—specific prohibitions of certain activities such as service of liquor within town boundaries—or the law of nuisance, e.g. dealing with excessively noisy activities or odor-producing activities. These public restrictions on land use are valid exercises of the state's power to protect the health and well-being of its citizens.

Right to Convey

Ownership of the fee brings with it the right to convey the fee or any other interest in the real estate. A property owner may convey the fee, his or her entire interest in the real estate, by sale or by gift or by leaving it in a will to his or her heirs.

The right to convey the entire fee gives the owner the power to convey lesser interests in the real estate as well.

Example ————————————————————

A, the owner of a three-family house, gives a lease for two years to the tenants of the other two apartments.

In this example, the landlord owner is conveying the right to occupy to the tenants, but only for a limited period.

SUMMARY

The first step in the real estate brokerage process is taken when the licensee is appointed agent for the seller for the purpose of selling his or her property. The appointment of agent is made with the listing agreement, a contract between the agent and the sellers that will provide, among other things, the amount of commission to be paid, the description of the property to be sold, the asking price, and the length of time the agreement is effective. Listing agreements are explained in greater detail later in the book in Chapter 6.

When the licensee has been appointed agent for the sellers, the listing process begins in earnest; it is here that the licensee's knowledge of real estate law becomes increasingly important because he or she must understand what is considered real estate, and therefore will be sold when a purchase and sale contract is signed, and what is not to be sold. A logical place for the listing process to begin is with the deed; the agent who has a copy of the deed with the legal description can walk the boundaries of the property and thus be able to show prospective buyers exactly what real estate is to be sold. The description will be a metes and bounds description or a reference to a lot on a plan or will use language of the rectangular survey system of land descriptions.

Real estate is the physical land within the property's boundaries, including the surface rights, subsurface rights, and air rights reasonably necessary for the enjoyment of the property, as well as any buildings or appurtenances on the land. The broker understands that it is not within his or her authority as a real estate agent to sell any personal property belonging to the sellers, such as garden tools, farm tractors, or livestock. However, there will probably be some items of personal property so attached to the real estate as to be a part of it or at least to raise the question as to whether it is intended by the sellers to be part of the real estate. Consider an above-ground pool or a television antenna strapped to the chimney: Do the sellers intend to take the pool and antenna with them when they leave? Will the buyers expect to find these items on the property when they move in? The real estate agent is expected to identify these fixtures, including the chandelier and door knocker, and if they are not to be sold with the real estate, they should be specifically excluded from the sale in the purchase and sale agreement.

Fixtures the seller takes along which the buyer expected to find when he or she moved in, can be a source of litigation. Where such issues are to be decided by a court, a judge looks at the objective evidence to decide what the apparent intent of the parties was concerning the fixture, including the method of attachment, the relationship of the parties to the property, the adaptability of the fixture to the real estate, and the relationship of the annexing party to the real estate. Brokers can help buyers and sellers avoid this kind of litigation through their thoroughness in the listing and negotiation process.

The ownership of real estate includes the ownership of rights to use the real estate. The largest collection of those rights, often referred to as the *bundle of sticks*, is called owning a *fee simple absolute*, or *fee*, for short, in real estate. Ownership of the fee gives the title holder the unfettered right to occupy, use, lease, and convey the property to anyone in accordance with any zoning or other lawful limitations on the use of land. Chapters 2–5 describe in further detail the nature of an owner's intangible rights in real estate and limitations on these rights, all of which a real estate agent must explain to prospective purchasers.

MULTIPLE CHOICE QUESTIONS ————————————————————

1. Which of the following is *not* a common method of describing the boundaries of a parcel of land?

    a. aerial photograph
    b. metes and bounds system
    c. reference to a map or plan
    d. rectangular survey system

2. Which of the following rights (is) are associated with ownership?

    a. the right to occupy
    b. the right to use
    c. the right to convey
    d. all of the above

3. A metes and bounds description must:

    a. have four perpendicular sides.
    b. enclose the land described.
    c. be used in the western U.S. only.
    d. all of the above

4. A metes and bounds description may begin with reference to a:

    a. landmark.
    b. surveyor's pin.
    c. stone monument.
    d. any of the above

5. Which of the following is an example of a public restriction on the use of land?

    a. riparian rights
    b. zoning
    c. affirmative easement
    d. restrictive easement

6. The basic unit in the rectangular survey system of land description is the:

    a. acre.
    b. township.
    c. meridian.
    d. base line.

7. Martha allows John to build a landing strip for his airplane across her field. John has _____ across Martha's property.

    a. an easement
    b. a crossing
    c. a restrictive agreement
    d. a mortgage

8. Ownership of real estate includes:

    a. rights to use the surface, subsurface, and air over it.
    b. fixtures.
    c. trees growing on the land.
    d. all of the above

9. Intangible rights in real estate include the right(s) to:

    a. convey it.
    b. use it.
    c. occupy it.
    d. all of the above

10. The right of a landowner and his or her heirs to occupy a parcel of real estate forever is called:

    a. a qualified estate.
    b. a life estate.
    c. an estate in fee simple absolute.
    d. an indeterminable estate.

11. Which of the following is (are) true?

    I. A gravel pit is real estate.
   II. A pile of excavated gravel is personalty.

    a. I only   c. neither I nor II
    b. II only   d. both I and II

12. By what authority may communities pass laws restricting land-owners in certain uses of their land?

    a. manifest destiny   c. the state's police power
    b. the law of nuisance   d. government fiat

13. Whether an item of personal property is attached to real estate so as to become part of it is determined by the:

    a. listing agreement.
    b. apparent intention of the party who attached it.
    c. sellers.
    d. buyers.

14. When a lease expires, trade fixtures belong to the:

    a. tenant.
    b. landlord.
    c. mortgagee.
    d. owner of the fee simple absolute.

15. If the sellers of a home want to take a fixture such as a Jacuzzi with them when they sell, they should specify this in their _____ with the buyers.

    a. deed
    b. mortgage
    c. contract
    d. all of the above

DISCUSSION QUESTIONS

1. Imagine that you are selling your home. Make a list of the personal property, particularly the fixtures to be sold with the property and the fixtures to be taken.

2. Assume that you are a real estate licensee taking a listing. What can you learn by walking the boundaries of the property? How can you determine what the boundaries are?

3. Bob Barber rents space for five years, which he uses as a barbershop. He installs a barber pole and other equipment. At the end of the lease, may he remove the built-in equipment? Why or why not?

2

The Estate Concept

───────────────── KEY TERMS ─────────────────

contingent	future estates
executory interest	nonfreehold estate
fee simple absolute	possibility of reverter
fee simple determinable	present estates
fee simple subject to	qualified fee
a condition subsequent	remainder
fee simple subject to an	reversion
executory limitation	right of entry
freehold estate	vested

A real estate broker's job is to represent owners of real estate by finding buyers to purchase what the sellers have to sell. Behind that very simple statement lurks a galaxy of concepts and terms pertaining to ownership and estates in land, which a competent professional broker must understand and be able to explain to prospective buyers and sellers alike.

Consider the concept of ownership for a minute, using the example of an automobile. What does a person who buys an automobile from a dealer get? First of all, the purchaser gets legal title to the car, which brings with it the right to possession and the rights to use the car, to lend it to a friend, and to drive it—with a license and according to speed limits and laws concerning inspections, insurance, driving under the influence of alcohol, etc. With these rights, the owner may borrow money and pledge the car as security for the loan; pledging the car as security for a loan means the owner is transferring the right to possession of the car to the lender if loan payments are not made on time. In other words, one of the rights of ownership of the car is the power to transfer some of those rights to others.

Example ———————————————————————————————

An auto-leasing company buys cars, and while it retains legal title to and ownership of the car, it transfers possession and the right to use it to someone else, for a day, week, month, or year.

———————————————————————————————

Ownership of real estate is similar to ownership of an automobile, as the owner will have both legal title and the right to possession, which means the right to lend it to a friend, to lease it, to pledge it as collateral for a loan. In other words, the owner will have all the rights that make up the bundle of sticks described in Chapter 1. However, because land is indestructible and will pass to future generations long after its current owner has died, and because it is susceptible to so many different uses—residential, agricultural, commercial, industrial, etc.— ownership of real estate is somewhat more complex than the automobile analogy implies.

The objective of this chapter is to describe the galaxy of ownership possibilities so that a broker working with sellers can find out exactly what rights, or what estate, it is that they have to sell, and then turn around and accurately describe it to buyers. The chapter also includes some examples of how Phillip and Elizabeth divided their land into different estates to provide for different people in their family.

THE NATURE OF ESTATES

An *estate* is an interest in land held by one or more people and consists of those rights and uses that the owners can make of the property and the time during which they can exercise those rights. Much of contemporary real estate law, including the concept of estates, is rooted in the history of land ownership in England in the Middle Ages.

In A.D. 1066, William the Conqueror crossed the English Channel and defeated the English armies. To reward his troops and to establish administrative control over the conquered land, he awarded to his generals the administrative control over certain portions of the country, for their lifetimes. The generals in turn gave administrative control to their sublieutenants for their life-times. At the bottom of the feudal pyramid were the English peasants who cultivated the land. For the privilege of cultivat-ing the land, the peasants gave a portion of their crops to their overlord and were available for conscription when he needed to raise an army. The overlord in his turn paid a portion of his crops to his superior in the feudal chain and, likewise, provided troops when necessary.

This arrangement was *tenurial* which meant that a tenant held the land on condition of good behavior—i.e. paying a portion of goods produced and availability for military service—and he held it for his lifetime only. When a peasant died, or when an overlord died, the right to cultivate the land or administer it was transferred to another. This system was dramatically differ-ent from our present concept of ownership, which involves legal title and the right to use, occupy, convey, pledge as collateral for a loan, etc.

It was from the tenurial system that the estate concept of prop-erty ownership developed. Rather than convey only administra-tive control to a sublieutenant, William's successors; as kings of England, began to convey control "to X and his heirs." This came to mean to X, and on X's death to his eldest living son, or to all of his daughters or, finally, to his collateral relatives and their heirs after them. Thus, a transfer to "T and his heirs" was potentially infinite in duration, and the concept of *general inher-itability* developed. This power to direct who would own real estate on the owner's death was essential to create the largest and most common estate in land, the *fee simple,* also called a *fee simple absolute.*

This is the estate that Phillip and Elizabeth have in Eagles' Nest and is by far the most common estate in land today. They received the property as a gift to own forever. They received all the rights possibly attributable to landowners, including the rights of inheritability—the right to leave it to future genera-tions by gift, deed, or will—and the right to sell it or any part of it. They own the largest possible bundle of rights with this prop-erty. There are no limits, other than zoning or environmental laws, on their use of the property and none on the duration of their ownership.

Estates in land—i.e. ownership of land—can be divided over time. In other words, two estates can be created in one parcel of land—one that exists today and another that will blossom in the future, on some future predetermined event.

Example

A rich uncle dies and leaves his home to his sister, Sally, for her life and on her death to the heirs of her son, Bob.

In the same home there are two estates: sister Sally has a present estate; Bob's heirs have a future estate in the same property. *Present estates* normally give the holder of the estate the right to present possession and use of the land. *Future estates,* on the other hand, involve a right to possession at some later date.

Future estates may be either *vested* or *contingent*. A vested estate is one that is guaranteed to the holder of the future interest. In the example above, the title to the land unquestionably will go to Bob's heirs on Sally's death. This is a vested remainder, one that is certain to take effect.

A contingent remainder is a future interest that may or may not take effect. Consider the following example.

Example

B dies and leaves his home to Sally for life, and on Sally's death to Nancy; if Nancy is not living at Sally's death, then to the heirs of his son Bob.

Nancy's future estate is a contingent remainder; it is not certain that she will take the property because she must survive Sally to take title. Her interest is contingent upon her surviving Sally.

A *remainder* interest is a future interest that is created in someone other than the grantor. In this example, the life estate goes to Sally and the rest, or "remainder," of the estate goes to

Nancy, if she survives, and ultimately to Bob's heirs. Another type of future interest is a *reversion*, a future interest that reverts to the original grantor.

Example ───

Rich Uncle Ted conveys a life estate to his Great Aunt Sally; when Sally dies, the property reverts to Ted; if Ted dies before Sally, then the property goes to his heirs or according to his will.

──

Legal limitations on certain future estates limit their duration or transferability. The Rule against Perpetuities limits how far in the future a present owner may control the ownership of property to a period measured by lives in being at the present owner's death, plus 21 years. In other words, a great-grandmother can leave Blackacre in her will to her great-grandson for life, and then to his children for 21 years, and the remainder to charity. In this case, if her great-grandson lives to be 100, she has controlled the property for 121 years; if the gift to her grandson's children was for more than 21 years, the disposition in the will would fail because it was a violation of the Rule against Perpetuities.

On the other hand, suppose a grandfather, G, leaves Blackacre to his grandson, S, for life, remainder to S's children. If the grandson is alive at the time of G's death, clearly the great-grandchildren will take the property within 21 years of the death of S, the lives in being at the time of G's death.

The owner of a future estate has additional rights, including a present right against the person now in possession to see that the value of the future estate is preserved.

Examples: ──

The person who has a future estate in a woodlot may have the right to prevent the removal of trees from the property by the present owner. At the same time, the present owner has the right to take as much wood as is reasonably necessary for the current enjoyment and use of the property.

Sister Nancy has a life estate in a 2,000-acre tree farm of valuable hardwood. Sound woodlot management practices dictate that a portion of the wood be harvested each year to generate income and promote future growth of the trees. Nancy is entitled to the income generated by the partial harvesting each year during her period of ownership. Obviously, if all 2,000 acres were cut to the ground, she could make a lot of money; however, this would be an abuse of her life estate; she has a duty to the future owners to preserve the underlying value of the property.

Duration

The duration of an estate is the length of time for which the holder of the estate has a right to legal protection of his or her interest.

Example

O, the owner of land, conveys it to A "for life." When A dies, the land passes back to O, or O's heirs, by *reversion,* a future interest. The duration of O's future interest is the span of A's life, since O or O's heirs have the right to prevent A from damaging the land during that time.

Sale of an Estate of Longer Duration

It may be important for a broker to determine the duration of an estate.

Example

Consider the situation in which a tenant who has a term of 20 years attempts to sell the property in fee simple absolute. The attempt to convey an estate of longer duration than the estate held by the seller will result in a valid conveyance only to the extent of the seller's own estate. Thus the grantee of the fee will receive only what the grantor had, the remaining term of the 20-year estate.

COMMON TYPES OF ESTATES IN LAND TODAY

The estate concept allows several people to hold interests in the same parcel of land at the same time. This section is an introduction to the various types of estates people may have in land. After reading it, licensees should be able to identify the types of interests in land and understand how the type of interest affects what a seller can do with it. They should be able to differentiate between interests that entitle a person to ownership of a property called *freehold estates* and those that entitle a person to temporary posession of property, called *leasehold* or *nonfreehold estates*. Finally licensees will understand that estates in land may vary greatly in value, depending on the type of estate a person holds in land.

Fee Simple Absolute

Phillip and Elizabeth have full title ownership and possession to Eagles' Nest and are completely free to do with their interest as they wish. They can sell part or all of their acreage outright. They can devise it in their wills to anyone. They can divide it into lesser estates, leasing some land for a period of years, granting parcels in life estates, and selling others subject to certain conditions. Their interest is called an estate in *fee simple absolute*, the most common interest in land and the one a broker will deal with most often. Because it is not subject to any conditions or limitations, it is potentially infinite in duration. It is the largest and most valuable estate recognized by law.

Qualified Fees

In contrast to the fee simple absolute, in which the holder is entitled to outright ownership for an unlimited duration, estates may be made subject to certain limitations or conditions; these are *qualified fee* estates.

Suppose Phillip and Elizabeth sold 40 acres to neighbor John on the condition that he continue farming the land. They conveyed the land to him in a deed by using this language: To John *so long as* the land is used for farming." John has a qualified fee, called a *fee simple determinable*. John owns the land and has all the privileges of ownership, including the right to sell, lease, or devise the land in his will as long as the land is farmed. If the farming activity ceases on the land, and someone decides to build an apartment complex, the land will automatically revert to Phillip and Elizabeth or to their heirs if Phillip and Elizabeth have died when the change in use occurs.

In theory, this restriction that the land be used only for farming would last forever. However, many states have enacted statutes that make such restrictions void after a period of years unless they are renewed.

Another kind of qualified fee is called *fee simple subject to a condition subsequent*. Suppose Phillip and Elizabeth want to grant 40 acres to their neighbor, Fred, reserving for themselves the right to terminate the grant if and when he stops farming.

The deed for this conveyance would state: "To Fred, *but if* the land is ever used for other than farming purposes, then we, the grantors, have the right to re-enter and repossess the land." Just as in John's case, Fred owns the land and has all the privileges of ownership until he stops farming. The difference between the two estates is that, in the first example, the land reverts automatically to Phillip and Elizabeth; in the second case, Phillip and Elizabeth must do something to recover the estate. Even if Fred stops farming, his estate will not end until the right of re-entry is exercised.

There is a third type of qualified fee, called a *fee simple subject to an executory limitation*. Suppose Phillip and Elizabeth want to see their son, Bob, continue farming the land, but know that their neighbor, a confirmed farmer, would certainly farm the land if their son would not. They might convey the 40 acres "to our son, Bob, but if within 20 years he stops using the land for farming, then to our neighbor Mark." Here, Bob has a fee simple absolute subject to an executory limitation. Note that there is no requirement here, as there was in the previous example, that the neighbors do something to regain possession. As in the example of the fee simple determinable, the estate will terminate automatically and go to Mark if Bob stops farming. The difference between a fee simple determinable and a fee simple subject to an executory limitation is that when the condition is broken in the later estate the estate goes to a third person and not to the grantor or his or her heirs.

It is not important that brokers memorize the subtle differences among a fee simple subject to an executory limitation, a fee simple subject to a condition subsequent, and a fee simple determinable. This is lawyer's work. It is sufficient to know that a property owner may create these private restrictions on the use on land when conveying an interest to another person and that the interest created in the new owner may be limited in both duration and use.

Estate for Life

Suppose that Phillip and Elizabeth want to provide for her octogenarian uncle, Henry, during his lifetime, but they want the land returned to son Bob after Henry dies. Drawing on an understanding of the estate concept, a broker might suggest that an estate for life be conveyed to Uncle Henry. A deed creating a life estate would read: "To Henry for life, *remainder* to Bob." At Henry's death, title to the land would fall to Bob, the remainderman. Henry would own a present estate, while Bob's estate would be classified as a future estate.

For the duration of his life, Henry takes title to and possession of the property together with the entire bundle of ownership rights, including the right to mortgage it, sell it, lease it, and use the profits from it.

Example

Henry may decide to retire in Florida. He needs the proceeds from the life estate to make a down payment on a house. Who would be willing to buy a life estate? Bob, the remainderman, might buy it because he has a future interest in the property. Another farmer might buy it if, based on Henry's life expectancy, he could make a profit growing crops or grazing animals.

There is one important restriction on Henry's use of his life estate: he may not abuse or destroy the property. He has an obligation to the remainderman, the future owner of the land, to maintain the property in reasonable condition for the future owner at the end of his life estate.

Future Estates

In the two previous sections, Phillip and Elizabeth made three conveyances of real estate. In each conveyance, they created present interests and future interests in the same land. In each example of qualified estates they granted:

a. "40 acres to John on condition he continues farming";

b. "40 acres to Fred, but if the land is ever used for other than farming, then we, the grantors, or our heirs shall have the right to enter and repossess the land";

c. "40 acres to our son, Bob, but if within 20 years he stops farming the land, then to neighbor Mark."

The estate of John, Fred, and Bob is subject to some condition or limitation. If the limitation is realized, what happens to the land? What kind of interest does the conditional owner have?

In the first example, John has an estate in fee simple determinable, entitling him to own the land as long as he continues farming, or to sell, devise, or lease the land. Only if the land is no longer farmed will Phillip and Elizabeth or their heirs be entitled to the land; until that time, they have only the possibility of ownership. Unlike John, who is entitled to possession now, Phillip and Elizabeth have an interest that may, at some future point, entitle them to ownership and possession of the land. They have a future interest in the 40 acres sold to John, an interest technically known as a *possibility of reverter*.

The broker should be aware that when a qualified fee—fee simple determinable, fee simple subject to condition subsequent, or fee simple subject to executory limitation—is conveyed, the condition named in the deed, will, or other legal conveyance document remains "attached" to the land. Subsequent purchasers will be bound by the condition.

Thus, in this example, John may decide after a year that farming does not agree with him, and he may wish to sell the land to Jones. Jones must also use the land for farming, or the estate will terminate and go back to Phillip and Elizabeth. This is a very effective way for a landowner to ensure that land sold is used in the manner desired.

Next, Phillip and Elizabeth granted 40 acres to Fred, reserving the right of re-entry. As in the previous case, they have a possibility of ownership, a future interest that will entitle them to repossess the land only if Fred stops farming and if they exercise their right to reenter. Their future interest in Fred's estate is called a *right of entry*.

Phillip and Elizabeth's deed to Bob had a provision that, if he stopped farming within 20 years, neighbor Mark would have the right to possession. This time it is not the grantors who have the potential right to future possession but a third party. Mark's interest is called an *executory interest*. Note that Phillip and Elizabeth have now given away all their interest in this 40-acre plot.

SUMMARY

This chapter has been about estates in land; an estate in land is a term used to describe the rights of people to occupy, use, or convey the real estate. The estate concept arose from the tenurial estates of feudal England where the right of possession for life grew into the right to occupy, use, and convey the land to provide for future generations of the landholder.

The largest estate in land is the fee simple absolute, which contains the fullest bundle of rights, each right giving the owner some power to use or dispose of the land. Estates in land can be present estates or future estates. Estates may be vested or contingent; they may be qualified by some restriction on their use or duration. Future interests include a remainder, a reversion, a right of entry for condition broken, and an executory limitation.

Phillip and Elizabeth carved Eagles' Nest into various smaller estates for various members of their family and used different types of estates to accomplish different objectives. Real estate brokers will be dealing most often with the fee simple absolute; it is possible that they will at some point encounter a life estate and, if involved with rental properties, leasehold interests that may last for a period of years. Landlord and tenant law will be considered more fully in Chapter 11.

This chapter on estates in land is intended to make the reader aware of how the sticks in the bundle called *fee simple* can be parceled out according to the needs of the property owner. The creation of qualified fees, various future interests, and their conveyance by deed or the writing of leases is complex and is regarded a lawyer's work. Because brokers are often called upon to counsel real estate owners about the use of their property, they should be conversant with these concepts but are not expected to be technically skilled in their creation.

MULTIPLE CHOICE QUESTIONS ————————————————

Questions 1-3 are based on the case below.

Brown grants 50 acres "to my niece, N, for life, and then to nephew, S." N plans to make huge profits by allowing the dumping of toxic industrial chemicals on the property.

1. Which of the following is true?

    a. S can prevent the contamination of the land.
    b. S has no recourse until N dies.
    c. Brown can seek protection for his reversion.
    d. all of the above

2. N has a:

    a. nonfreehold estate.
    b. fee simple determinable.
    c. life estate.
    d. fee simple subject to an executory limitation.

3. S has a:

    a. reversion.
    b. remainder.
    c. qualified fee.
    d. none of the above

4. Farmer Brown conveys land "to sister Sarah for life." When Sarah dies, the land will:

    a. revert to Farmer Brown.
    b. go to Sarah's children.
    c. pass to the state.
    d. none of the above

5. Jones granted an estate "to my daughter Jane for life." Jane later sold her interest to Anne. Anne's estate:

    a. is in fee simple absolute after Jane dies.
    b. is in fee simple absolute after the father dies.
    c. ends when Jane dies.
    d. ends when Anne dies.

6. Suppose Brown conveys a building "to my niece, N, but if she ever uses it for selling liquor, then I, the grantor, have a right to re-enter and repossess the land." N has a:

    a. fee simple absolute.
    b. fee simple determinable.
    c. fee simple subject to a condition subsequent.
    d. none of the above

7. A, the owner of Promenade Apartments, gives B the right to occupy an apartment for three years. B has a:

    a. freehold estate.
    b. nonfreehold estate.
    c. right of entry.
    d. none of the above

Questions 8 and 9 are based on the situation below.

O conveys Blackacre to A for life, then to B for life.

8. What type of interest does O have in the property?

    a. a reversion
    b. a remainder
    c. a right of entry
    d. no interest

9. If O dies before A and B, who gets Blackacre?

    a. B's heirs
    b. the heirs of A or B, whoever survives
    c. O's heirs
    d. It can't be determined without additional facts.

10. O has a fee simple interest in Blackacre. He conveys "to A for life and to B for life." If B dies before A, what happens to title to Blackacre?

    a. B's remainder goes to B's heirs.
    b. O has the right of re-entry.
    c. Blackacre reverts to O.
    d. none of the above

Questions 11 and 12 are based on the following case:

Jay conveys land to M for life, remainder to B if B survives M, but if B predeceases M, then to Q.

11. What is B's interest in the property?

    a. a contingent remainder
    b. a vested remainder
    c. a contingent reversion
    d. none of the above

12. If B predeceases M, what kind of interest does Q have?

    a. an alternative contingent remainder
    b. a vested remainder
    c. a fee simple determinable
    d. a reversion

13. If Brown conveys land "to sister Sarah for life," who takes title to the land when Sarah dies?

    a. Brown
    b. Sarah's children
    c. the state
    d. Sarah's heirs at law if she has no children

14. Which of the following is not a future interest?

    a. a reversion
    b. a remainder
    c. an executory interest
    d. a determinable fee

15. A owns Blueacres, a valuable parcel of shorefront property. She wants the land to remain in the family forever. A deed for this purpose:

   a. would violate the rule against perpetuities.
   b. should be made to a guardian of the youngest family member.
   c. must state "to her heirs and assigns forever."
   d. must be a warranty deed.

DISCUSSION QUESTIONS

1. O wishes to specify in his will that nephew N will inherit O's home. At the same time, he wants to make sure that W, his wife, can remain there comfortably if she survives him. Without assuming any specific rights of spouses, set up the manner in which O could achieve the desired result.

2. Peter conveyed a downtown office building to David for life with the remainder to Jeff if Jeff survived David, but if Jeff predeceased David, then to Ellen. Assume that David is 60 years old and in good health, that Jeff is 55 and in moderate health, and that Ellen is 30. The office building has no mortgage on it and generates a net monthly income of $12,000.

   If you were a banker, would you lend money to David on the strength of his interest in the office building? Would you lend money to Jeff on the same basis? Would you lend it to Ellen?

3. Pastor Paul has 25 acres that he wants to convey to his son Nathaniel. What language would Paul use in the deed to make sure that if Nathaniel ever opened a bar on the premises the acreage would immediately belong to the local church?

3

Forms of Ownership

─────────────── KEY TERMS ───────────────

community property
concurrent ownership
condominium
cooperative
curtesy
dower
inchoate dower
interval ownership
joint tenancy

partnership
right of descent
severance
tenancy by the entirety
tenancy in common
testator
testatrix
vests

Legal title to property may be held by one person alone or concurrently by two or more individuals. Multiparty ownership, called *concurrent ownership,* has several recognized forms. The forms are tenancy in common, joint tenancy, tenancy by the entirety, tenancy in partnership, community property, condominium and cooperative ownership, and timesharing or interval ownership.

Licensees must realize that the laws of concurrent ownership, like the laws affecting other aspects of real estate, vary from state to state. Nevertheless, to practice real estate brokerage, it is essential that real estate licensees understand concurrent ownership and its implications for the transfer of ownership from sellers to buyers.

In our example, Phillip and Elizabeth are contemplating the sale of Eagles' Nest. Because Phillip and Elizabeth are equal owners of the property, both of them must sign the deed to convey title to the purchaser. Each owner must convey his or her interest in the property; only with the signatures of each owner can the purchaser acquire the interest of each.

When Phillip asks a broker to handle the sale of Eagles' Nest, the broker must ask whether he is the sole owner of the property. If Elizabeth is also an owner, the broker will need to ask if she too wants to sell. Further, does she want the broker in question to handle the sale? Clearly, the broker cannot offer to sell Eagles' Nest with a good title if one of the owners doesn't want to sell or if one of them doesn't want to hire him.

Thus, in order for a broker to facilitate a sale where there is concurrent ownership, he or she must know who all the sellers are, if there is more than one, and must secure their signatures on the proper documents in the transaction. Failure to do so can mean no sale, loss of commission, possible censure by the state regulating agency, or even loss of license.

This chapter explains the different types of concurrent ownership and how they are created.

Creation of Interests

A person most commonly acquires an interest in real estate by purchasing it or receiving it as a gift. When the land is purchased or received as a gift, the seller or donor will convey title to the property by signing and delivering a deed. If two or more people are to take title, the deed will read: "We, Phillip and Elizabeth, husband and wife, owners of Eagles' Nest, hereby grant to John and Joan the property known as Eagles' Nest...." The deed will be more precise in its description of the property and in stating exactly how John and Joan will take title. Whether the land is acquired by purchase or by gift, the deed will state who the new owners of the property are and what kind of concurrent ownership they enjoy.

Not all property is conveyed by purchase or gift; property of deceased persons passes to new owners who are specified in the deceased's will or, when there is no will, according to the laws of the state in which the land is located.

A person who dies without a last will and testament is said to have died *intestate*. Imagine the problem that would arise if Phillip predeceased Elizabeth and left all his property to her by his will, and Elizabeth then died intestate, leaving an estate of Eagles' Nest and also four children and two grandchildren born of her fifth child, who was now also deceased.

At Phillip's death, his will governs the distribution of his property. But what happens on Elizabeth's death, with no will to direct the distribution of her estate? Intestacy is sufficiently common that state legislatures have enacted laws, called *statutes of descent*, that dictate the distribution of the estate of an intestate decedent.

The distribution of the decedent's estate depends on who the heirs are. In many states, the Uniform Probate Code has been enacted. The code provides for both the surviving spouse and other heirs and, if there is no surviving spouse, for the remaining heirs in another manner. For example, the estate of the deceased is divided among his or her heirs as follows if there is a surviving spouse:

a. If there is no surviving issue or parent of the decedent, the entire intestate estate goes to the spouse.

b. If there is no surviving issue, but the decedent is survived by a parent or parents, the surviving spouse gets the first $50,000 plus one-half of the balance of the intestate estate.

c. If there are surviving issue, all of whom are issue of the surviving spouse also, the first $50,000 plus one-half of the balance of the estate goes to the spouse.

d. If there are surviving issue, one or more of whom are not issue of the surviving spouse, the spouse gets one-half of the intestate estate.

The remainder of the estate, or the entire estate if there is no surviving spouse, is divided among the heirs as follows:

a. It goes to the issue of the decedent, to be distributed per capita at each generation.

b. If there is no surviving issue, it goes to the decedent's parents equally.

c. If there is no surviving issue or parent, it goes to the issue of the parents or either of them, to be distributed per capita at each generation.

d. If there is no surviving issue, parent, or issue of a parent, but the decedent is survived by one or more grandparents or issue of grandparents, half of the estate passes to the paternal grandparents if both survive, or to the surviving paternal grandparent, or to the issue of the paternal grandparents if both are deceased, to be distributed per capita at each generation. The other half passes to the maternal relatives in the same manner. If there is no surviving grandparent or issue of grandparents on either the paternal or maternal side, the entire estate passes to the relatives on the other side in the same manner as the half.

To inherit from the deceased's estate, the heir must survive the decedent. *Per capita* means that, if a grandparent dies, leaving one son and two grandchildren who survived another child, the daughter of the deceased, then the surviving son gets one-half, while the two grandchildren share the other half the daughter would have received, or one-quarter each.

What happens to the title of the real estate the deceased owned in his or her name at the time of death if he or she died intestate? Does it spring to the heirs of the deceased? What if there is no surviving issue, parent, or issue of a parent and the situation described in item *d* above applies?

The answer is that the title to the real estate *vests*, that is, passes to, the heirs of the deceased. When there is no will, this situation can become quite sticky; in order to sell the real estate, each of the heirs of the deceased must sign the deed to convey his or her interest in the real estate in order to convey a clear title to the buyers.

Example ——————————————————————————

M dies, leaving four living children and two grandchildren, daughters of a child who died earlier. According to the law of the state where M died, the four children each get 20 percent and the two grandchildren get the share their parent would have taken, or ten percent each. Six people now own the property that M once owned alone. Six people now must sign the deed, each to convey his or her interest in the real estate.

———————————————————————————————————

The wisdom of having a will should be apparent from the example of how complex the laws of intestacy can make the distribution of the estate of an intestate. In real life, the administration is often made more complex by family feelings about the sale of property and by the common problem of heirs who cannot be located to sign a deed.

Where a *testator* or *testatrix,* a deceased person who leaves a will, provides in a will for the passing of title to the real estate, the administration of the estate can be much simplified. For example, the testator may provide that the real estate pass to one particular heir, or to two or three heirs. In any event, by specifying in the will who will take title to the real estate, the problems of the missing heirs can be prevented.

Example ——————————————————————————

M dies and leaves "my home on Main Street to my three children, O, P, Q." O, P, and Q each have a one-third interest in the house formerly owned by M alone. Thus concurrent ownership is established by will. In order for Z to purchase the house for himself, O, P, and Q all must sign the deed to Z.

———————————————————————————————————

Concurrent interests are created by deed or by will or by the laws of intestacy of the state where the landowner dies without a will. The balance of this chapter will explain the different types of concurrent interests and the importance of these differences.

When listing property for sale, a broker must know which, if any, of the forms of concurrent ownership exists and must be aware of how the law treats such property. This is important because, when concurrent ownership exists, all owners must sign the listing agreement and the deed.

Tenancy in Common

The form of concurrent ownership called *tenancy in common* gives each owner a separate and distinct interest in property with the right to possess and enjoy all the property, not just a percentage of it. No owner can claim a particular portion as his or her own. Although the law presumes that the concurrent owners have equal shares, unequal shares may be conveyed by the grantor or created by unequal investment of the purchasers.

Example

A, B, and C buy Silversands, a piece of shorefront property to be developed for recreational purposes. A contributes $100,000 of the purchase price, B contributes $400,000, and C pays $500,000. Their ownership is proportional to their contributions to the investment so that A has a 10 percent interest, B has a 40 percent interest, and C has a 50 percent interest.

A tenant in common can freely sell, give, devise, or mortgage his or her undivided interest. If one tenant dies, that share passes to devisees under the will of the owner or to heirs, who become tenants in common with the other owners.

A buyer of property currently held by tenants in common must get the signature of each on a deed to receive a 100 percent interest in the property. In our example, if Z wants full ownership of Silversands, he must get the signatures of A, B, and C on a deed. A separate deed from A, a deed from B, and a third deed from C, whereby each conveys his or her interest in the property, would be equally satisfactory.

Joint Tenancy

Two or more people can own property as joint tenants. The single most important feature of a joint tenancy is the right of survivorship. If one joint tenant dies, the remaining owner or owners take title to the interest of the deceased.

Examples ————————————————————————————

Charles and Diane are married; they take title to their home as joint tenants. When one spouse dies, the other automatically gets title to the entire piece of real estate owned by them as joint tenants.

Assume that there are three joint tenants—Arthur, Barbara, and Carrie—each having a one-third interest in Weathering Heights. Upon Arthur's death, Barbara and Carrie absorb his interest so that each of the women now owns an equal half-interest in the property. When Barbara dies, Carrie gets title to the entire parcel.

A joint tenancy has other features to distinguish it from a tenancy in common. A *joint tenancy* is characterized by what lawyers call the *four unities*:

a. unity of time;

b. unity of title;

c. unity of interest;

d. unit of possession.

This simply means that; in a true joint tenancy, the owners acquire the same interest (c), at the same time (a), and have the same title (b) and the same right of possession (d). In a joint tenancy, therefore, the joint tenants will take title by deed or by will simultaneously. If there are two joint tenants, they each have a 50 percent interest; if there are five joint tenants, each will have a 20 percent interest; and so on. They acquire the same title and have the same right to possession, and each has the opportunity to acquire a greater interest by surviving the others.

Contrast the joint tenancy with the tenancy in common, in which the concurrent owners may have unequal interests, they may acquire their interests at different times, and none of the tenants has a right of survivorship over the interest of the other tenants. Tenants in common share only one of the unities, the right of possession.

To create a joint tenancy, specific words are required in the deed or will creating the tenancy.

Example

"To Adam and Alfred as joint tenants with the right of survivorship and not as tenants in common."

If a conveyance to two or more people leaves any doubt as to which type of tenancy is intended, the tenancy in common results. Some states have enacted laws that specify the exact language to be used to create a joint tenancy.

Where the right of survivorship exists, a joint tenant's interest cannot be devised by will. Upon death, the joint tenant's interest merges with the interests of the remaining tenants. Only the last living joint tenant has sole ownership of the property and, therefore, may leave the interest in his or her will.

Severance

A joint tenancy may be terminated by a process called *severance*. A joint tenant may convey his or her interest by deed, and the new owner's interest will be *severed* from the joint tenancy; he or she will receive a tenancy in common with the remaining joint tenants. Readers should note, however, that many states require the selling joint owner to get the permission of the other joint tenants in order to sell his or her interest.

Example ─────────────────────────────────────

Blackrock is owned by A, B, and C as joint tenants; C conveys her interest to D, who now has a one-third interest, but as a tenant in common with A and B, who remain joint tenants with a right of survivorship with respect to each other. D's one-third interest has been severed from the joint tenancy.

───

Consider the following scenarios for the future of the ownership of Blackrock:

- If A dies first, B will take A's interest by right of survivorship. D's interest will be unaffected by A's death. B will own two-thirds; and D will own one-third.

- If B dies first, A will take by survivorship and own two-thirds; D will still own one-third.

- If D dies, his third will go to his heirs or by his will; A's and B's interests will be unaffected.

Partition of Joint Tenancy or Tenancy in Common

Joint tenancy, with its four unities and right of survivorship, and tenancy in common are both forms of concurrent ownership. Concurrent ownership is not always a happy arrangement since disagreements may arise as to the use and management of the property. But the law of real estate provides a mechanism for resolution of these situations. An unhappy owner, or all the owners who have reached an impasse over the use of the property, may bring to court a *petition for partition* of the real estate.

A partition is a physical division of the property. Instead of concurrent undivided ownership in the entire property, partition creates a divided ownership in the property, with each person owning a separate parcel.

Physical partition gives each cotenant a separate geographic portion of the property. This separation can occur in a court action, resulting from a suit for partition, or in a voluntary action agreed upon by the cotenants. Where physical partition is not practical or wise, a court may order the sale of the entire property with a division of the proceeds between the parties.

Example _____

Alex, Betty, and Chris hold a joint tenancy, each having one-third interest in a lakefront piece of property. A dispute arises when the three cannot agree on its optimum use. Alex prefers a golf course; Betty, a driving range; and Chris, a marina. Because their goals are different, the three seek a physical partition of the land into three equal portions.

_____

Partition differs from severance. Severance does not alter undivided ownership but merely eliminates the element of survivorship. Following severance of their interests, joint tenants become tenants in common. There is no concurrent ownership after a partition.

Simultaneous Death in a Joint Tenancy

What happens if joint tenants die at the same time, for example in a car accident? The Uniform Simultaneous Death Act, the law in almost all states, provides that when joint tenants die under circumstances where the order of death is impossible to determine, courts will consider them as having died as tenants in common.

Tenancy by the Entirety

Tenancy by the entirety, a form of ownership specifically for married persons, is like joint tenancy in that the right of survivorship exists. However, unlike joint tenancy, one spouse cannot sever his or her interest in the property. Any conveyance requires the signatures of both spouses.

Example _____

Mr. and Mrs. Hayfield took title to a summer camp by deed that read: "To Harry and Joy Hayfield, husband and wife, as tenants by the entirety." After a couple of years of marital stress, Harry tried to sell the property. Because he could not get Joy's signature on the deed, releasing her right of survivorship, he could not convey a clear title to a new buyer.

A tenancy by the entirety may be terminated by a deed from one spouse to the other. It is also terminated when the marriage ends, as in divorce or annulment. The tenancy by the entirety ends with the death of one spouse as well, leaving the survivor with sole ownership.

In some states, a deed to a married person is automatically construed to create a tenancy by the entirety. In other states, the deed must designate that such a tenancy is intended: "To A and B Briggs, husband and wife, as tenants by the entirety with the right of survivorship." In still other states, this form of concurrent ownership has been abolished.

Risks of Joint Tenancy and Tenancy by the Entirety

A joint tenancy or tenancy by the entirety can occasionally result in an undesirable diversion of wealth to unintended recipients. Suppose that Elizabeth, after 40 years of marriage to Phillip predeceases him, leaving him widowed with four grown children, all of whom were born and raised at Eagles' Nest. Later, Phillip decides to remarry. Suppose that either his new bride, years his junior, persuades him that the family homestead should be in their joint names or they buy a new residence as tenants by the entirety, using the proceeds of the sale of Eagle's Nest.

If Phillip spends a great deal of money on this new residence, and he predeceases his new bride, her right of survivorship means she will take title to the entire value of the joint real estate. It may be the result Phillip intended; on the other hand, that asset is diverted from Phillip and Elizabeth's children through his bride's right of survivorship. When Phillip's bride dies, her heirs, not his, will take the property.

It is important for both purchasers to understand the implications of the title they hold in property: whether there is a right of survivorship and whether each has the power to decide by will who will inherit their interest in the event they should die.

Real estate brokers should understand the implications of each form of joint ownership and, if appropriate, suggest that the buyers consult with an attorney on how to take title. Advice of this nature is lawyer's work and should not be undertaken by a real estate agent.

Community Property

Several western and southwestern states have adopted the community property concept from their Spanish heritage. None of these states allows tenancy by the entirety. The community property concept recognizes the husband and wife not as a unity, but as individuals who may own property either separately or jointly. Community property laws recognize that, regardless of who earns the money, marriage is a joint venture and each spouse contributes equally. Therefore, acquisitions made with earnings during the marriage automatically become *community property*, each spouse owning an undivided one-half interest, regardless of the name on the title. A deed or mortgage of community property requires the signatures of both parties. One spouse can convey his or her one-half share to the other, making the property the sole holding of the other spouse. Also, each spouse can devise his or her share of the property at death because there is no right of survivorship.

Example ——————————————————————————————

Harold and Wendy own a $50,000 sailboat acquired during their marriage. Harold can assign his undivided one-half interest to Wendy, making the vessel entirely hers. If Harold decides to convey his one-half interest to his brother, Wendy can void the transfer if she did not sign it. If Harold and Wendy should ever divorce, they will automatically become tenants in common so that each spouse can dispose of the property as he or she desires. Because there is no right of survivorship, the death of either Harold or Wendy during the marriage would cause the deceased's one-half interest to go to his or her heirs or as directed by the deceased's last will.

Note that the principles of community property law apply to

both real estate and personal property and that property acquired before marriage, or during marriage by gift, inheritance, or will, is separate property.

Partnership Realty

Nearly all states have adopted the Uniform Partnership Act. According to this statute, when business partners become co-owners of specific partnership realty, each person holds as a tenant in *partnership*. The partners enjoy an equal and undivided right to the possession of partnership property, but only for the purposes of that partnership. Upon the death of a partner, his or her right to the partnership realty vests in the surviving partner or partners, with reimbursement to the estate of the value of the partnership share.

Example ────────────────────────────────

Mike and Peter, real estate brokers, form a partnership to go into business. For $100,000, they buy for the partnership a small office building, which they put in the business name M & P Realty. When Peter is killed in a plane crash a year later, his estate is entitled to one-half the value of the building. Pete's wife has *no* interest in the property, which would cloud the title. And Mike is not unjustly enriched by Pete's death.

───

A partnership interest may not be conveyed without the consent of the other partners, but a partner in the conduct of business may buy and sell real estate for the partnership.

CONDOMINIUMS AND COOPERATIVES

Many people today are moving away from traditional individually owned, freestanding houses and are choosing to live in *condominiums* and *cooperatives*. Statutes have been adopted in all states authorizing the creation of condominiums by defining new concepts in joint ownership.

Students will notice that, in the discussion of condominiums and cooperatives, the expressions *joint ownership* and *common ownership* are used. The words *joint* and *common* in this section of the chapter are not to be confused with joint and common tenancies. In referring to condominiums and cooperatives, the words *joint* and *common* mean multiple ownership, where many parties own and share parts of the same property.

Condominiums

Traditionally, the owner of a single-family home is the owner in fee simple of the land upon which it stands, and use of the house is merely one of the ways in which the person enjoys the use of the land. How do a condominium owner's rights differ from those of an ordinary homeowner?

An owner of a condominium, whether the unit is in a freestanding house or is a townhouse or an apartment, has a fee simple title to the unit—a 100 percent interest in the unit, but only a percentage interest in the common with the other unit owners in certain "common areas."

Example ───

Alex purchased a 12th-floor, two-bedroom condominium unit for $80,000. The value of this apartment was three percent of the total condominium complex. Alex's deed gives him a 100 percent fee simple absolute interest in his apartment and a three percent fee simple interest in the "common areas," which include the land, hallways, driveways, and tennis courts.

───

Although ownership rights are limited by statute, a condominium unit owner has the same rights as the owner of a single, freestanding home. That is, the unit owner can sell and devise the unit and the percentage interest in the common areas. The owner also can take advantage of tax laws that encourage home ownership.

One of the most important rights of the owner is the right to mortgage his or her unit. A mortgage on one unit in a condominium is totally independent of the titles and mortgages held by owners of the other units and can be enforced by foreclosure only against the one fee simple title to which it is attached. Should any one of the owners in a condominium complex be unable to meet the mortgage obligation, only his or her particular unit, and not any unit that is owned by another, can be taken and sold to satisfy the debt.

Because the owners in a condominium do share many responsibilities—maintenance, snow removal, painting, etc.—certain obligations are imposed collectively on the owners to ensure that the complex will run in the interests of all the owners. Most condominium agreements specify that all exterior maintenance of common areas in the complex will be the sole responsibility of the association, which is composed of all the owners. An individual owner is not free to make changes and improvements to the exterior of his or her own unit without the express authorization of either the association or its governing board or a certain percentage of the owners of the condominium. These restrictions, while they are meant to protect the interests of all the owners, can cause dissatisfaction, especially when individual aesthetic taste is involved, such as in the choice of paint colors, the erection of television antennas, or the planting of shrubs in the yard.

Another potential trouble spot is the decision by the association of owners to add improvements, such as a swimming pool; each unit owner will be compelled to pay a pro-rata share of the cost for any improvements whether or not he or she voted for the improvement itself. For many people, this final aspect of condominium ownership is its least attractive feature.

Cooperatives

Unlike traditional home ownership or ownership of a condominium, ownership of a cooperative does not include individual fee simple absolute title to a unit. Most frequently, ownership is achieved by the organization of the cooperative as a corporation. Upon its formation, the corporation acquires either a fee simple absolute title to or a long-term lease on an apartment complex. The organizers of the cooperative sell shares of the cooperative's corporate stock to interested buyers. Shares are allocated to each living unit according to a formula based on the value of a unit to the value of the entire complex. A buyer of a unit in a cooperative does not acquire title to a unit; instead, the buyer acquires ownership of the shares of the cooperative's stock allocated to a specific unit. Therefore, a unit owner in a cooperative is, in reality, not a unit owner at all but rather a *shareholder* in the corporation that owns the complex in which the unit is located.

As a part of the cooperative agreement, each shareholder automatically becomes entitled to a lease to the specific unit to which his or her shares of stock are assigned. This lease in turn gives the exclusive right to occupy a unit.

A co-op owner is somewhat like an owner of a condominium in that he or she lacks certain freedoms of the traditional homeowner. This lack of freedom occurs because all shareholders are interested in the operation and maintenance of the complex. Therefore, an individual cooperator may not, in most instances, make any major structural changes within a unit or change its exterior appearance without first obtaining the permission of the governing board.

Like any property owner, however, the owner of a cooperative acquires an owner's equity in the held shares of the cooperative's stock, and, should their market value increase, he or she will reap the profits at the time of sale.

While living in a well-run cooperative has many advantages, it also has some disadvantages. One major disadvantage of cooperative ownership is the undivided joint ownership and resulting financial interdependence of cooperators. The obligations of the corporation for property taxes, mortgage payments, and other expenses are the legal responsibility of the corporation only. To pay them, the corporation uses the maintenance fees paid by its cooperators. If some cooperators are unable to pay their fees, or if some units are unrented, the fixed obligations of the corporation become unpaid debts. Creditors can attach assets, force their sale, and thereby receive satisfaction of their claims. Although the creditors may not collect corporate debts from shareholders, individual cooperators may lose the money invested in stock in the event of corporate bankruptcy. In addition, as a part of the bankruptcy process, the cooperators' leases would be cancelled, and their rights to occupancy would be lost. The forcing of a cooperative corporation into liquidation because of uncollectible maintenance fees is a risk for the shareholder.

Another disadvantage is the right of the corporation to refuse to approve transfers of stock when a shareholder decides to move out. A potential purchaser of cooperative shares should always investigate the financial history and strength of a cooperative corporation before deciding to invest.

Timesharing

As the price of real estate has escalated, especially in the resort areas of Europe, real estate entrepreneurs have developed a new form of real estate ownership, called *timesharing* or *interval ownership*. In almost all respects, timesharing is comparable to condominium ownership. Each owner of a unit in a timesharing resort has sole ownership of his or her unit and yet shares ownership of common areas such as the hallways, lobbies, tennis courts, pools, golf courses, parking facilties, etc., as a tenant in common with other unit owners.

The significant difference between interval ownership and condominiums is that ownership is sold in units of time, usually a week. Thus, a purchaser might acquire the first two weeks in August for a resort in temperate climates and two weeks in February at a resort in the tropics. Resorts generally sell 50 weeks of time each year and close for two weeks for maintenance.

The 50 weeks are divided into three classes of desirability: high season when the demand for units is greatest, low season when demand is at its nadir, and shoulder time, weeks between high and low season. The price of the units varies according to the demand; many timesharing resorts will assist purchasers in the financing of their week or weeks.

The nature of the estate sold by timesharing resorts varies. Many resorts sell a fee simple interest in the unit for the week or weeks acquired. This allows the purchasers to leave it in their will to their heirs or whomever they wish. Other resorts sell weeks of time for a period of years, perhaps 20 years, after which the unit owners are given the option of purchasing their week outright in fee for an additional charge.

Additional privileges for timesharing owners are available. International clearinghouses have made it possible for unit owners to exchange their weeks with other unit owners worldwide. The lure of vacations in faraway places has become an important selling point for the timesharing industry.

The phenomenon of timesharing is growing rapidly in this country and in Europe. Whether or not licensees ever become involved with the marketing of timesharing, they will, as real estate professionals, undoubtedly be asked to explain it to a client at some point in their careers.

MARITAL PROPERTY RIGHTS

Although a married person is not precluded from holding property under his or her own name, the mere fact of marriage gives a spouse an interest in the realty individually held by the other. The existence of this marital property interest has implications of which brokers must be aware. Before a married person can sell his or her own real estate, he or she must secure the spouse's "release" of this marital property interest. This release is normally obtained by having the spouse "join" in the transfer of the property by cosigning the listing agreement, the purchase and sale contract, and the conveying deed.

This section of the chapter explains the nature and extent of the marital property interest today, as well as the methods by which it may be released. A background in the historical origin of the marital estate is also provided.

Estate by the Marital Right, Curtesy, and Dower

Under the common law of feudal times, a married woman's legal identity was merged into that of her husband; she was not permitted to acquire or dispose of any land. During marriage, her husband was entitled to the occupancy and profits of any land she may have owned. Her husband's interest in the possession and profits of her land was referred to as his *estate by the marital right*, which continued until the marriage ended in death or divorce.

The estate by the marital right lasted only as long as the marriage. However, if a child was born of the marriage, the husband's estate by the marital right was enlarged to an estate for his entire life so that, upon the death of his wife, he could continue to occupy the premises as a life tenant. This life estate, said to be granted to the husband "by the *curtesy* of England," attached to all of the land the wife held at any time during the marriage.

The common law also provided a widow with a means of support, maintenance, and security after her husband's death. *Dower*, as it was called, entitled the wife to a life estate in an undivided one-third of the realty that the husband held at any time during the marriage that was inheritable by issue. During her husband's life, the wife's right consisted solely of the possibility that she might outlive her spouse and become entitled to the dower interest. Until her death her dower was said to be *inchoate*. She could not sell her inchoate dower, nor could she be forced to pay her debts with it. The right was well protected; her husband could not defeat her dower by conveyance or will, nor could the interest be impaired by her husband's creditors upon his death. Her right of dower in land owned by her husband was released only when she joined in the sale of the property.

If she predeceased her husband, her dower right was automatically extinguished. If she survived her husband, her dower became consummate. However, one-third of the land held by her husband during their marriage, which was not released by her dower interest, was apportioned for her by relatives or by court order. She received a life estate in this land.

Example ────────────────────────────────

Henry and Wanda Smith were married in 1940. In 1945, Henry acquired a 40-acre tract that he sold in 1950 without the approval and signature of his wife. Brian, the buyer, resold the land to Sam Jones in 1960. Upon Henry's death in 1970, Wanda claimed her life estate in the one-third interest in the land to which dower entitled her. Sam had no recourse. Wanda's inchoate dower interest, which attached to the land when Henry purchased it, became an actual interest upon Henry's death.

Marital Rights Today

Today married men and women enjoy identical rights with respect to their own real estate—each may buy, sell, mortgage, inherit, and devise as freely as the other.

With the exception of most southern states, which continue to recognize the common law notions of curtesy and dower, many states have passed statutes that give a minimum percentage of the decedent's estate to the surviving spouse. Moreover, the property in many states comes to the survivor as absolute ownership, not as a life estate.

The extent of this marital property interest is determined according to the statute of descent and distribution, and the interest itself is often referred to as the spouse's *right of descent.* The exact percentage guaranteed under the rules of descent is calculated as if the deceased had died intestate, that is, without a valid will. Even if the deceased had drawn up a will, his or her spouse would be protected against exclusion from the will to the level established by the rules of descent.

The fact that the surviving spouse's right of descent attaches to all of the realty individually owned by the other at any time during marriage also means that a spouse must obtain a release of his or her spouse's right of descent to convey real estate free from that potential encumbrance.

Example ————————————————————

Mrs. Smith sells a piece of land that she holds in her own name to Murphy without first securing Mr. Smith's release of his right of descent. Murphy receives the property subject to Mr. Smith's potential claim of descent. If Mr. Smith survives his wife, he becomes entitled to a portion of Murphy's land.

Spousal release of right of descent usually is not a problem in selling real estate. In all but very few cases, a spouse will agree to release his or her right of descent so that a clear title can be conveyed to the purchaser. Normally, release is accomplished by securing the signature of the spouse with the right of descent on the listing agreement, the purchase and sale contract, and the conveying deed. Signature of release is also obtained when mortgaging property.

SUMMARY

The first two chapters explained the laws that define the different interests and estates in land that people may own. This chapter has explained the laws that define how more than one person may own the same parcel of property at the same time. Concepts of joint ownership, tenancy in common, and tenancy in partnership have evolved to meet the needs of persons who are living, working, or investing together. The law also has responded to changing needs with the creation of new land ownership concepts, especially the condominium, which enables people to live in apartment-type communities yet continue to take advantage of homeowner tax laws.

The feudal society in England provided for the social security of spouses through laws creating the rights of dower and curtesy. Today, the laws of our 50 states provide spouses with rights in the property of the other spouse through the laws of descent, another example of how two or more people can have rights in the same property.

It is important for real estate licensees to understand the various types of concurrent ownership and joint interests that can arise. Whenever land is sold, clear title can be delivered to a buyer only if all parties who have an interest have signed the deed.

MULTIPLE CHOICE QUESTIONS

1. If three individuals are joint tenants of a piece of property, and one of the joint tenants dies, the remaining two tenants take what was owned by the deceased because of:

    a. survivorship.
    b. unity of title.
    c. coparcenary.
    d. the intent of the common grantor.

2. If two parties are tenants in common, and one of the two dies, then:

    a. the property owned by the deceased is subject to the Simultaneous Death Act.
    b. the remaining cotenant takes through survivorship.
    c. the heirs of the deceased take what belonged to the deceased.
    d. none of the above

3. A, B, and C are joint tenants. C sells his interest to D. Which of the following is (are) true?

    a. A and B remain joint tenants.
    b. D stands as a tenant in common with A and B.
    c. Should D die, his heirs will stand as tenants in common with A and B.
    d. all of the above

4. Which of the following is (are) true?

    I. A joint tenancy must reflect the four unities.
    II. A joint tenancy can exist only between spouses.

    a. I only   c. Both I and II
    b. II only   d. Neither I nor II

5. Partners M, N, and O buy a shoe store. All three are married. When M dies, his surviving spouse will not get title to the store because of the:

    a. operation of common law dogma.
    b. Uniform Partnership Act.
    c. spouse not signing the deed.
    d. accepted practices in today's business community.

6. Abe owns an undivided interest in a piece of property with two other individuals, with no right of survivorship. Abe holds the real estate as a:

    a. year-to-year tenant.
    b. shareholder.
    c. tenant in common.
    d. joint tenant.

7. A person who owns in fee simple absolute an apartment in a building that has other unit owners is probably living in:

    a. a condominium.
    b. a cooperative.
    c. a mortgaged building.
    d. a subleased dwelling.

8. Should the owner of a unit in a condominium complex be unable to meet his or her mortgage payments, the bank's foreclosure action will:

    a. not affect the other owners in the condominium complex.
    b. force the other unit owners to come up with the money in order to protect their investment.
    c. become a liability of the condo developer.
    d. both A and C

9. The status of a person living in a cooperative is similar to that
    of:

    a. an ordinary tenant.
    b. a traditional homeowner.
    c. a fee simple title owner.
    d. a tenant in common.

10. Which of the following is (are) true?
    I. A unit owner in a condominium holds a percentage in-
        terest in the common areas as a joint tenant with the
        other unit owners.
    II. An owner of a week of timesharing holds a percentage
        interest in the areas in common as a tenant in common
        with the other owners of timesharing units.

    a. I only   c. Both I and II
    b. II only   d. Neither I nor II

11. In a condominium, who is responsible for paying property
    taxes?

    a. the individual unit owner
    b. the governing board
    c. the trustees
    d. all of the above

12. If a deed to two or more owners does not specify which type of
    co-ownership is created, the law presumes that the parties in-
    tended to create:

    a. joint tenancy.
    b. tenancy in common.
    c. tenancy by the entirety.
    d. unit ownership.

13. Tom, Dick, and Harry are brothers who own a beach resort motel as joint tenants, with the right of survivorship. While Tom and Dick are returning from a conference of motel operators on the West Coast, their plane crashes and they are killed; it is impossible to determine who died first. Who owns the motel?

    a. Harry
    b. Harry and the heirs of Tom and Dick
    c. the heirs of the brothers
    d. none of the above

14. A tenancy by the entirety may exist between:

    a. sisters.
    b. siblings.
    c. spouses.
    d. sons.

15. Which of the following types of co-ownership apply to spouses only?

    a. cooperatives and condominiums
    b. joint tenancy and tenancy in common
    c. freehold estates and remainders
    d. tenancy by the entirety and community property

DISCUSSION QUESTIONS

1. Emily and Julia are sisters. They live together, sharing expenses and income. They have agreed that when one dies all property will go to the survivor. Explain how they should hold title to real estate and why.

2. Assume that you are a licensed real estate broker and that you are showing a young, inexperienced couple a condominium and a cooperative. Explain to them the legal differences between these two forms of ownership.

3. Two brothers go into business together by purchasing an ice cream store. Should they hold title as joint tenants, tenants in common, or tenants in partnership? Discuss the differences and possible advantages of each form of ownership, taking into account their potential business objectives and family circumstances.

4

Easements, Profits, and Licenses

There are several ways in which a person may acquire a limited interest or right in land owned by another. The interests to be discussed in this chapter—easements, profits, licenses, and historical preservation easements—give flexibility to the ownership of land, enabling owners to manipulate the bundle of rights belonging to one parcel to make its use compatible with neighboring parcels. Each of the limited interests discussed in this chapter affords its owner certain privileges; each must be created and terminated in very specific ways.

Real estate brokers need to understand and be able to explain these miscellaneous property interests. For example, prospective homebuyers might ask for explanations about any utility easements, shared driveway agreements, or other restrictions that affect most residential real estate. The owner of a large parcel of shorefront property might ask for suggestions as to how to subdivide the parcel and still provide all new owners with access to a dock or beach. Someone who owns a property of historical significance may need to know how to protect the property's historic value and thereby maximize the potential sale price. While it is beyond the scope of this introductory text on real estate law to qualify the licensee to advise comprehensively on these and other matters, it is important for salespeople and brokers to understand the potential significance of these miscellaneous interests.

EASEMENTS

An _easement_ is a right to use the land belonging to another for some specific purpose.

Example ──────────────────────────────────────

A public utility company owns the right to lay pipes across a homeowner's front yard to supply water and gas. If the pipe breaks, the company can come onto the land, dig up the pipe, and repair it.

This is a _utility easement_. When showing property, a broker will explain to prospective buyers all utility easements affecting the property and explain their legal ramifications. For urban and suburban properties, typical utility easements will include those for water, sewer, electricity, and natural gas. Rural properties may have their own wells and septic systems and thus no easements for these utilities; however, they may have electrical and gas utilities.

There are two types of easements: _easement appurtenant_ and _easement in gross_.

Easement appurtenant

The term _appurtenant_ means "belongs to." An easement appurtenant is one that belongs to a parcel of land that benefits from the easement. The benefited land is called the _dominant tenement;_ the land burdened by the easement is referred to as the _servient tenement_.

Example ———————————————————————

Smith owns Lot 1 with frontage on Round Pond. He conveys an easement to Jones; who owns a back lot with no lake frontage, so Jones can reach the lake. Smith's land is the servient tenement, burdened by the easement; Jones's lot is the dominant tenement, which is benefited by the easement.

An easement appurtenant is so closely connected with the dominant tenement that it will pass with title to the dominant estate if the property is sold, even if the deed fails to mention the easement. The easement appurtenant "runs with the land," and whoever owns the dominant estate also owns the easement. When selling real estate, a broker must learn if the lot is benefited by or subject to any easements and be able to pass this information to prospective buyers.

Easement in Gross

An easement in gross does not benefit any piece of land; it exists independently of other land and is a personal right or privilege to use the land of another in some way. Thus, it has a servient tenement but no dominant tenement.

Example ———————————————————————

A couple is building a home on a vacant lot. They grant an easement in gross to the local electric company to install power lines from their poles on the street across their land to service their house. The vacant lot is subject to this utility easement. There is no parcel of land that is the dominant tenement; the beneficiary of the easement is the power company.

Commercial easements in gross are generally transferable; however, noncommercial easements in gross are transferable only if such intention is indicated at their creation. Most noncommercial easements in gross are construed to be exclusively personal in nature and thus nontransferable.

Creation of Easements

Express Grant

A landowner may create an easement over his or her land by *express grant* to another. Often the grant of an easement will be incorporated into a deed that also conveys land. Since an easement is an interest in land, a grant of an easement should contain all the formal requisites of a deed. It should be in writing, should sufficiently describe the easement and the land subject to it, and should be signed, acknowledged, and recorded in accordance with local rules governing deeds. No particular words are necessary to create an easement, but failure to comply with these formal requirements results in the creation of a revocable license, described later in this chapter, instead of an easement.

Example ————————————————

S owns Lots 1 and 2. He sells Lot 1 to Jones. After the property description in the deed, the following clause is inserted: "The grantor hereby conveys to Jones as an easement appurtenant to the premises a right-of-way across the southern ten feet of Lot 2 for purposes of ingress and egress to Lot 1." The deed thus conveys both ownership of Lot 1 and an easement appurtenant.

Reservation of an Easement

A landowner may, in conveying a portion of his or her land, reserve or except an easement in the conveying deed in favor of the land retained.

Example ————————————————

S conveys Lot 1 to Jones, "excepting or reserving an easement in the most easterly 12-foot strip to be used as a roadway to Lot 2, which S retains."

If, in the above example, the deed had stated "excepting a 12-foot strip running along the eastern boundary" (without the words of purpose), the court might construe the words as fee simple absolute exception rather than as an exception creating an easement. Words of purpose are crucial to the creation of an easement.

As with creation of easements by express grant, the local formal requirements respecting deeds must be followed in creating *easements by reservation* or exception.

Prescription

Easements may be created by long-continued use of another's land for a particular purpose. These easements are known as *easements by prescription.*

A prescriptive easement is acquired only by a continuous use for a certain period of years fixed by each state. The use must be adverse under a claim of right, which means simply that the user must be acting inconsistently with the property rights of the owner; the use must not be permissive. In addition, the use must be with the owner's knowledge and acquiescence or so open, notorious, and visible that knowledge and acquiescence will be presumed. Where the use has been open and notorious for the required number of years with the knowledge and acquiescence of the landowner, it will be presumed to have been adverse unless contradicted or explained.

Example ――――――――――――――――――――――――――――――――――――――

J has been walking across S's property to reach a public beach for 25 years. Such a use of S's lot is open and notorious, and thus J will be presumed to have used S's land adversely under a claim of right for that period of time. However, S can rebut this presumption by producing evidence that he had granted J oral permission to walk across his property to the beach.

The use must be continuous, but it need not be constant; repeated periodic acts or uses are sufficient so long as they are of a nature that the owner should reasonably be put on notice that his property is being used adversely. In the last example, even if Jones proceeded across Smith's land only on sunny summer days for the purpose of sunbathing, his use would be considered "continuous" if Smith should have recognized that use. The use must be with the owner's knowledge and acquiescence.

Anything that disproves acquiescence stops the running of the prescriptive period by rebutting the presumption that a grant was made.

Example

In the illustration above, S sends Jones a letter informing him that he will no longer be allowed to walk across his land to the beach. Smith no longer "acquiesces" to Jones's use of the land.

Similarly, if the landowner posts notice on the property of his or her intention to prevent the acquisition of an easement by prescription, the required element of acquiescence is lacking.

Implication

An *easement by implication* or necessity may be created by operation of law rather than by written instrument or continuous adverse use. These easements may be created when an owner conveys one or more lots out of a larger parcel of land and may be implied in favor of the grantor or grantee. They are based on the *presumed intent* of the parties at the time of the conveyance. In some states, an easement will be implied only if it is "strictly necessary" for the beneficial use of the land conveyed or retained.

Example

S owns two adjoining lots, both square, which form a rectangle from north to south. On the northern boundary of the lots is a public roadway; the south boundary borders on the Atlantic Ocean. To the east and west are other lots, privately owned. When S deeds the southern lot to J, J receives no implied easement over S's retained property to the roadway because J can exit by the Atlantic Ocean, and an easement here is not strictly necessary. Such an easement would be a mere convenience. Had J been totally landlocked, an easement of necessity would have been implied.

Note that some state courts have implied easements in cases where the grantor had made certain continuous use of the property before selling a portion of it. These courts infer that an easement permitting the continuation of the use was intended, particularly where it has been reasonably necessary to the enjoyment of the dominant tenement.

The Extent of Easements

The extent or scope of an easement depends upon its type: express, prescriptive or implied.

Express easements

In determining what uses are permissible under an express easement, one must first examine the language of the grant. If the uses are described in detail, the matter is resolved accordingly.

The uses to which an express easement are put may change with the normal development of the dominant estate. It is assumed that the parties intended the easement to meet the needs of the dominant estate not only at the time of its creation, but also in the future, to accommodate increased needs resulting from development of that land.

Example ───────────────────────────────

Sixty years ago, Smith granted an access right-of-way over his Lot 1 to Jones's predecessor in title. Jones may drive his automobile over this right-of-way today, even though his predecessor utilized a horse and buggy.

As a general rule, if the dominant estate is divided, each transferee acquires a right to use the easement appurtenant, provided that this use does not expand the burden on the servient estate beyond that contemplated at the creation of the easement.

Example ───────────────────────────────

S and J are adjacent landowners. S conveys to J an easement to draw water from a well located on his land. At the time of the conveyance, J is using his land as a private residence. J later divides his land and sells the uninhabited half to M. M builds a residence and wishes to draw water from S's well. If S and J could have contemplated such a division of J's land at the time of creation of the easement, M should be allowed to draw the water. If J had instead destroyed his house and erected a hotel, leaving an inadequate water supply for S, his use of the water would be prohibited as a surcharge or overburdening of the easement.

Prescriptive Easements

Where an easement has been created by prescription, courts are hesitant to enlarge the scope of its use. It is normally fixed by the use for which it was created. Recall the illustration of prescriptive easement above, in which J established an easement by prescription to the beach over S's land by his continuous use of a footpath for a period of 25 years. J claimed an easement by prescription. To establish this easement for all future owners of his land, he will, unless S willingly agrees that an easement has been created, go to court for a decree that the easement is valid.

Under such circumstances, a court might award J a decree stating that the easement is valid but only for use by pedestrians; the court would not enlarge the easement to permit cars and trucks to pass on a prescriptive easement established as a footpath.

Easements by Implication

In the case of implied easements by necessity, the extent of the necessity determines its scope.

The Termination of Easements

1. **Expiration.**   If an easement is created for a specific purpose, it expires when that purpose is accomplished. Similarly, an easement of necessity ends when its necessity ceases. Most easements, however, have potentially unlimited duration, and an affirmative act is required to extinguish them.

2. **Releases.** An easement may be terminated by written re-

lease from its owner to the owner of the servient tenement, so long as the release conforms to the formal requirements, i.e. as long as it is in writing, is signed by the owner of the easement, and is a proper conveyance of the rights.

3. Unity of Title. By definition, an easement is an interest in the land of another. If that other land is acquired by the owner of the easement, the easement is automatically merged into the dominant estate.

Example ——————————————————————————————

S has granted J, his nextdoor neighbor, a right-of-way. If J subsequently buys S's lot, the easement is extinguished because title to the two lots is merged into one owner. There is no longer a dominant tenement or a servient tenement; both lots are now one.

4. Abandonment. If the holder of an easement intends to abandon the easement and there is some act evidencing such intent, the easement may be extinguished.

Example ——————————————————————————————

J owns an easement to cross S's land to reach a lake. J has not used the easement in years and has surrounded his own property with a six-foot fence. His easement may be abandoned.

5. Estoppel. The legal doctrine of *estoppel* holds that anyone whose promise, or act leads other people to respond to their detriment must abide by the consequences of the misleading act or promise. Estoppel is a doctrine that the law applies in many situations, including the establishment and termination of easements.

Example ——————————————————————————————

Jones, the owner of the dominant estate, informs Smith, the owner of the servient estate, that he will no longer use the right-of-way over the easterly 20 feet of Smith's land. In reliance on Jones's statement, Smith builds a house on the very land that was subject to Jones's easement. In this case, Jones is barred or estopped from claiming he had an easement because Smith acted in reliance on Jones's statement that he would no longer use the easement.

Estoppel is the term that describes a legal defense or argument that S would make if J sued him to reopen the easement.

The doctrine of estoppel could also be used to create an easement.

Example ─────────────────────────────────────

John has a 2,000-acre dairy farm. Access to one of his pastures is difficult through his own property but much easier over the land of a neighbor. The neighbor gives John permission to cross his land. Over the years, John builds a dirt road, then a paved road, then some outbuildings in the distant pasture to which access is possible by the road only. John may have established an easement by prescription; the neighbor, because of his inaction over the period of time, may be barred, estopped from contesting the existence of the easement.

---

6. Prescription. Use by an owner of his land in a manner adverse to the interest of the easement holder can extinguish the easement; for example, permanently fencing off a right-of-way. For an easement to be extinguished by prescription, there must be a continuous and uninterrupted interference with the easement for the period of years required in the particular state.

PROFITS

An easement confers the right to use another's land; a *profit* grants the right to take away a particular substance from the servient land. Profits may be created only by express grant or by prescription, not by implication.

Example —————————————————————————————

S sells J the timber growing on Lot 1. J has a profit to extract the timber.

An *exclusive profit* gives its owner the sole right to take something from the land. The servient owner has no right to the substance, nor can he or she grant a right to anyone else. If a *nonexclusive profit* is conveyed, the grantor may utilize the substance or grant similar rights to others.

Example —————————————————————————————

Phillip and Elizabeth granted a profit to Sam's Sand and Gravel Company for ten years to take sand from the property. If they retained the right to take sand and gravel for their own use as well, the profit is nonexclusive. If only Sam's Sand and Gravel can take the stuff, then the company has an exclusive profit.

Like easements, profits may be either appurtenant or in gross. Unlike easements in gross, however, profits in gross are freely assignable.

Example —————————————————————————————

Smith, owner of sandy beach property, grants to Jones Cement Company an exclusive right to extract as much sand as the company wishes. Jones Cement Company now has an exclusive profit in gross, since the profit is not for the benefit of any particular piece of Jone's land. The profit may be sold by Jones.

Smith, owner of a lake, grants to Jones, owner of a camp on the lake, the privilege of drawing water from the lake for drinking and bathing purposes only. Jones has a nonexclusive profit appurtenant, since it aids in the use and enjoyment of his lakefront property as owner thereof. Smith may grant similar rights to others.

If the holder of a nonexclusive profit unreasonably increases the taking of water, timber, or cement beyond the intention in the original conveyance, the servient tenement is _surcharged_, and the profit is extinguished.

Example ─────────────────────────────

Smith grants Jones, owner of a private residence having several fireplaces, a nonexclusive right to take timber from his land. Jones enters the lumber business and sells Smith's timber commercially. The profit is extinguished because it is the presumed intent of the parties that Jones take only enough for the fireplaces.

Divisibility of Profits

1. Exclusive Profits. The courts normally infer an intention of the parties that an exclusive profit be divisible. Therefore, if the exclusive profit is in gross, it may be sold by its owner to others; if it is appurtenant, it passes to all owners of the dominant estate if that estate is divided. Often the inference of divisibility works to the benefit of the servient owner.

Example ─────────────────────────────

Smith grants Jones the exclusive right to remove timber from Subdivision 1. Smith is to receive a certain sum per board foot of extraction. Jones may divide this profit in gross between himself and another or others to the benefit, (in terms of compensation per board foot), of Smith.

2. Nonexclusive Profits. A nonexclusive profit in gross is *not* divisible. The grantor of such an interest retains the right to create similar rights in other persons. If the profit holder could divide the profit, he or she could create rights inconsistent with the grantor's retained rights. An attempt to divide a nonexclusive profit in gross may be treated as a *surcharge* that will extinguish the profit.

A nonexclusive profit appurtenant, like an exclusive profit appurtenant, passes with title to the dominant tenement, and where the dominant estate is divided, it normally may be used by each of the transferees. However, if the servient land is surcharged, the profit will be extinguished.

Example ————————————————————————————

Smith conveys to Jones, a neighboring householder, the right to take timber off his land. Some time later, Jones divides the land and erects 50 houses, all with fireplaces. He purports to assign the timber profit for the benefits of all 50 houses. The profit is extinguished unless it is limited to the amount of wood that Jones alone would have used so that Smith's land is not unduly burdened.

LICENSES

A *license* is simply permission to enter and do certain acts on another's land. It is revocable at the will of the licensor and is regarded by the courts as too slight to be considered an interest in land. Licenses may be created orally, in writing, or by failure of the parties to comply with the formalities necessary for the creation of an easement or profit. A license is automatically extinguished by the death of the licensee or by an attempt to transfer the license to someone else.

Example ————————————————————————————

Smith, a landowner, gives Jones permission to hunt and fish on his land. Jones has a license. Smith may change his mind and revoke permission at any time.

HISTORICAL PRESERVATION INTEREST

Some states have enacted statutes permitting nonprofit historical organizations to acquire preservation interests in properties of historical value. The nature and scope of this *historic preservation interest* are explicitly set out in a *preservation agreement,* which the owner of historic property signs voluntarily. The agreement may forbid certain activities that might alter the historic property's special character. For example, the stripping of ornamental wood may be prohibited. The agreement may require certain duties such as structural maintenance and landscaping.

Like easements, the preservation interest has potentially infinite duration, which is extremely important since it ensures the future historical integrity of properties that hold this interest. Any future owner of the property would have notice of the restriction because all preservation agreements are recorded at the registry of deeds.

Example

Smith is owner of a pre–Revolutionary War mansion. He voluntarily conveys a preservation interest to the local historical society and agrees to maintain the exterior of the building in its present condition. The historical society is entitled to inspect the building periodically to ensure compliance with the agreement, even after Smith sells the property to a new owner.

SUMMARY

This chapter introduced the concept of carving property rights from a fee simple to maximize the utility and hence the value of real property. Easements, profits, licenses, and historical preservation interests are among the most common legal tools that give landowners the flexibility to maximize use and enjoyment of their real estate.

Virtually every residential property that enjoys service by a public utility company or town water or sewer system is subject to an easement giving the company or municipality the right to maintain its service to the property. Easements may be created by formal grant and recorded in the registry of deeds. The recording gives future owners of the land formal notice of the existence of the easement and serves to make the easement permanent. Easements also may be created by continuous use over an extended period of time, or they may be created by necessity, as where there is no other access to the property.

While easements are legally enforceable rights to a limited use of land belonging to another, a license is merely permission to use someone else's land and can be revoked at any time the landowner changes his or her mind.

Profits are the right to harvest crops or take minerals from land belonging to another. A profit may, however, be limited by the parties' agreement. The owner of the profit may not take more from the land than the agreement permits.

Many states have enacted statutes that permit a homeowner to convey rights to a nonprofit historical preservation group. The owner of the historical preservation interest rights can force any subsequent owner of the fee to maintain the property according to historical standards.

MULTIPLE CHOICE QUESTIONS ————————————————

1. Which of the following is (are) true?

    I. An easement is an interest in land that may be created by express grant in a deed.
    II. The extent of a prescriptive easement is normally limited to use made of the property over a required statutory period.

        a. I only   c. neither I nor II
        b. II only   d. both I and II

2. Parties who wish to create an easement appurtenant but do not comply with the formal requirements in fact are creating

        a. a profit.
        b. an easement in gross.
        c. a license.
        d. none of the above

3. Which of the following is (are) true?

    I. When a parcel of land with an easement appurtenant is conveyed, the grantee who is unaware of the easement will not be entitled to its benefits because of the doctrine of estoppel
    II. An owner of historical property in some states may grant a preservation interest to a local historical society, after which the society can regulate the manner in which the landowner uses and maintains the property so that none of the historical value will be lost.

        a. I only   c. neither I nor II
        b. II only   d. both I and II

4. Which of the following is (are) true?

    I. A profit is automatically extinguished when the owner takes more of the particular substance than was intended in the original grant.

   II. A license to hunt on someone else's land may be transferred by the hunter to a friend.

     a. I only   c. neither I nor II
     b. II only   d. both I and II

5. Sam has an easement across Ned's land for drawing water at a nearby spring. Sam's house, of course, has running water. Sam buys Ned's land in 1978; in 1980, Sam conveys his former lot to Anne but keeps Ned's lot. The broker should tell Sam that:

     a. Anne will have no easement to draw water.
     b. Anne will automatically receive his former easement.
     c. Anne has a prescriptive easement.
     d. none of the above

6. For several years, neighborhood youngsters have crossed your backyard to reach their school bus stop. You like children and therefore have not opposed this. The law recognizes the youngsters' right to pass as:

     a. a revocable license.
     b. an easement in gross.
     c. an easement by implication.
     d. an easement appurtenant.

7. Which of the following is (are) true?

   I. An easement will always be implied from a conveyance so long as the grantor has made a particular use of the land on a continuous basis prior to the transfer of title.

  II. The scope of extent of a prescriptive easement is normally limited to the adverse use made of the property over a required statutory period.

    a. I only   c. neither I nor II
    b. II only   d. both I and II

8. An easement may be terminated by

    a. written release to the grantor of the easement.
    b. prescription.
    c. acquisition of the servient tenement by the owner of the dominant estate.
    d. all of the above

9. Which of the following is (are) true?

   I. A nonexclusive profit appurtenant is divisible by the grantor.

  II. A license is a strictly personal right that may be revoked at any time at the grantor's will.

    a. I only   c. neither I nor II
    b. II only   d. both I and II

10. A license may be terminated:

    a. orally.
    b. by the death of the licensee.
    c. by the death of the licensor.
    d. all of the above

11. When a landowner sells Blackacre, which has an easement appurtenant across Greenacre, the new buyer

    a. must talk to the owner of Greenacre to purchase the same easement.
    b. acquires the easement appurtenant automatically.
    c. acquires the easement appurtenant only if the deed so provides.
    d. none of the above

12. When a landowner sells Blackacre, which is subject to an easement which benefits Greenacre, the buyer acquires Blackacre

    a. free of the burdensome easement.
    b. subject to the easement.
    c. subject to the easement only if the deed so provides.
    d. none of the above

13. The easement of a water company to maintain water pipes to a building is an example of

    a. an easement in gross.
    b. an easement appurtentant.
    c. a license.
    d. an exclusive profit

14. John owns a house with a garage on a small lot. To reach the garage, his driveway crosses land of his neighbor, a right created by the developer of the subdivision. John has an easement

    a. appurtenant.
    b. by prescription.
    c. by necessity.
    d. in gross.

15. John's lot, described in the question above, would be character-
    ized as the

    a. dominant tenement.
    b. servient tenement.
    c. prescriptive tenement.
    d. none of the above

DISCUSSION QUESTIONS

1. Myrtle Myers, a client you have helped buy a 125-year-old
    townhouse, is considering conveying a preservation interest to
    the local historical society and asks you to explain the conse-
    quences. Give her a general outline of what she can expect.

2. A client, Andy Anders, is thinking of selling the rights to re-
    move oak trees from his farm. Advise him as to the varying
    consequences of granting an exclusive or nonexclusive profit.

3. Jones granted Smith an easement to cross the Jones property
    to fish in a lake. Several years later, Smith said that his wife
    refused to cook fish ever again, so he wouldn't be using the
    road. Jones subsequently built a garage that extended over the
    road. Smith conveyed his property to Elliott, suggesting that
    the premises include the easement. Discuss whether or not
    Jones will have to move his garage.

5

Zoning
and Other Limitations
on Land Use

KEY TERMS
---

affirmative covenant
benefited land
building codes
burdened land
Clean Air Act
certificate of occupancy
Coastal Zone
   Management Act
eminent domain
housing code
National Environmental
   Policy Act
negative covenants
Noise Control Act

nonconforming use
Occupational Safety and
   Health Act
permitted use
prohibited use
property tax
restrictive covenant
special exceptions
tax base
variance
Water Pollution
   Control Act
zoning

In colonial times, landowners could generally make whatever use of their land they wanted. Unoccupied land to the "west" was seemingly limitless, and the sparse population was so widely dispersed that what owners did with their land had little impact on the lives of their neighbors. Even into the early years of the 20th century, cities and towns had relatively small populations and plenty of vacant land; development, whether of a residential or commercial nature, was welcomed.

However, with rapid growth of cities and towns from the 1950s on, people began to realize that uncontrolled development led to undesirable results. Homeowners, for example, found their houses surrounded by industrial and commercial buildings, while owners of factories located in residential areas began experiencing opposition to their plans for expansion. With this increasing need for planning, public and private mechanisms for controlling, limiting, and channeling growth evolved.

Public mechanisms for controlling landowners' use of their property are inherently part of the government's *police power,* the right of government to act for the welfare of society as a whole. Perhaps the most visible exercise of the police power to regulate land use is *zoning*; that is, designating different parts of a town or city for development as residential, commercial, or industrial.

Other examples of police power include *eminent domain*, the right of government to take private property for a public purpose; the right to enact building codes establishing minimum construction standards for the safety of the inhabitants; environmental laws governing clean air and water and noise limitations; and the power to tax property owners.

With the development need for planning, states passed zoning enabling acts, which empowered local communities to adopt zoning ordinances to control growth by restricting or limiting the uses property owners could make of their land.

Private land use restrictions also evolved to limit and control the use of land. Private limitations are those imposed by individual landowners through the creation of limited fee estates discussed in Chapter 2, through easements discussed in Chapter 4, and through the use of private deed restricitons and covenants, to be covered in this chapter.

Anyone concerned with the sale or lease of residential, commercial, industrial, or undeveloped property will need to understand and be able to explain to prospective buyers both the public and private restrictions that affect land being listed and sold. The following sections of this chapter describe the most commonly used restrictions on land use.

PRIVATE RESTRICTIONS

A *covenant* is a promise one landowner makes to another regarding the use of the land. As a result, the burdened owner's use of the property is limited. Covenants fall into roughly the same classifications as do easements and profits. The promise may be *affirmative*, whereby the landowner is required to perform a particular act, or *negative*, whereby the landowner must refrain from using land in a certain way. *Restrictive* or negative covenants such as the one in the following example are more prevalent.

Example

S and J are adjoining hillside landowners. Smith; situated below, promises to Jones that he will not construct a house higher than 20 feet above his building pad so the Jones's view will not be impaired. J pays $2,000 for this promise. The covenant is made and conveyed in the format of a deed and recorded in the registry of deeds so that S's land is subject to a covenant that restricts his use of land.

Covenants may be created only by an express grant that conforms to the formal requirements of deeds. A buyer who accepts a deed with a restriction agrees that he or she will limit the use of the newly acquired land as agreed for the benefit of the grantor. For example, the buyer will agree to use the property solely for residential purposes. Between the grantor and grantee a contractual relationship is established, and if the grantee violates the covenant in some way, the grantor may enforce the promise by bringing a legal action.

Like the dominant and servient tenements of easements and profits, covenants have *benefited* and *burdened land*. The promisor/grantee normally incurs a burden on the land, while the promisee/grantor receives a benefit.

Covenants can be written to limit the use of a parcel to conform to almost any plan of the seller. Examples of common covenants include agreements to build a house exceeding a certain value, to join a neighborhood association, to refrain from cutting trees and shrubs, to restrict a house to a certain elevation, and to have the seller approve the design of a house to be built.

Example

Arthur owns a large tract of land, half of which he sells to B. In the deed is a restrictive covenant prohibiting B from raising pigs on the parcel he buys. When B later sells the land to C, C is also bound by the restrictive covenant not to raise pigs. The restriction attaches to and passes with the land. Arthur's parcel is the benefited parcel; C's parcel is burdened because a possible use of the property is prohibited.

The most widespread use of the private covenant today is in land development. For example, a land developer will dedicate an entire 30-acre subdivision to residential housing. When the developer filed his plan for the subdivision, showing all the lots, he would also record the restrictions that would affect the entire subdivision: "Each home to be constructed on lots in this subdivision must be at least 2,300 square feet in size." As the developer conveys each lot to an individual buyer, the deed contains the restriction, and the law permits any buyer of a lot within the subdivision to enforce the restriction against all other purchasers of lots in the development. It would not be fair for one person to buy a lot and build a cheap 800-square-foot home in a neighborhood that was designed for more majestic housing.

When all of the lots in the subdivision have been conveyed in this manner, the entire area is effectively *restricted* to homes of this size. Because the restriction is spelled out in each deed and because the deed is recorded in the registry of deeds, as discussed in Chapter 10, each purchaser knows that the use of the land is subject to the restriction.

Termination of Covenants

Covenants that are not limited in time may last forever; however, occasionally convenants may be terminated in the same ways that easements may be terminated. For example, if the titles to the parcels of benefited land and burdened land come into the hands of one person, the merger extinguishes the covenant.

If a developer abandons a plan to create residential housing, any promises that were secured become unenforceable.

Example ───────────────────────────────────

S, a land developer, conveys Lots 1–5 in a 40-lot subdivision sub-ject to a restriction to residential use. He then conveys Lots 6–18 without any restrictions. S has abandoned the neighborhood scheme, and the restriction on the first five grantees is unen-forceable.

───

Similarly, if the character of the restricted neighborhood has changed so substantially that it is no longer possible to secure the benefits of the restrictions to a substantial degree, the cove-nent may be deemed inoperative.

Example ───────────────────────────────────

In 1950, a land developer placed residential restrictions on a 40-acre parcel of land. Over 20 years' time, the restrictions were ig-nored, and incompatible, nonresidential uses including a gas station, restaurant, and several retail establishments—were lo-cated within the block. Smith wishes to open a variety store on his lot. Jones sues to enforce the covenant that the land can be used for residential purposes only. The court may rule that the change of conditions in the neighborhood has effectively terminated the covenant.

───

Some states have statutes whereby covenants terminate auto-matically after a period of years unless they are formally renewed.

PUBLIC RESTRICTIONS

Although an individual may have complete ownership of a piece of land in fee simple absolute, the government also has the power to control the use of that property. The state's power in-cludes the right to tax, to enact zoning ordinances and building and housing codes, to exercise the right of eminent domain, and to enforce environmental protection regulations. The govern-ment's power supersedes an individual's control of his or her property.

Zoning

Recognizing that growth and development should be controlled, officials of cities and towns began developing plans to regulate land use within municipal boundaries in the early 20th century. In 1926, the Supreme Court ruled that communities could control land use by passing zoning ordinances that were aimed at reasonably improving the general health, safety, or welfare of the citizenry.

Today, zoning and regional planning regulations are common throughout the country. In all states, the legislatures have passed land use control laws authorizing cities and towns to develop comprehensive development plans and to adopt zoning ordinances to provide for the general welfare of their inhabitants.

This section will explain the reasons for zoning and the ways in which communities may be zoned. How zoning ordinances operate, including the way decisions affecting a landowner's use of land may be appealed and the significance of special-use exceptions and variances, will also be covered.

Development of the Zoning Ordinance

All states have enacted legislation authorizing municipalities to develop a comprehensive plan. A comprehensive plan is an assembly of maps, data, policy statements, and standards prepared by a planning board that sets guidelines for housing, land use, resource use, transportation, and other municipal concerns. When completed, the comprehensive plan consists of a package of interrelated plans, including a zoning ordinance, a community facilities plan, air and water pollution plans, and a park or open-space plan. Zoning is simply one of the tools used to reach the goals of the comprehensive plan.

The zoning process begins with the creation of a planning board, appointed by a local legislative body such as the town council. The local planning board takes an inventory of every parcel of land within the town boundaries. After considering such factors as population growth and density, availability of municipal services, and growth patterns of the area, the planning board assembles a first-draft zoning plan and submits it to the city or town council for review.

After reviewing the proposed plan and conducting public hearings for feedback from the community residents, the council returns the plan to the planning board with comments and suggestions for change. When the plan has been revised and meets the final approval of the council, it is formally adopted as the land use law of the community. One of the principal aims of zoning is to ensure the future isolation of incompatible uses. To do so, most municipal zoning ordinances established zoning districts. They are typically:

1. residential;

2. commercial;

3. rural/agricultural;

4. industrial.

For each of the districts, the zoning ordinance contains regulations that may specify:

a. permitted uses;

b. special exceptions;

c. prohibited uses;

d. minimum lot size requirements;

e. minimum yard requirements;

f. general requirements;

g. nonconforming uses.

The following paragraphs describe how these regulations operate.

Permitted uses. Uses listed under this heading in the district regulations section of the ordinance are *permitted* "as of right." An applicant for a building permit must be given the permit if the use is permitted and he or she meets the other regulations pertaining to the district, such as lot size, yard, and setbacks. Thus, the owner of residential property will receive a building permit for the construction of a family home as long as the owner conforms with the other regulations affecting residentially zoned property.

Suppose, instead, that an owner wanted to construct a private club on residential property. The district regulations state that a private club is not a permitted use within the district. In such a case, a prospective builder would probably apply for a special exception.

Special exceptions. A _special exception_ is a use that would not be appropriate to allow as of right in the zoning district. If controlled as to number and location, however, it would be both compatible with neighboring uses and of convenience or necessity to the permitted uses. A municipality, for example, might wish to permit hospitals in residential zones as special exceptions rather than face the possibility of too many hospitals if they were permitted as of right.

Zoning ordinances provide for special exceptions to ensure that plans for growth and development will be flexible enough to meet the changing needs of the community. Thus, just as an ordinance would list permitted uses for each district, it might list special exceptions for each district.

In the example above, the owner might receive a building permit for a private club because "a private club on at least five acres" is one of the special exceptions for the district. However, the local board will grant the permit only if the owner can prove that such a club is convenient or necessary to the neighborhood and is compatible with existing uses. In addition, the board might require the owner to meet certain other requirements; for example, the structure might have to be a particular size or height, or it might have to be built on the edge of the district.

Note that, unlike the case of permitted uses, the board does not have to issue a permit just because the owner's use is listed in the ordinance. The board will look at each application for a special exception on a case-by-case basis and will issue a permit only if it decides that the use is convenient or necessary and is compatible with existing uses.

Prohibited uses. Some ordinances contain absolute prohibitions against certain uses in an incompatible district. Single-family residences being completely forbidden in commercial districts and industrial plants being completely prohibited in residential districts are examples of *prohibited uses*.

Minimum lot size requirements. Zoning ordinances usually contain provisions for minimum lot sizes for residences or structures to be built on any lot within a district. The minimum lot size will vary from district to district and from town to town.

Minimum yard requirements. Zoning ordinances usually contain provisions for depth of front and rear yards and width of side yards. Like minimum lot sizes, these will vary from district to district and from town to town.

General requirements. Unlike the district regulations discussed, general regulations do not vary; they apply to all districts within a given municipality. A typical zoning ordinance would contain general regulations relating to such activities as excavation of minerals, posting of signs, off-street parking, water recreation, and storage facilities, as well as to subdivision and cluster development.

Nonconforming uses. When an existing town enacts a zoning ordinance to control its future growth, the ordinance will identify certain areas as single-family residential, others as multifamily residential, some as retail, others as industrial, etc. At the time of adoption, there are likely to be certain properties that do not conform to the zoning law as written. For example, there may be a two-family home in an area that is zoned for single-family residences, or there may be a convenience store in a residential area. These are examples of *nonconforming uses*, a technical term for properties whose incompatible use predates the adoption of the zoning law.

Nonconforming uses are *grandfathered* under new zoning laws, which means that their current use may be continued, in fairness to the current owners. However, the right to the nonconforming use is lost if that use should ever terminate. If a nonconforming two-family residence were ever converted to a single-family home, the property could never be reconverted to use as a two-family. Similarly, if a nonconforming corner convenience store were destroyed by fire, the property would thereafter be classified as residential.

Operation of the Zoning Ordinance

The mere existence of a municipal zoning ordinance does not ensure compliance by local landowners. Ordinances provide for enforcement and interpretation by a zoning officer, or the code enforcement officer (CEO) as he is called in some places, and the zoning board of appeals.

The zoning officer. This administrative official enforces the zoning ordinance on a day-to-day basis—answering questions, interpreting the zoning map, maintaining records, and carrying out the decisions of the board of appeals. In addition to keeping a current copy of the official zoning map and text, the *zoning officer* may also maintain detailed maps of nonconforming uses, special exceptions, and variances for quick reference and effective enforcement. Other records detailing such variables as population density and street and sewer plans may also be kept.

The building permit application is the CEO's primary enforcement tool. Each application for a building permit is reviewed to make sure that all district and general regulations are met. If the application is for a permitted use and all the requirements are met, then the CEO will issue the building permit. The CEO will deny each application for special exception, enlargement of nonconforming use, or variance and will refer the application to the board of appeals for review. A landowner who has been denied a particular use by the CEO may also attempt to convince the town council to amend the ordinance to permit the proposed use.

Periodically, all uses authorized by the CEO or the board of appeals are inspected. After a structure is completed, the CEO will conduct a final inspection to make sure that the structure conforms to all regulations and issues a *certificate of occupancy* if all conditions and requirements have been satisfied. Occupancy of the structure without receipt of the certificate of occupancy is illegal. In addition, if a citizen complains of a particular violation of the ordinance, the CEO will investigate the allegation and initiate the proper legal action if a violation is not corrected.

The zoning board of appeals. This supervisory board is created to deal with specific conflicts as they arise by hearing appeals cases. Thus, any interpretation of the ordinance by the CEO is appealable to the *board of appeals.* However, the most important and controversial prerogative of the board is its power to grant a variance from the zoning law, a process described below.

• *Appeal of special-exception application.* Almost every zoning ordinance contains a provision that authorizes the board of appeals to issue use permits for particular purposes such as public utility structures, hospitals, churches, and cemeteries if the proposed use is compatible with the present use of the area. Most ordinances list allowable special exceptions in the district regulation section. Obviously, uses of this sort must be located somewhere, but discretion must be exercised by the board to minimize the adverse effects on neighboring property owners. The decision as to whether a particular special exception should be granted is left for the zoning board of appeals on a case-by-case basis. Some zoning ordinances provide specific guidelines and standards that aid the board in reaching a conclusion. Others offer no guidance and open the door to attacks of arbitrariness, favoritism, and self-service by adversely affected citizens. A special-exception proposal may be approved outright or may be approved subject to certain conditions.

• *Appeal of variance application.* Even a well-written zoning ordinance may cause unintentional hardship to certain tracts of land. In such cases, the board of appeals may exercise discretion and allow a <u>variance</u> in the strict terms of the ordinance. This adjustment device should be utilized sparingly, or the zoning plan soon may be in shambles. Some boards have used this device extensively to, in effect, amend the ordinance, even though amendment of the zoning ordinance is the responsibility of the town council, not the board of appeals.

Amendment of the Zoning Ordinance

No zoning ordinance can be drafted that will satisfy the requirements of a developing community forever. Zoning is a continuing process, and zoning ordinances and the comprehensive plans of which they are a part are meant to be revised periodically.

Normally, amendments are adopted by the town council upon the recommendation of the planning board. The council will amend ordinances cautiously and only after a full consideration of the numerous factors involved.

Plans for land use may be subject to local, regional, or state regulations, which may have substantial effects on a broker's transactions. Knowing that the local zoning ordinances prohibit the type of use a buyer is contemplating, or knowing that plans for development or subdivision of land require approval of the board of environmental protection or, in some cases, the approval of the municipality may save the principal and the sales agent both time and money.

It is not important to memorize a local zoning ordinance or the regulations concerning subdivisions. It is important to know *when, where,* and *how* to get the information needed to assist clients and/or buyers in their land use plans.

Building and Housing Codes

Like zoning, the government has the rights under the police power to regulate health, safety, and general welfare, to enact and enforce building and housing codes concerning private property.

Building Codes

Building codes regulate safety by setting standards for materials to be used in construction. The state or municipality may set up standards for plumbing, electrical wiring, load and stress, ventilation, number of exits, types of structural materials, and so on. Sometimes wiring and plumbing requirements are set forth in separate codes.

Enforcement of the codes is achieved through the permit system. Before a new structure can be built, the contract must apply for a building permit. When the applicant demonstrates that code specifications will be met, a permit is issued. Inspectors check during construction to see that codes are being observed. Finally, the contractor must obtain a certificate of occupancy before allowing the new building to be used.

Housing Codes

Housing codes seek to enforce minimum standards in existing dwellings. The codes set out requirements for sanitation, repair, space per person, ventilation, heat, fire protection, and other comfort and safety provisions. Some states have enacted codes for statewide application; most cities adopted codes after the enactment of the Housing Act of 1954, which required cities to have codes to be eligible to apply for federal urban renewal assistance.

Power of Eminent Domain

Eminent domain is the power of federal, state, and local governments to take property and convert its use for the public welfare.

Example

Fred owns a farm along a riverbank. The public power company decides that a hydroelectric dam would serve the public good by reducing consumer charges, and it chooses a site downstream from Fred's acreage. Although the utility has the power to effectively "take" Fred's property by flooding it with the new dam, Fred must be fairly compensated.

Land may be acquired through eminent domain for public purposes such as schools, parking, highways, parks, and urban renewal. Licensed public utilities such as electric power companies, telephone companies, natural gas companies, and railroads can also obtain property through use of eminent domain proceedings. The constitution provides that there shall be compensation for the taking of property for public purposes.

Power of Taxation

Another public limitation on an individual's property ownership is the government's right to tax. This power traces its history to the feudal lord's right to demand contributions from his tenants for community defense and other benefits they received from using the king's lands. Today, local governments act under delegated powers of the state to impose *property taxes* to provide for local services. Local property taxes are an important source of revenue for such community services as schools, libraries, parks, and police and fire departments.

A property owner pays these taxes according to the property's assessed value and the municipality's tax rate. In some localities, assessed values are related to market values, whereas in other localities a fractional system is applied.

Example ───────────────────────────────

John Smith owns a home with an assessed value of $50,000. The market value is $100,000. The local tax rate is $30 for every $1,000 of assessed valuation, or 30 mills, making Smith responsible for an annual property tax of $1,500.

───────────────────────────────

The mill rate is determined by first evaluating the community's *tax base*, which is the total value of all property in the community. City officials then estimate the amount of money required to provide local services for the year. Say the tax base is $100 million, and the amount necessary to operate municipal services is predicted to be $3 million. The mill rate results from dividing the amount required by the amount of the tax base. In this case 30 mills, or $30 for every $1,000 of assessed valuation, is the resultant figure.

The power to tax carries with it the power to seize property for which taxes have not been paid. The local government can then sell the property to realize the unpaid taxes, as discussed in Chapter 8.

Environmental Controls

It is estimated that in the United States the land, with its buildings and improvements, accounts for 75 percent of the country's wealth. The federal, state, and local governments have recognized that real estate is a significant economic resource and have enacted laws promoting sound land use policies to protect the environment.

A broker, especially when dealing with commercial and industrial property, must be well-informed of such laws in order to explain restrictions on the use of land to potential purchasers.

Example ──

Ricardo approaches Bob Broker about buying a vacant riverside factory to set up a small, self-contained furniture plant. In discussing financing and total cost of converting the structure, Bob reveals to Ricardo the effects of local, state, and federal environmental and workplace laws. For example, noise from shaping the metal frames must be controlled. No wastes from fabric treatment can go into the river. Air pollution laws influence the use of chemicals for processing fabrics. In addition, other federal and state standards will demand that certain measures be taken to provide a safe and healthful job site for workers.

National Environmental Policy Act

Passage of the 1969 *National Environmental Policy Act* (NEPA) was the first step in a series of acts to control the impact of a development project on the environment. The NEPA applies to federal actions such as construction projects, highway building, pest control, waste disposal, and even federally permitted major private projects if they will significantly affect the environment. NEPA requires developers of these projects to file *environmental impact statements* with the Federal Council on Environmental Quality. The statements will help the council weigh the benefits against the drawbacks of a project being considered. For example, if a major housing development is being planned, its effects on energy consumption, sewage systems, school population, drainage, water facilities, and other environmental, economic, and social factors must be estimated. Where a proposed project is found to have an adverse impact on the environment, the project will not be approved.

Many states have passed statutes patterned on the NEPA.

These laws, sometimes called *little NEPAs*, require states and sometimes individuals to file environmental impact statements.

Clean Air Act

Several acts passed since 1969 have detailed measures to ensure other kinds of preservation. In 1970, the *Clean Air Act* gave states the responsibility of controlling air pollution within their boundaries. The state measures must be acceptable to the federal Environmental Protection Agency. Air pollution control, of course, is a limitation on land use. Air quality that is above national standards may not be allowed to deteriorate because of any proposed project. A broker should be able to inform clients of local clean air standards.

Federal Water Pollution Control Act

In 1972, additional environmental laws were enacted. The federal *Water Pollution Control Act* was amended to restore chemical, biological, and physical cleanliness to the nation's waters. Primary goals of the act are to protect wildlife, to prohibit discharge of toxic wastes, and to give assistance to waste treatment plants. A permit is now required for everything that goes into a navigable stream from a point source. States may administer the permits so long as their standards are as high as federal standards.

Noise Control Act

The *Noise Control Act*, also passed in 1972, required the EPA to set noise pollution standards that cannot be violated by federal projects. Airplane noise was a major target, but other noise pollution is included. For example, any project using federal funds may not be built near a facility where noise exceeds federal standards.

Coastal Zone Management Act

The *Coastal Zone Management Act* was also passed in 1972. States having shorelines were encouraged by federal matching funds to preserve and protect their coastal areas. The act has had a great effect on real estate use because the use of both the public and private oceanfront and Great Lakes shoreline is governed by applicable standards. The state must consider ecological, historic, and aesthetic preservation when reviewing an application for use of shoreline property.

Occupational Safety and Health Act

Another federal law that can significantly affect a purchaser's use of property is the *Occupational Safety and Health Act* of 1970 (OSHA). The act provides health and safety standards for employees in their work environment.

It applies to three-quarters of the civilian labor force and empowers the secretary of labor to set mandatory health and safety standards for the workplace, to encourage research and training to prevent accidents, and to enforce the standards. States are encouraged to take the responsibility for enforcement of the law; severe criminal penalties may result from breaches of standards.

When a broker is dealing with industrial or commercial property, knowledge of OSHA standards is very helpful. If a purchaser were planning to convert a warehouse to industrial use, for example, and that warehouse had an asbestos covering on the ceiling, the broker should be able to advise the client of the significant expense, over and above the cost of purchasing the building, that would be required to meet OSHA standards for a safe workplace.

State Laws

In addition to state versions of the federal acts such as NEPA and OSHA, states have enacted other laws concerning sanitation, safety, and environmental control. These limitations on property use should be familiar to the broker.

SUMMARY

When the New World was colonized in the 1600's, the abundance or resources, particularly land, meant there was little need for restrictions on land use. By the late 1900's, population densities had radically changed that situation creating a great need for land use laws. Licensed real estate brokers and salespeople should be able to explain the limitations that will affect the use of property under consideration for purchase.

Limitations on land use may be private, in the form of convenants, or public, such as local zoning ordinances and building and housing codes. Every broker's office should have the local zoning maps and regulations available as a reference tool, and a careful agent would check the zoning district of listed properties. Federal laws also limit land uses to those that are safe, clean, and quiet—in other words, compatible with environmental conditions.

Governments have a responsibility to protect the public welfare and have the power to take a private landowner's property or tax it to pay for public services. The competent real estate broker will understand all these limitations on land use and will be able to find out whether a piece of real estate conforms to the law.

MULTIPLE CHOICE QUESTIONS ————————————————

1. Which of the following is (are) true?

    I. Zoning is an example of the police power of government.
    II. Deed covenants are enforced by the Code Enforcement Officer of the town where the affected land is located.

       a. I only
       b. II only
       c. neither I nor II
       d. both I and II

2. Samuel, owner of a hillside tract of land, conveys the lower half to Shelley. There is a restrictive covenant in Shelley's deed preventing her from building a house over 20 feet tall. Five years later, Shelley, having built no house, reconveys the land to Samuel. Which of the following is true?

       a. Merger of the two tracts of land extinguishes the covenant.
       b. Samuel or his subsequent grantee will be bound by the covenant.
       c. If Shelley's deed reconveying to Samuel did not contain the covenant, it may be extinguished.
       d. none of the above

3. Which of the following is (are) true?

    I. Land may be acquired through the power of eminent domain for private uses such as paper mills and gas stations.
    II. When land is taken through the power of eminent domain, the government and the landowner may reach an out-of-court agreement on compensation.

       a. I only
       b. II only
       c. both I and II
       d. neither I nor II

4. Which of the following is (are) true?

   I. The community tax base is the valuation of all industrial and commercial property in the municipality.
   II. The power to tax gives a local government not only the right to compel payment, but also the right to seize property to realize the unpaid taxes.

   a. I only
   b. II only
   c. both I and II
   d. neither I nor II

5. Which of the following is (are) true?

   I. The 1969 National Environment Policy Act requires filing of an environmental impact statement for all state projects that may significantly affect the environment.
   II. The Federal Water Pollution Control Act does not require permits for wastes disposed of in small brooks.

   a. I only
   b. II only
   c. both I and II
   d. neither I nor II

6. Sarah owns a small apartment house in an area recently zoned for single-family houses. Consequently, Sarah will:

   a. have to apply for a variance.
   b. have to forgo renting the apartment, but she will be compensated by the town.
   c. have to apply for a special exception.
   d. be permitted to continue renting the apartment.

7. The district regulations of the town of Smithville list tennis clubs as one of the special exceptions in residential districts. Bobbi Jean wants to build a club in a residential district. Which is true?

   a. Bobbi Jean will have to build the club in a commercial district.
   b. She will automatically be granted the exception.
   c. Bobbi Jean has to apply for a variance.
   d. She will be granted a special exception only if she proves the club is convenient to and compatible with the neighborhood.

8. Middletown's zoning ordinance contains a list of prohibited uses in some districts. Single-family houses are prohibited in industrial zones. Rufus, who owns property in an industrial zone, wants to build a house there. Rufus will:

    a. have to get a special exception.
    b. have to get a variance.
    c. not be permitted to build.
    d. be able to build the house only if the land complies with the minimum lot size requirements in the district.

9. Which of the following is (are) true?

    I. The code enforcement officer has the power to grant special exceptions to the local zoning ordinance.
    II. The zoning board of appeals may grant zoning variances when the zoning ordinance causes real hardship to a party.

    a. I only   c. both I and II
    b. II only   d. neither I nor II

10. Which of the following is (are) true?

    I. The Clean Air Act requires that air quality that exceeds national standards be maintained.
    II. Plans for federally funded subdivisions must generally file an environmental impact statement.

    a. I only   c. both I and II
    b. II only   d. neither I nor II

11. Which of the following is (are) true?

    I. The zoning ordinance for a particular town may be found in that town's municipal offices.
    II. A town may regulate land use type but may not regulate minimum lot size or maximum building height.

    a. I only   c. both I and II
    b. II only   d. neither I nor II

12. Which of the following is (are) true?

    I. Deed covenants are an example of the police power of government

    II. A non-conforming use under a town's zoning laws may nevertheless be permitted to continue.

    a. I only   c. both I and II
    b. II only   d. neither I nor II

13. Which of the following is (are) true?

    I. A decision regulating land use by the local code enforcement officer may always be appealed.

    II. A variance is granted only when the strict application of the ordinances would cause undue hardship to the landowner.

    a. I only   c. both I and II
    b. II only   d. neither I nor II

14. You are assisting a buyer who wants to develop a region of land located in more than one town. In order to advise her more effectively, you might consult:

    a. ordinances of the towns involved.
    b. the local council of governments.
    c. the regional planning commission.
    d. all of the above

15. Before a developer constructs a large commercial development, he or she ought to:

    a. check the local zoning ordinances.
    b. contact the state board of environmental protection for approval.
    c. obtain a conversion permit.
    d. A and B only

DISCUSSION QUESTIONS

1. Explain the difference between building codes and housing codes.

2. Describe how one would achieve a zoning variance.

3. Check your local zoning map and find the zones for:

    a. high-rise apartments.

    b. large industrial plants.

    c. single-family houses.

6

Listings
and Agency Relationships

KEY TERMS
---

agent
co-brokerage agreement
commingling
conflict of interest
contingency clause
disclosure
dual agency
earnest money
employee

exclusive agency
exclusive right to sell
fiduciary
independent contractor
net listing
open listing
principal
ready, willing, and
    able buyer

Thus far in the book, the broker has visited Eagle's Nest, secured a legal description, identified the boundaries, and talked with the owners about the fixtures they want to keep (door knocker and chandelier), the estates they want to create for members of the family and neighbors, and the easements affecting their property. The broker now has a firm idea of what it is that Phillip and Elizabeth are selling.

The next step is to have them sign a listing agreement by which they will authorize the broker and his or her company to act as their agent in the advertising, showing, and selling of their property. This chapter focuses on the three types of agency relationships between the seller and broker and how each is created and terminated. The chapter also discusses the broker's duties and legal obligations to the seller, the buyer, and his or her supervising broker and what the broker must do to earn a commission.

ESSENTIALS OF LISTING AGREEMENTS

Like any other agreement, the listing agreement has certain essential elements. The listing agreement shown below contains the six key elements. The letters in the column to the left of the agreement correspond to the lettered paragraphs below, which explain each of the elements.

BLUEBERRY REAL ESTATE AGENCY

EXCLUSIVE RIGHT TO SELL AGREEMENT

In Consideration of the sales efforts and advertising of the above named Agency or Broker (herein called Broker)

A to effect a sale of (my) (our) real estate at _____

and consisting of _____

_____

_____

B to which (I) (We) have a good and merchantable title, (I) (We) hereby give to said Broker the exclusive right to
    sell above mentioned property at the price of _____ Dollars
C for the term of _____ months from _____ termination on_____
    Said Broker shall receive a commission of _____ per cent of the sale price of the said property by whom-
D soever sold. This agreement shall hold good whether the property is sold at the above price or any other price
E which may be acceptable to (me) (us). (I) (We) agree that, if a prospect with whom the said Broker or associates
    have been negotiating purchases the said property within six months after the temination of this agreement, the
    commission shall be due and payable. All inquiries shall be Referred to said Broker.
F SPECIAL CONDITIONS: A "For Sale" Sign may be placed on the property (yes_____ no_____). A key to the buldings
    will be on file with said Broker (yes__,no__). Property will be listed with Maine Multiple Listing Service, Inc.
    (yes__,no__).

A COPY OF THE CONTRACT IS TO BE RECEIVED BY ALL PARTIES AND BY SIGNATURE:
RECEIPT OF A COPY IS HEREBY ACKNOWLEDGED

Dated _____ Owner _____

Accepted By _____ Owner _____
              Broker

A.   The listing agreement includes a brief description of the property; often the street address is used because, at the time the listing is taken, neither the seller nor the broker has yet secured a copy of the deed from the registry of deeds. The description should be legally precise, including if possible a reference to the deed by which the sellers took title, showing exactly what the sellers have agreed to sell and exactly what the agent is showing for sale.

It is also appropriate to list here exceptions to the property to be sold; i.e. "the real estate at Eagles' Nest Road, being the property conveyed to us by Elizabeth's parents in a deed recorded in Book 3,452 Page 267, Oxford County Registry of Deeds, and consisting of all the buildings, tennis court, etc., but *excluding* the door knocker and chandelier in the dining room."

B.   The listing agreement states the price at which the sellers will agree to sell the property. In the buying and selling of real estate, many, if not all, of the terms of the transaction are subject to negotiation between the buyers and sellers. It is common practice for the price stated in the listing agreement to be somewhat higher than the sellers might in fact accept if a good offer were forthcoming.

C.   This section of the listing agreement states for how long the agent's authority is to last and specifies the date upon which the agreement is to terminate. In many states, the real estate licensing laws, discussed at greater length in Chapter 12, require that the listing agreement specify its date of termination. Again, this helps the seller and the agent avoid misunderstanding about the agent's authority. Where the listing agreement terminates prior to the sale of the property, the agent and sellers may have to sign a new agreement if the agent's authority is to be renewed.

D.   This exclusive-right-to-sell agreement entitles the broker to a commission no matter who sells the property. The licensing law of some states requires that the listing agreement specify who is entitled to a commission if and when the property sells. While it may be clear to the experienced broker who is to be paid a commission, it may not be clear to an inexperienced seller who signs a listing unless it is spelled out in detail.

E.   This clause of the agreement is designed to protect the broker's right to a commission if the property is bought within six months by one of the broker's customers. If the broker showed couple A the property one week before the listing expired, and the next week they buy the house, it is only fair that the broker be paid his or her commission. When a listing agreement has a clause of this type, the broker should make sure the sellers know the names of each of the people who have seen the property through his office.

F. Paragraph F of the listing gives the broker special powers to act on behalf of the seller. The licensing laws of some states require written authorization from the seller to place a sign on the property. Signs on property are generally acknowledged to be the most cost effective form of advertising. There may, however, be several reasons why sellers do not want to attract attention to the fact that their house is for sale, including the intrusion of strangers who, seeing the sign, ring the doorbell to inquire about the house. The listing agreement is also an appropriate place to indicate other special conditions such as "the house will be shown after 5:00 P.M. on week nights only, and 24 hours' notice to the sellers is required."

TYPES OF AGREEMENTS

The six elements described above are common to all listing agreements. It is paragraph D that will determine the type of agreement the broker secures from his sellers.

The three generally recognized forms of listing contracts are:

    a. open listings;

    b. exclusive-agency listings;

    c. exclusive-right-to-sell listings.

Although each agreement appoints an agent to market the property, each one is different with respect to who is authorized to act for the seller and who is entitled to earn a commission.

Open Listings

The *open listing* is the form of agency agreement by which a seller hires a broker, for a fee, to find a buyer for his or her real estate. The unique characteristic of this listing is that the seller can engage as many brokers as he or she chooses. A commission is paid to the first broker to procure a qualified buyer.

In addition, the seller is free to sell the property independently of any broker. The seller does not have to pay any commission if he or she sells the property before a broker produces a buyer.

Example

Ann Brown has given an open listing to five different real estate agencies: Big Red's Real Estate; Running Brook Realty; Acres Agency; Best Brokers Associates, Inc.; and Landmark Associates, Inc. When Ann subsequently sells her home to her second cousin, Ellen, none of the agencies will receive a commission although each may have spent time and money looking for a buyer for the property.

The licensing laws of the states differ as to whether an open listing should be in writing or whether a verbal agreement is legally adequate for a broker to claim a commission in the event that he or she finds a ready, willing, and able buyer. Although a written agreement may not be required as a matter of law, a broker benefits significantly from having the agreement on a signed document. Consider the following example.

Example

Big Red of Big Red's Realty was at a dinner party last Saturday night, where he met John and Jane Doe. In the course of conversation, the Does mentioned their plan to sell their house and, in the euphoria of the evening, casually inquired if Red could help them. The next day, a customer walked into Red's office, asking about a property, and the Does came to mind. Red phoned for an appointment to show the house, a sale was concluded and the Does refused to pay a commission, arguing they had never listed the house with Red. Red should have had a written agreement to prove that he was the Does' agent.

Exclusive-Agency Listings

The *exclusive agency* is a brokerage relationship in which the seller agrees to list the property with one broker; this is the only broker who has the authority to advertise and show the prop-

erty and thus is assured of a commission if he or she finds
a buyer.

However, under an exclusive-agency listing, the seller retains
the authority to sell the property independently of the broker
and avoid paying a commission. Since the seller has retained the
authority to sell the property, he or she may not get the broker's
best efforts in finding a buyer because the broker fears losing a
commission to the owner.

The license law of most states requires that an exclusive-agency
agreement be in writing to be enforceable. Furthermore, it must
also contain at least the elements of the listing agreement on
page 116. An exclusive-agency agreement can be identified by
its title, under the name of the company where the words
Exclusive-Agency Agreement will appear. In addition, where
paragraph D appears, the agreement will read: "Said Broker
shall receive a commission of _____ percent of the sale price of
the said property," in contrast to the exclusive-right-to-sell
agreement, which goes on to say "by whomsoever sold."

Exclusive-Right-to-Sell Listings

The *exclusive right to sell* is a relationship in which the broker
obtains from the seller the exclusive and only right to list the
property and procure a buyer. No matter who finds the buyer,
the broker gets a commission because he or she has the exclusive right from the owner to market and sell the property.

The difference between the exclusive right to sell and the exclusive agency is that the owner cannot save a commission by finding a buyer for the property under the exclusive right to sell.
The broker collects a commission, regardless of how much or
little he contributed to the sale of the property; that is the legal
nature of the exclusive right to sell. As a practical matter, buyers who purchase property directly from sellers without the
services of a real estate broker generally discount their offer to
reflect that there is no commission to be paid. There is therefore
some question as to whether a seller actually saves the commission.

Brokers prefer an exclusive-right-to-sell listing of property. They are more willing to spend money and time showing and advertising property when they know they will receive a commission if a buyer is found during the term of the listing agreement.

COMMISSION EARNINGS AND NET LISTINGS

The sample listing agreement contains a blank in which the broker and seller enter an agreed commission rate. Real estate brokerage commissions are negotiated for each transaction. Suggestions that commission rates are fixed by agreement of all brokers in a community is an issue to which the real estate brokerage industry is very sensitive. Price fixing of any kind, whether by large national corporations or by brokers in a community, is a violation of antitrust law, as discussed in Chapter 13.

Commissions for real estate brokerage services tend to be six to seven percent for residential properties and ten percent for raw land and commercial transactions. The apparent consistency of commissions reflects the margins needed by brokers to maintain a profitable business. Much as grocery prices are similar from supermarket to supermarket, so are brokerage commissions consistently within the six- to ten-percent range.

There is a slowly growing trend nationwide away from charging a fixed commission for brokerage services. More and more, brokers want to be compensated for work performed on an hourly basis, as other professionals such as doctors, lawyers, and CPAs are paid. A broker might charge for different services: one fee for listing the property, another fee for each showing, another for advertising, and an additional sum for being involved in the negotiations and financing. Brokers who are charging for their brokerage services in this manner, should incorporate their fee schedule into the listing agreement, along with an indication from the seller as to which services are being selected.

NET LISTINGS

A *net listing* is a form of negotiated compensation for a real estate broker. Brokers need know only two things about net listings: what they are and that they are illegal in most states.

A net listing is an agreement between a broker and seller that states that the seller wants to "net" a certain sum from the sale of his or her property; whatever the broker can get for it above that net figure will be the compensation for the sale.

Example

Seller Sam is transferred to a new job out of state and is in a hurry to sell his house. He tells Broker Brown that all he wants is $40,000 net for the property, he doesn't want to bother with a lot of negotiations. He signs a listing agreement and leaves town. Buyer Baker purchases the house for $55,000, which nets Sam his $40,000 and gives broker Brown $15,000. A year later, Sam returns to the house to pick up some tools he left and learns from Baker the actual sale price of the house. Broker Brown will be accused of failure to represent the best interests of seller Sam.

The basic problem with net listings is that they pit the interests of the agent—a willingness to wait for a sale in order to maximize a commission—against the seller's interests, which is to sell the property quickly, regardless of the commission. Even where net listings are legal, they are fraught with pitfalls, and it is simply poor professional practice to consider them.

WHAT CONSTITUTES PERFORMANCE BY A BROKER

The listing agreement on page 116 provides "in consideration of the sales efforts . . . by the broker to effect the sale of my real estate . . . said broker shall receive a *commission* of X percent of the sale price . . . ." The seller has made a promise to pay a commission to the broker who effects the sale. What must the broker do to earn the promised commission?

- Must the broker spend hundreds of dollars in advertising?

- Must the broker show the house to all customers?

- If a buyer walks into the broker's office the next day and offers to purchase the property before the broker has advertised the property, is the broker entitled to a commission?

The answer to these questions is: to earn a commission, the broker must simply find a buyer who is *ready, willing, and able* to purchase the property on the seller's terms. To be entitled to the agreed commission, the broker need only perform by finding the buyer, regardless of how much money, time, or effort was spent to find that ready, willing, and able buyer.

Procuring the Purchaser

A broker earns nothing until this buyer is produced. It is crucial to realize that the contract between the broker and the seller becomes legally binding when the broker has fully performed his or her side of the contract, i.e. when the broker has produced the purchaser or when the buyer has in fact purchased the real estate. Although a listing contract can be drawn to make the broker's commission contingent upon the actual sale of the property, the usual agreement requires merely that the broker procure a ready, willing, and able buyer.

Seller's Terms

The purchaser must be ready to buy the property on the exact terms given by the seller.

Suppose the seller simply told the broker the lowest price he or she would consider for the property, and the broker procured a buyer who would pay that lowest price but insisted on a warranty deed. The buyer would not be considered ready, willing, and able if the seller's terms were to convey a quitclaim deed. Because the buyer has not agreed to all the terms of the seller's offer, the broker would not be entitled to a commission.

This harsh rule of law applies only when the seller is unwilling to accept any terms offered by the buyer that differ from the original terms in the listing agreement. It is more common that the seller is willing to negotiate with the buyer and perhaps accept different terms. For instance, the seller may say in the listing agreement that the bottom price is "$33,000." Often the seller will accept a lower price when negotiating with the buyer. When the seller is willing to deal with a buyer who offers terms other than the original terms of the listing contract, the broker *is* entitled to a commission.

The correct rule of law is that a broker must have completed performance of the listing contract to be entitled to a commission, that is, when he or she has procured a purchaser who is ready, willing, and able to buy on the exact terms of the listing or on any other terms acceptable to the seller.

Given that the purchaser must always be ready, willing, and able to buy on terms acceptable to the seller, there are three situations in which a broker may be said to have procured a qualified purchaser.

Placing Buyer and Seller in Contact

In the typical situation, the broker has placed a purchaser in communication with the seller. If a qualified buyer is put in contact with the seller as a result of the broker's efforts, the broker is eligible for a commission, even if the sale is not consummated because the seller refuses to deal with the qualified purchaser.

Whether or not the broker has placed a qualified buyer in contact with the seller can be the subject of litigation. A situation that gives rise to lawsuits is one in which the broker contacts a prospective buyer to spark interest in the client's real estate. The buyer declines to buy through the broker but later contacts the client directly or is contacted by the client or another broker. The prospect then decides to buy.

Has the original broker produced a ready, willing, and able purchaser? To establish the broker's right to a commission, the courts will require the original broker to prove that he or she was the effective and producing cause of the sale, or the primary cause, and not merely a contributing cause. If the broker awakened and cultivated the buyer's interest, so that it appears that he or she played the primary role in effecting the sale, the broker will be entitled to a commission.

Obtaining the Written Offer to Purchase

The broker also has completed performance of the listing contract and is entitled to a commission when he or she obtains from the buyer a written offer to purchase on the precise terms set by the seller. The written offer is proof that the broker has in fact produced a qualified buyer. Whether the seller accepts the buyer's offer, thereby creating a binding contract for sale between the two parties, or the seller refuses to offer is irrelevant with respect to the broker's right to a commission.

Procuring a Mutually Binding Contract

The third situation in which the question arises of whether a broker has completed performance of the listing contract is when the agent causes the parties to enter into a mutually binding contract. Where a seller signs a document accepting a buyer's offer with terms different from his original conditions of sale, an enforceable contract is created between the buyer and seller. Where the broker has been the procuring cause of the contract, he has performed according to the terms of the listing contract and is entitled to a commission. The point here is that the buyer and seller have a mutually binding contract.

Many, if not most, real estate contracts are signed subject to certain conditions. That is, they are not mutually binding at the moment of signature, but will become binding if certain conditions are met. The most common *contingency clause* in a residential real estate contract is one that makes it "subject to the buyer's obtaining a first mortgage of $XX,XXX at Y percent for 30 years." In other words, the buyers will buy if they can get the money to pay for the house. A contingency clause of this type will generally give the buyer ten days to two weeks to find financing. If the buyer obtains financing within that period, the contract becomes mutually binding; if not, then the contract is void and the broker is not entitled to any commission.

Proof of Express Agreement

In many states, listing agreements must be in writing. In the few states in which open listings need not be in writing, legal problems can arise.

To earn a commission, a broker must have been hired by the seller to find a buyer. The hiring agreement, the listing, is the basis of the agent's right to a commission. Clearly, if there is a written agreement that explicitly states the percentage of the price that will be paid on the sale of the house, a seller cannot easily dispute the agent's right to a commission.

When listing agreements are not in writing, the broker's right to a commission becomes less certain.

Example

A neighbor casually asks broker Brown if she thinks she could find a buyer for his $80,000 home. The next day, Brown mentions to a friend that her neighbor wants to sell; Brown's friend signs a purchase and sale agreement with her neighbor. Is Brown entitled to a commission? Clearly, she was the predominating and procuring cause of the sale. But was she hired?

Implied Listing Contract

The above example typifies a situation in which there has been an honest misunderstanding between the parties. The seller thought he was asking the broker a personal favor, while the broker thought that she was hired as an agent. In this and similar cases, courts have held that a contract may be implied from facts and circumstances if it appears that the broker rendered services for a client who knew of and consented to the services.

What is important about the formation of the listing contract is that such services must be rendered for the benefit of and with the knowledge and consent of the client. The essential basis of a court's determination that a contract has arisen by implication is whether or not the parties to the contract have acted in such a way that it is reasonable to infer they had, in fact, reached an agreement. When the client accepts the benefits of the services performed by the broker, and when he or she knows or has reason to know that the broker was actively seeking to procure a buyer and consents to the broker's efforts, an *implied contract* exists between the parties.

The burden of proof, however, lies squarely on the broker's shoulders. He or she must show that the services rendered were actually beneficial to the client and that the latter accepted those benefits. The broker might also have to show that the client knew or had reason to know that the broker's services were rendered in expectation of payment. For this reason, courts are reluctant to declare that a contract exists unless the broker has presented a very clear and compelling case. The safest way for the broker to avoid this problem of proving that he or she was hired is to get the listing contract in writing.

TERMINATION OF THE LISTING CONTRACT

There are four ways to terminate the agency relationship of the real estate broker to his or her principal. One way occurs when the listing agreement expires; the other three ways are by operation of law in specific circumstances.

Termination by Expiration

The agency will automatically terminate upon the date specified in the listing contract in those states that require a written instrument with a specified termination date. In the states in which no listing period need be specified, a listing is considered to be effective for a "reasonable" period of time.

Termination by Operation of Law

The agency may also be terminated by operation of law in three different situations.

• It may be terminated when a change in the law makes the required acts illegal.

Example ─────────────────────────────────

Seller contracts with broker to find a buyer for a bar and lounge with gambling slot machines. The seller intends that the gambling operation continue, and the sale is to be contingent on that. Then the legislature passes a law prohibiting the use of slot machines and all forms of gambling. The agency automatically terminates when the new law takes effect.

* It may be terminated when there is a change in the subject matter of the contract, such as the destruction of the property.

Example ————————————————————————

Seller lists his house with broker. A plane attempting to land at a nearby airport crashes into the seller's house and destroys it. The agency automatically terminates.

* It may be terminated when there is a change in the condition of the parties, such as death or insanity.

Example ————————————————————————

Seller lists a parcel of land with broker. Seller dies before a buyer is found. The seller's death terminates the listing.

Termination and the Listing Type

Open Listings

Generally, if the client has an open listing with one or more brokers, the listing is revocable at any time before a qualified purchaser is found. It does not matter that the broker has spent time and money looking for a buyer; the seller can revoke the offer to pay a commission and thereby terminate the agency at any time before a buyer is found.

Exclusive Listings

Suppose a homeowner gives a broker a 90-day exclusive right to sell a residence because he is being transferred out of state. After 45 days, the seller learns that he will not be moving out of state after all. The seller calls the broker and terminates the listing. Meanwhile, the broker has spent $400 for advertising, plus time showing the property to prospective purchasers. Can the seller back out of the listing contract?

Clearly, if the broker had presented a buyer who was ready, willing, and able to purchase the property before the listing was terminated, the broker would be entitled to the commission. After all, the broker did what was promised in the listing agreement. But what happens when the seller terminates the listing before its expiration date?

In some states, if the broker has begun performance of the unilateral listing contract, the contract will remain enforceable until it expires or until the broker finds a buyer, whichever comes first. Although this legal reasoning favors the broker, it could have the harsh result of forcing the seller's family out of its home.

Alternatively, some jurisdictions permit the seller to terminate a listing contract at any time before the broker has found a buyer. The seller who does so, however, must be ready to reimburse the broker for the costs incurred in performance of his or her obligations under the listing contract.

BROKERAGE

The first part of this chapter explained the creation and termination of the real estate broker's agency relationship with the seller. This part of the chapter focuses on the nature of the brokerage relationship and the basic rights, duties, and obligations of the licensee and the seller to each other and to the buyer.

Broker's Duties and Legal Obligations

The typical brokerage relationship involves a property owner and a real estate broker. Legally, the landowner alone holds the right to sell his or her land. However, agency law, as applied to real estate, is founded on the principle that whatever a property owner may lawfully do on his or her own behalf he or she may also appoint an *agent* to do. Thus, real estate owners retain brokers to help in the marketing and sale of their property.

The establishment of a brokerage relationship creates only a limited agency. The broker is not authorized to do all of the things a landowner may do; he or she may perform only those duties that are specifically assigned. For example, if the broker is hired to find a ready, willing, and able buyer, he or she holds no authority to bind the seller to a contract for the sale of the land. The broker's authority and responsibilities extend no further than those expressed in the listing agreement.

Broker's Fiduciary Responsibilities

In the world of professional relationships, the lawyer, doctor, accountant, banker, and clergy share a special responsibility to their clients. Individuals entrust their legal rights, health, assets, and spiritual well-being to members of these professions and accept on faith that their representatives in each of these areas will devote the utmost of professional skills to the nurturing and promotion of their interests. This special relationship is called a *fiduciary* relationship, one based on trust.

In each case, our law and the ethics of our business communities demand the highest standards of these professionals; the law will strip the privileges of the profession from the fiduciary who abuses the trust placed in him or her by a vulnerable client. Attorneys are disbarred, doctors are disenfranchised, and clergy are defrocked for their abuse of their responsibilities and for bringing disrepute to their profession.

The relationship of real estate broker's to their seller's is a fiduciary relationship, which demands the same high degree of loyalty and trust exacted of doctors, attorneys, and the clergy. The law imposes the highest professional standards on real estate agents because, for most people, the purchase and sale of real estate, particularly a home, is the most significant financial decision they make in their lifetimes. No other decision so affects lifestyle, standard of living, and often the ability to finance college educations and retirement. With so much at stake for both the unsophisticated homebuyer and the seller liquidating such a significant asset, it is proper that the law be uncompromising in its high expectations of real estate agents.

The real estate agent's job in devoting his or her professional skills to promote the interests of the seller is potentially compli-

cated by two factors. First, unlike the other professional fiducia-
ries who are paid on an hourly basis and whose compensatory
arrangements promote quality service, real estate agents are
paid on a commission basis. Thus, the more transactions that
are closed, the more money there is to be made. In an economic
recession, when closings are few and far between, a real estate
broker's integrity may be tested when a seemingly small digres-
sion from the seller's best interests may help close a sale and
put food on the broker's table.

The second factor that complicates the broker's fiduciary responsibility is the question: For whom does the broker work? To
whom does the broker owe this fiduciary duty? The answer is
clear and unequivocal: the duty is owed to the person who hired
the broker, to the person who is paying for the broker's loyalty.
In the majority of cases, this is the seller.

A broker's fiduciary duty is to the person who hires him or her;
but this point is sometimes clouded by the nature of the real
estate business. Consider the typical situation in which a real
estate agent opens an office that attracts prospective buyers
looking for a home. A good broker will secure the buyer's personal trust and confidence; the broker will ask the buyer to provide personal information concerning income, debts, and
lifestyle. Many buyers are lulled into the assumption that the
broker works for them and is in fact their agent. Unless the
buyer is paying for the services of the broker, the licensee is the
seller's agent and owes his or her fiduciary responsibilities to his
or her principal.

In many real estate transactions, more than one broker is involved. There will be a listing broker, who was hired directly by
the seller, and a selling broker, who has a buyer for the property.
In these cases, the brokers will enter into a *co-brokerage agreement* where by they agree to split the commission if the prospective buyers buy the house. In this case, to whom does the
selling broker owe his or her fiduciary loyalties? The answer is:
to the seller. Although the selling broker has worked with the
buyers, it is still the seller who is paying the commission. By
entering into a co-brokerage agreement with the listing broker,
the selling broker becomes the sub-agent of the seller. Both the

agent and the sub-agent are hired by the seller and owe their duties to that individual.

The real estate broker's duties to the buyer are generally spelled out in the license law of the state where he or she is practicing. A real estate agent must deal fairly and honestly with the buyer at all times. A broker must take care not to misrepresent the property to be sold and in fact has an affirmative obligation to the buyers to disclose to them any known defects of the property.

Example ───────────────────────────────────

Sally gives broker Smith an exclusive right to sell her antique home in the country. In heavy spring rains, the cellar floods and the roof leaks. She tells Smith about the problems and asks that he show the home on sunny days only. Smith's obligation is to tell prospective buyers of both the cellar and roof problems, particularly since they may not be able to identify these problems on their own.

──

The fact that the brokerage relationship is based on such principles imposes on the real estate agent special duties, including the following.

Duty of Full Disclosure

A broker fails to satisfy the legal mandate of the agency relationship unless he or she makes a complete and timely *disclosure* to the seller of all facts that might affect the client's interests. Consider the following situations.

• If, after an agency relationship is established, the broker learns that a major corporation will be moving to the area, which will have an impact—either beneficial or adverse—on the value of the client's land, the broker is bound to disclose it.

• If a broker is aware that a prospective purchaser is prepared to offer a higher price than that which was originally offered, this must be communicated to the seller. At no time can the broker's interest in earning a commission interfere with his or her promotion of the seller's best interests.

• If, while a seller is contemplating accepting an offer on his or her property, the broker learns that other offers may be submitted, this must be disclosed to the seller.

• The broker is obligated to submit all offers to the seller as they become available and should be available to consult with the seller on the relative advantages and disadvantages of each.

• The broker is under an obligation to see that all terms of the buyer's offer are understood by the seller and, similarly, that all of the seller's terms are understood by the buyers. Misunderstanding resulting from incomplete disclosure of information to all parties can torpedo a sale.

• In many states, real estate license law requires the broker to disclose to buyers and sellers what the closing costs will be and which costs each party will pay.

• The license law of some states requires the broker, after the closing, to give a written statement showing how all the money was disbursed. If this statement is provided by a lending institution, the broker may be relieved of the responsibility.

• If the buyer does not have cash for a down-payment, and instead gives a promissory note, the broker must advise the seller of this fact; it may have a bearing on whether the seller accepts the prospective buyer's offer.

Conflicting Interests

A broker's professional loyalties belong to the seller. Any time the broker's loyalties may be suspect, he or she is under an obligation to tell the seller of the potential *conflict of interest*. Consider the following situations.

• If the broker decides to purchase the seller's property for his or her own account, the seller must be told. Clearly, a broker cannot be expected to get the best price for the seller if he or she is negotiating to buy the property for a personal account.

• Similarly, if the person making an offer to buy the property is related to the broker, the seller must be advised of this relationship. A broker cannot be expected to represent the best interests of the seller when negotiating a sale for a relative.

Dual Agency

An agent may not act in dual capacity, representing the buyer and seller of property, unless each party has full knowledge of the *dual agency* and assents to it. In most cases, the interests of the buyer and seller are in direct conflict.

While the buyer hopes to minimize his or her expenditure for the property, the seller hopes to obtain the highest possible price. Since the broker is duty-bound to secure for the seller the most advantageous agreement possible, it is clear that the broker cannot serve both the buyer and seller without compromising his or her fiduciary responsibility to one.

Example

Agent Agee has been discussing with his friend the possibility of selling an abandoned building he has just inherited, but they have not signed a listing agreement. The BIM company calls from out of state and makes a contract with Agee to find a suitable building for a new factory. It will be very difficult for Agee to strike the best bargain for both parties.

Binding the Principal

Ordinarily, the real estate broker is an agent hired by the seller and is given only limited authority. Unless it is expressly stated otherwise in the listing agreement, the broker is presumed to be vested with the implied authority to perform those acts that are reasonably necessary to the accomplishment of the agency purpose. Consequently, the innocent representations of a selling broker with respect to such matters as lot size, boundary lines, water supply, soil condition, and the status of land title are usually binding upon the principal.

While the *principal* generally assumes responsibility for the acts of the broker done within the scope of his or her agency, the broker is obligated to act responsibly and professionally on the principal's behalf. The broker is legally bound to exercise a reasonable degree of care and skill in the performance of his or her duties. In the event that the broker acts negligently or incompetently, he or she forfeits any claim to a commission and becomes personally liable to the principal for any resulting loss.

It is important to point out that misrepresentation is the single largest source of complaints filed against real estate agents. Licensees who are anxious to persuade buyers to purchase may risk careless representation of specific facts about a property. For example, an item often misrepresented to buyers is the septic or sewage system for a home. The buyer wants to know whether the property is on town sewage; the licensee, anxious to reassure the buyer that all systems are in good order, carelessly or ignorantly, gives the assurance. When, after the buyer moves in, the septic tank needs replacement, the buyer will sue broker and the seller for misrepresentation. Often the seller has moved out of the state and the licensee is left to defend the suit and pay the judgment. The lesson for licensees is: Make representations of fact that can be documented. If a licensee does not know about the sewage system, it promotes the buyer's confidence to say, "I don't know, but I will consult an expert." It minimizes the risk of later suit and may shift the liability to an expert if the expert makes an error.

If the broker exceeds the authority conferred in the listing agreement, he or she risks becoming personally liable to the principal for any losses incurred. For example, if a broker who has found a buyer attempts to draft a purchase and sale agreement, and the transaction fails because of the broker's error, he or she may be held liable for the damages sustained by the principal.

Earnest Money Deposits

A real estate broker has the authority to accept an earnest money deposit on the purchase price, if the power is expressly conferred in the listing agreement. The laws of most states require a broker to keep such deposits separate from personal funds. Mixing earnest money deposits with personal funds, called *commingling*, is punishable by license suspension or revocation in states that forbid it.

Trust Accounts

Of the many fiduciary responsibilities imposed on the real estate professional, few are greater than the proper handling of money that belongs to other people. Brokers handle money belonging to others both in their capacities as property managers, where they may accept tenants' payments of rent and security deposits, and as sellers' agents when accepting buyer's *earnest money* deposits. Earnest money is money submitted by a buyer with a written offer to purchase real estate as proof of honest and serious intent to purchase. Real estate license laws are universally strict about the broker's handling of the funds.

Because of the importance of trust accounts, a broker should know how to:

1.   open a trust account properly;

2.   maintain records that properly document trust account transactions; and

3.   keep separate accounts for sales and rental business.

The key difference between the broker's business account, from which he would pay all his office expenses—including secretary's salary, rent, utilities, sales associates' commissions, etc.—and the trust account is that the *trust account* holds *other people's money.* The license laws of most states specifically prohibit the broker from commingling more than a nominal amount of his or her own money—usually $25; needed to open the account and pay service charges—with that of clients.

There is a very practical reason for this. Assume that Fraudulent Fred, a real estate tycoon of dubious reputation, had failed to file tax returns with the Internal Revenue Service for years. The IRS has finally caught up with him and files a lien on all his property, including all bank accounts in his name. A trust account with the broker named as trustee only, with none of the broker's funds in the account, is established so that the trust account money will remain beyond the reach of plaintiffs in the case that the broker is sued by the IRS or by other creditors who attach his property. The broker's problems thus will not prevent the clients business from being transacted.

The requirements for opening and maintaining the broker's trust account and documenting the transactions involving it are found in the real estate licensing laws of each state. A thorough reading of this chapter should be augmented by reference to the license law of the reader's state.

The Broker/Salesperson Relationship

Most real estate offices are made up of a broker or group of brokers who own and run the office, along with several sales associates. Generally, the broker provides each salesperson with a desk, office space, perhaps secretarial help, forms, and other tools of the business. In turn, the salesperson pays a percentage of any commission he or she earns to the sponsoring broker and/or a flat fee for other services provided.

The exact nature of the business relationship between the broker and the sales associates is an interesting and important topic. The legal status between them determines such important things as the type of employer taxes a broker must pay, if any, and determines the extent to which the broker is responsible for the actions of salespeople.

Generally speaking, a salesperson is either an *employee* of the sponsoring broker or an *independent contractor*. A broker is far more responsible for the associate who is an employee than for the associate who is an independent contractor. In addition, the broker must pay additional taxes if sales associates are characterized as employees rather than as independent contractors.

Tax Implications

As a general rule, the more *direct control* the broker has over the salesperson, the more likely it is that that person is an employee of the broker. Conversely, the more independence the associate enjoys, the more likely it is that he or she will be

considered an independent contractor. Consider the following
examples.

Example

Salesperson Sally has a desk in broker Ken's office. Broker Ken
provides her a telephone, paper, and typing services. Sally is paid
only when she makes a sale, and she receives 50 percent of the
commission. Sally is not required to attend any meetings called by
Ken, and there is an agreement that she need not be in the office
for any particular number of hours.

Broker Ken provides a new sales associate, John, with the same
telephone, desk, forms, and typing services as Sally in the example
above, but also requires John to attend weekly office meetings, to
report to work at 9:00 A.M., to contact specific people every day,
and to maintain and turn in a daily log of activities.

Clearly, Sally is much more independent of her broker than John
is. In effect, Sally in self-employed. She decides how to spend
her day, whom to see, and when to report to work. She is truly
independent of her broker; she has a contractual arrangement
with the broker, who provides her with essential forms and services for a fee.

By contrast, John is under the full control of his broker. Although John may spend much of his day out of the office, his
daily routine is directed and monitored by his broker. He lacks
the independence and opportunity to exercise initiative and is
thus, for legal purposes, defined as an employee.

When the sales associate is an employee, the broker incurs liability to pay certain taxes; for example, the broker must pay with-
holding and social security taxes to the federal government.
Since most states follow the tax definitions of the federal government, the broker must also withhold the employee's state
taxes and pay worker's compensation and unemployment insurance premiums. The sales associate who is an independent contractor, on the other hand, must arrange for and pay these taxes
and insurance premiums. In addition, if the broker has any

profit-sharing plans, he or she will have to include employees but not independent contractors. Thus, most brokers prefer to have their sales associates characterized as independent contractors.

It is important to understand that there are no absolute definitions of *employee* and *independent contractor*. The Internal Revenue Service has issued two rulings to help brokers and sales associates understand how the service views this issue.

Revenue Ruling 76-136 states that real estate salespeople who are:

> . . .remunerated solely on a commission basis, who are provided office facilities and supplies, are required to pay their own expenses, but are not required to work under supervision, attend meetings, or work specified hours, are not employees.

Revenue ruling 76-137 describes a more common situation. It states:

> [R]eal estate salespeople, remunerated solely on a commission basis, who are registered by the state in the name of the company, may receive a draw against commissions, may be required to submit reports and attend sales meetings, and may be discharged for failure to sell a minimum amount of property *are employees* of the company.

A comparison between the two rulings shows that it is indeed a fine line that separates the status of and employee and that of an independent contractor.

A final important concept in defining the relationship is that a salesperson must be sponsored by a broker to collect a commission legally. The IRS ruling states that:

> . . .the fact that the [broker's] sponsorship is essential to the salesperson's ability to perform in the industry . . . should be heavily emphasized in favor of ending an employer—employee relationship.

Thus, in those states requiring sponsorship, it will be difficult to argue an independent contractor relationship between a salesperson and a broker, at least for federal tax purposes.

Tax matters of this sort are difficult for a layman to judge. If there is any doubt as to the status of a salesperson, a tax expert should be consulted.

Broker Liability

Another difficult area of law is the extent to which a broker is liable for the acts of sales associates, acts that inflict some physical or monetary damage upon third persons. This indirect responsibility that the broker may have is referred to as *vicarious liability*.

Many states have statutory provisons that a broker is responsible for the acts of sales associates committed while they represent the broker as agents. These regulatory statutes, enacted to protect the public against incompetence and dishonesty, usually specify that the broker supervise and control employees because he or she has superior skill in and knowledge of real estate. In supervising the sales staff, the broker will be held to a reasonable standard of care, which may extend to hiring competent and trustworthy individuals, making sure all salespersons maintain their licenses, and ensuring that personnel perform only the acts for which they were licensed.

If a broker does not properly carry out these supervisory duties, he or she may be disciplined or lose his or her license. Usually a broker will be disciplined only for some occurrence over which he or she could have exercised control. The wise broker may want to follow regular office reporting procedures to keep abreast of the employees' activities.

Generally speaking, an employer is liable for acts that employees carry out as a normal part of their employment. Important here is the question of whether a real estate salesperson is considered a broker's employee. Assuming such a relationship exists, the following examples of vicarious liability may arise.

Example —————————————————————————

Salesperson Jake is showing a piece of commercial property to buyer Ben. At Jake's instruction, Ben steps through a door that Jake says leads to a hallway. It is actually an open elevator shaft.

Jake's showing of property is a normal part of his employment, so Ben or his survivors can argue strongly that broker Brian, Jake's boss, is liable for Jake's negligent act.

Salesperson Jake tells buyer Ben that the undeveloped property he was shown is zoned for industrial use. Ben relies upon that representation and spends considerable money purchasing the property. After the sale, Ben discovers the property is zoned residential or farm use only. Since Jake's representation of zoning is a normal part of his employment, Ben can argue strongly that broker Brian may be vicariously liable for the damage caused by his salesperson's negligent misrepresentation.

Again, this is a complicated area of the law. The moral of the story is that a broker must be confident of the sales staff's competence not only for reasons of profitability, but also for self-protection from possible lawsuits arising from their negligent acts.

SUMMARY

This chapter explained the basic legal principles of the brokerage business: the appointment of the broker/agent, the kinds of agency relationships, the agent's commission, the agent's authority, and the agent's responsibilities to the seller. A real estate licensee is in a position of great responsibility and trust concerning the seller of real estate. As such, the agent is required to be licensed by the state, which proves that he or she possesses at least a minimal knowledge of the business and that he or she is a person of moral and trustworthy character. The licensing of the agent is covered more fully in Chapter 12.

MULTIPLE CHOICE QUESTIONS ─────────────

1. Sandy Seller hires three brokers to find a buyer for her home. Sandy and her agents agree that she will pay a commission to the first broker to procure a ready, willing, and able buyer. Which type of contract does Sandy have with the agents?

    a. a net listing
    b. an open listing
    c. an exclusive agency
    d. an exclusive right to sell

2. Sandy Seller gives an open listing to three brokers to sell her home. When her cousin Alice decides to purchase a home, Sandy negotiates with Alice and sells her the home. Which of the following is true?

    a. In selling before the listing agreements with her brokers terminate, Sandy breaches the contracts.
    b. The brokers divide the commission three ways.
    c. The brokers earn no commission because Sandy has the right to sell her home.
    d. The sale cannot go through before the termination of the contracts.

3. Sandy Seller hires Bob Broker to sell her home; they draw up an exclusive-agency contract. A month later, Sandy sells her home to Aunt Esther. Which of the following is true?

    a. Bob will receive no commission.
    b. Sandy may sell, but Bob will receive the commission.
    c. Sandy may not sell until the listing contract expires.
    d. Bob will receive one-half of the agreed upon commission.

4. When Sandy Seller hires Bob Broker to sell her home, their listing contract gives Bob an exclusive right to sell. Two weeks later, Sandy sells the home to her friend Frank. Which of the following is true?

    a. Sandy will owe Bob one-half of the agreed upon commission.
    b. Sandy may not sell until the contract expires.
    c. Bob will receive no commission.
    d. Although Sandy has sold the house, Bob will receive his commission.

5. Which of the following listing agreements is generally preferred by brokers?

    a. net listings.
    b. open listings.
    c. exclusive agency agreements.
    d. exclusive right to sell.

6. Sandy Seller owns a small restaurant. After she and Bob Broker enter into a contract giving Bob an exclusive right to sell, a kitchen fire destroys the property. Which of the following is true?

    a. The contract is terminated by operation of law.
    b. The exclusive agency will terminate only upon the expiration date.
    c. The contract will terminate only if both parties agree.
    d. The contract will terminate at Bob's option.

7. Listing agreements should be in writing to establish

    a. the amount of the broker's commission.
    b. that the broker was in fact hired.
    c. the expiration date of the agent's authority.
    d. all of the above.

8. When Sandy Seller hires Bob Broker to sell her home, she suggests that she wants a price of $45,000 for the house and that any money he can get above that amount is his commission. Bob refuses because:

    a. net listings are illegal or unwise due to conflict of interest.
    b. he wants an exclusive agency, and a net listing cannot be an exclusive agency.
    c. he wants an exclusive right to sell, and a net listing cannot be an exclusive right to sell.
    d. Sally wants an open listing, and an open listing cannot be a net listing.

9. Sandy Seller has an open listing with three brokers. A month after she made the contracts, Sandy decided to refuse the new job offer in city X and remain in her present home. Which of the following is true?

    a. Sandy can revoke with any broker who agrees.
    b. Sandy can revoke only if all the brokers agree.
    c. Sandy can revoke the listing contracts if no broker has found a purchaser.
    d. Sandy will have to let the contracts terminate at the agreed upon dates.

10. Sandy Seller hires Bob Broker to sell her house. Bob finds a buyer who wants to purchase Sandy's home but wants to vary the terms of her offer. The buyer wants Sandy to leave the major kitchen appliances in the home and to reduce the price by $4,000. While Sandy and the buyer are negotiating, she tells Bob that he will not be entitled to his commission. Which of the following is true?

    a. If Sandy and the buyer reach an agreement, Bob will be entitled to his commission.
    b. Bob is not entitled to his commission because the buyer was not ready, willing, and able to purchase on Sandy's terms.
    c. Bob may be entitled to part of his commission for producing a buyer who was willing to negotiate.
    d. Bob is entitled to all of his commission for producing a buyer who was willing to negotiate.

11. If a broker accepts deposit money toward the purchase price without specific authority, the:

    a. broker will be responsible.
    b. principal will be responsible.
    c. contract will be formed.
    d. all of the above

12. A broker who is dishonest with a principal:

    a. has violated the broker's fiduciary duty.
    b. may be held liable for a violation of a state real estate licensing law.
    c. risks bringing on legal action by the principal or by the real estate commission.
    d. all of the above

13. A broker has performed his or her part of the listing contract when:

    a. an optional contract to buy has been signed by the buyer and seller.
    b. sale of the real estate is completed.
    c. he or she has produced a ready and able buyer who is willing to purchase on the exact terms or terms acceptable to the seller.
    d. none of the above

14. A real estate sales associate may be an employee or an independent contractor. This classification is important to the:

    a. sales associate.
    b. hiring broker.
    c. Internal Revenue Service.
    d. all of the above

15. The most important factor in determining whether a sales associate is an employee or an independent contractor is:

    a. the employer's control.
    b. the employment contract.
    c. the amount of money earned.
    d. whether the employee has a separate office.

DISCUSSION QUESTIONS ——————————————————

1. Bob Broker and Sandy Seller sign a listing agreement whereby Bob acquires an exclusive right to sell Sandy's home. A month later, Bob agrees to act as Bill Buyer's agent to find Bill a home. Discuss the duties Bob owes to each party and the possible legal problems.

2. Discuss the ways in which a listing contract may terminate by operation of the law.

3. Discuss the reasons why a net listing is often illegal and always unwise.

7

Contracts

acceptance   offer
breach of contract   offeree
consideration   offeror
contract   option
counteroffer   rescission
encumbrance   specific performance
infant (minor)   statute of frauds
liquidate damages   time is of the essence
marketable title

The single most important document in a real estate transaction
is the purchase and sale contract. The agreement contains all
the terms and conditions upon which the seller agrees to sell
and the buyer agrees to buy. These are all terms negotiated by
the real estate broker who brought the parties together. Before
examining a real estate contract in detail, this chapter provides
an overview of the general law of contracts. While negotiating a
real estate agreement, a real estate broker will need to understand the elements of a valid contract—offer, acceptance, and
consideration—and be able to recognize when the terms to which
the buyer and seller have agreed are sufficient to form a legally
binding contract. Once the agreement in a real estate transaction is made, it becomes the road map for the transaction. It
will specify the price of the sale, the time for the closing, the
date of occupancy of the new buyers, the type of deed the sellers
will give, the down payment, and which fixtures are not to be
sold with the property. Because the real estate broker is very
often the negotiator for these agreements, it is critically important that he or she understand the implications of each item of

the agreement. The second part of this chapter focuses on standard clauses in purchase and sale contracts for real estate.

This chapter will also cover the very important statute of frauds, which requires that contracts for the sale of real estate be in writing. Oral agreements are legally unacceptable for real estate transactions, a rule of law to which the exceptions are very rare.

COMPONENTS OF A CONTRACT

A _contract_ is legally enforceable agreement or promise between two or more parties. There are three basic components of a contract: (1) the _offer_, (2) the _acceptance_ of the offer, (3) and the _consideration_.

Offer

To form a contract, the parties must reach an agreement to which they mutually assent. This mutual assent is reached through the offer and the acceptance. This means that one party proposes a bargain and the other party agrees to this proposed bargain. The person making the offer is known as the _offeror_; the person receiving the offer is called the _offeree_.

What is an offer? In most cases, an offer contains a conditional promise and proposes that the other party accept the offer by making a promise in return. If a contract consists of an exchange of promises, it is called a _bilateral contract_, as discussed in Chapter 6. Most contracts are bilateral, since both parties usually promise to perform some act.

Example ────────────────────────────────

Jones says to Smith, "I promise to pay you $50,000 if you promise to sell me your home and the lot on which it sits." Smith answers, "It's a deal." A bilateral contract has been formed—there has been a mutual exchange of promises.

──

A person wishing to contract may make a statement, which is not an offer but rather an invitation for bids. Such statements cannot be accepted, but merely serve as a basis for preliminary negotiations. Statements made with merely the intent to open negotiations, which might later lead to a sale, do not constitute an offer. An advertisement in a newspaper for a piece of real estate is an example of an invitation for offers, an invitation to open negotiations. By contrast, for a statement to be viewed as an offer, it must be clear and definite and such that the offeree can meet its terms by acceptance.

Termination of Offers

When an offer is made, either it will be accepted or it will terminate. There are four ways in which an offer is typically terminated:

a. lapse of time;

b. revocation by the offeror;

c. rejection or counteroffer by the offeree;

d. death or incapacity of the offeror or the offeree.

Consider the following examples of offers that terminate by operation of these four rules.

Lapse of Time. Suppose a seller of real estate is asking $85,000 for his property. A buyer offers $79,500 and gives the seller four days in which to consider the offer. If the offer is not accepted by that time, it will terminate automatically. The buyer can make another offer or move on to look at other real estate.

Revocation. Suppose that, in the example above, after two days the seller has not replied to the buyer, who then changes his or her mind and decides that the property is too expensive. May the buyer withdraw or revoke the offer? Yes—until the offer is accepted, the buyer has the right and opportunity to revoke the offer. There is no reason to require the buyer to leave it open.

Rejection/Counteroffer. Within the four-day period, the seller does not accept the buyer's offer of $79,500 but makes a *coun-*

teroffer of $82,500. What is the status of the offer for $79,500? Very simply, it is dead. The buyer's offer terminates when the seller either rejects the offer or decides to make a counteroffer. The seller's counteroffer will remain open until the buyer accepts it, or the seller withdraws the offer, or the counteroffer lapses because the time for its acceptance runs out.

Death or Incapacity. The fourth circumstance that terminates an offer is the death or incapacity of either the offeror or offeree.

If either the offeree or the offeror dies, or if either party loses the legal capacity to enter into a contract by becoming insane or senile, the power to accept is terminated. This is so even if the offeree does not learn of the offeror's death or incapacity until after the acceptance has been sent. The legal capacity of people to enter into a contract is discussed in more detail in later sections of this chapter.

Acceptance

An offer alone does not make a contract. The legal effect of an offer is to give the offeree the opportunity and power to make a contract by accepting the offer. To be effective, the acceptance must be made while the offer is open.

An offeror may require that the offer be accepted in a certain way. For instance, the offeror may insist that the offer be accepted by "telephone before noon the following day," or by "letter no later than Wednesday next," or "by telegram," or "by signature on the enclosed letter." In such a case, if the offeree does not accept in the manner prescribed, there will be no contract. If an offer does not specify the method of acceptance, the acceptance may be given in any reasonable manner.

The Acceptance Must Be Communicated

To make a contract, the offeree must communicate unequivocal acceptance to the offeror. Without communication of the acceptance there can be no contract. Such communication must reach the offeror either within the specified period of time or, if no deadline is given, within a reasonable time.

Traditionally, when an offer is received through the mail, it is customary to accept through the mail. Of course, an offer may be received through the mail, specifying that the acceptance be made in some other way—by phone, telex, etc. In such a case, the offeree must accept as requested.

Consideration

To create a binding contract, the promises exchanged between the parties must be supported by consideration. Consideration is something of value, usually but not necessarily money.

Examples ───

A agrees to purchase, and B agrees to sell, a property at 19 Broadway for $20,000. The consideration for this contract is $20,000.

A agrees to purchase, and B agrees to sell, the 19 Broadway property, if A will transfer his antique auto to B. The consideration for this contract is the antique car.

───

As a general rule, a judge will not listen to a suit by a buyer or seller who complains that he or she paid too much or received too little for a piece of real estate. Imagine the blossoming of lawsuits if every time someone felt he or she had overpaid or undersold an item there was an opportunity to correct the situation in court. The law does not review the adequacy of consideration in contracts unless the plaintiff can prove that there was fraud or a mutual mistake about the property that was sold. In most cases, the law places the burden on the contracting parties to look out for themselves.

The Option: A Special Kind of Offer

An *option* is a special contract often used by real estate investors and developers, which is best defined as an agreement between the developer and the landowner that gives the developer the right to buy the seller's property at any time within a certain time period, six months for example. For this right the developer pays the seller an agreed sum, say $1,500.

The developer is paying the seller to keep the land available while he or she talks with an architect, secures a building permit, and arranges for financing for the project. The developer may or may not exercise the option within the time period specified, depending on how plans evolve during the option period.

Example ———————————————————————————

Al offers to sell Joe his hunting camp for $50,000 at any time during the next two weeks. Joe pays Al $500 to keep the offer open for two weeks. The option operates not only as an offer of sale, but also as a contract binding Al to keep the offer open for that period of time.

The option can also be viewed as paying the seller to keep his or her offer to sell open for a prolonged period of time. However, an option is more than just an extended offer; it is a true contract in which there has been an offer, acceptance, and consideration, $1,500.

Right of First Refusal

A *right of first refusal* is another contract form, erroneously confused with an option. With a right of first refusal, the contracting parties agree that, if A decides to sell Blackacre, or if A gets an offer for the property from any source, B will have the right to buy the property, usually at a fair market price established at the time of the sale. In other words, A may not want to sell at this time, but if A ever does want to sell, then B gets the first opportunity to meet A's terms. Because a right of first refusal is a contract, there will be an offer, an acceptance, and consideration.

Example ———————————————————————————

A owns two adjacent lots on Silver Spring Lake. He has a cottage on one; the other is vacant and lies between his cottage and that of his neighbor, B. B would like to own the lot and build on it. A doesn't want to sell until his children reach college age, in three years. B, to assure that he will have the right of first refusal, pays

A $1,000 for a contract guaranteeing him the right to buy it if A decides to sell. The written contract is recorded in the registry of deeds so all future potential buyers know of B's rights.

Parties Must Have Contractual Capacity

Certain classes of persons have only limited power to contract. The most important of these classes are *infants,* or *minors,* and the mentally handicapped.

The age at which a person reaches adulthood, or majority, is determined by statute in each state. The most common ages of majority are 18 and 21. Generally speaking, an infant may not enter an enforceable contract unless it is for necessities, including food, clothing, medical care, shelter, and education.

Example

Sonny, a minor, contracts with Honest John to buy a special-order new car. When the car arrives, Sonny decides he does not want it. He can cancel the contract and walk away—Honest John cannot hold him to the contract. Sonny has the power to void the contract.

A minor can generally enter into contracts to buy and sell real property. In most instances, the infant may disaffirm or void the contract at any time. However, once the minor reaches the age of majority, he or she has only a reasonable time within which to void any agreements made as a minor. After that, the contracts becomes legally enforceable.

Mental incompetents—including not only the insane but also those who are senile, mentally retarded, or under the influence of alcohol or other drugs—are treated the same way minors are. That is, they are recognized as having limited contractual capacity. In many cases, a party's mental state may be less than alert, yet not so diminished as to allow automatic withdrawal from the contract, as is the case with a legally insane person. The contracting party may, for instance, be only slightly intoxicated or dull-witted, but not retarded. In such a situation, if the other party took advantage of the slight infirmity, the court may allow the party to withdraw on the grounds of either infirmity or fraud.

Legality of Object or Purpose of Contract

The object or purpose of a contract must be legal if the contract is to be enforceable. A contract is illegal, if its purpose violates state or federal statutes or the all-encompassing domain of public policy.

Example ─────────────────────────────────────

A contract between two thieves to rob banks is unenforceable, because robbing banks violates state and federal laws.

Uncle John makes a contract with his niece Jenny to pay her $10,000 if she remains unmarried until age 40. After her 40th birthday, Jenny sues to recover the $10,000, which Uncle John is refusing to pay. Although Jenny has fulfilled the requirements of the contract, the court will not enforce Uncle John's promise. The contract is invalid, despite Jenny's sacrifice, because public policy supports marriages. Contracts to inhibit marriage are against public policy.

───

A quick review of the essential elements of a contract may be useful. Legal, enforceable contracts must meet the following tests:

1. The parties must have legal capacity, i.e. that adults be of sound mind.

2. The object or purpose of the contract must be legal.

3. There must be an exchange of consideration, or something of value, usually money.

4. There must be an offer and a proper acceptance of the offer before the specified period of time ends.

5. The parties must agree to at least the essential terms, which the law defines as:

a. the identity of the parties;

b. the subject matter of the contract;

c. the prices; and

d. the time period for performance.

A valid contract must pass these five tests of validity. It is an attorney's job to determine whether each of the tests is successfully met. However, since a broker is the agent who negotiates most, if not all, of the terms between the parties, he or she must understand the kinds of terms to be considered to secure a valid contract. In some states, it is a broker's function to fill in the blanks on a written purchase and sale contract; in other jurisdictions, brokers work with attorneys who are responsible for reducing the buyer's and seller's agreement to writing.

Statute of Frauds Requirements

The following paragraphs describe why real estate contracts must be committed to writing and what elements need to be included in written contract.

In general, many contracts are valid despite the fact that they are made orally. Certain types of contracts, however, are unenforceable unless they are in writing. The rules requiring certain kinds of contracts to be in writing come from an old English statute known as the *statute of fraud*. This statute is so named because its primary purpose was to prevent fraudulent claims by requiring written evidence to prove the claim.

Example

Em Bezzler decides that he wants Vic Tem's spectacular 100-acre property, Mountain-View. Vic refuses to sell, so Em brings a lawsuit in court, falsely and fraudulently claiming that Vic agreed to sell him Mountain-View. To prove his case, Em bribes his unscrupulous friends to lie to the judge, saying that Vic had agreed to sell the property. Clearly, if Em's friends are successful liars, Vic will lose his property. Thus, to prevent this wrongful theft of property, courts require a written contract or memorandum as evidence of the agreement.

The statute of frauds has the following effects on contracts for the sale of real estate. A typical statute of frauds provision, reads:

NO ACTION SHALL BE MAINTAINED...UPON ANY CONTRACT FOR THE SALE OF LANDS, tenements or hereditaments, OR OF ANY INTEREST IN OR CONCERNING THEM, UNLESS THE PROMISE, CONTRACT OR AGREEMENT on which such action is brought, or some memorandum or note thereof, IS IN WRITING AND SIGNED BY THE PARTY TO BE CHARGED.... (Me. Rev. Stat. Ann., Title 33, § 5164) (1964)

As the law states, a promise to transfer or buy any interest in land falls within the realm of the statute of frauds, and thus *must be in writing and must be signed by all parties against whom one would want to enforce the contract.*

Interest in Land

An interest in land is anything the law designates as real estate, including such rights in land as easements, profits, mortgages, and leases.

A real estate broker's job is to list, market, and sell various interests in land. Thus, virtually all transactions with which he or she is concerned will involve contracts subject to the statute of frauds' requirements of a signed written agreement or memorandum. An interest in land is any one of the topics defined and discussed in Chapters 2, 3, and 4 in this text: fee simple absolute, qualified fee, life estate, future interests, the interest of a concurrent owner easements and profits.

Options, rights of first refusal, trust deeds, installment land sale contracts, leases, and mortgages are the most common contracts concerning an interest in land, all of which the statute of frauds requires be in writing to be enforceable.

Satisfaction of the Statute of Frauds

When the contract, meaning the entire agreement of the parties, is in writing, the statute is obviously satisfied. But the statute of frauds may also be satisfied by something less than the complete written agreement of the parties; a note or a *memorandum* of the agreement may be enough to satisfy the statute's requirements.

To satisfy the statute of frauds, a memorandum or note must:

1. reasonably identify the subject of the contract;

2. indicate that a contract has been made between the parties;

3. state with reasonable certainty the essential terms of the contract; and

4. be signed by or on behalf of the party to be charged, i.e. by the person against whom the contract is to be enforced or by his or her authorized agent.

The memorandum required by the statute of frauds need not be contained on a single sheet of paper or as part of a whole document. It may consist of several writings, such as an exchange of letters, office memos, or telegrams; two or more memoranda together may satisfy the statute of frauds. The requirements as to contents and signatures, however, must be satisfied.

For separate writings to be considered together, their relation to each other must be clear. For example, in an exchange of letters, one letter may state: "in reply to your letter of September 1." Note that not all separate writings need be signed. An unsigned writing may be considered together with a signed writing if by express reference or sufficient internal evidence the unsigned paper is connected with the signed paper(s).

Exceptions to the Statute of Frauds

On very rare occasions, it is possible to enforce an oral contract for the sale of land, even though the statute of frauds requires that a contract for sale of land be in writing to serve as evidence of the existence and terms of a contract. If there is no written contract, but there is other compelling evidence that a contract exists, courts will sometimes enforce the agreement. For instance, a purchaser of real estate under an oral contract may, in reliance on the contract, take actions that serve as evidence that a contract was made.

Example ——————————————————————————

Laura agrees to serve as Ben's nurse and housekeeper for the remainder of his life. In return, Ben promises to leave one-half of his real estate and personal belongings to Laura. Acting in reliance on Ben's promise, Laura leaves her home in Michigan, moves to Maine, and serves as Ben's nurse for the next six years. When Ben dies without a will, Laura attempts to enforce the promise. The court is willing to override the statute of frauds stipulation because Laura has fully performed in reliance on Ben's promise.

Although reliance on an oral contract sometimes overrides the statute of frauds, the broker should accept as law that all contracts for the sale of an investment in real estate must be in writing. Only occasionally have courts issued orders to convey real estate without a written contract.

STANDARD CONTRACT CLAUSES

The sample contract for the sale of real estate on the facing page is keyed with letters to match references in the text. This sample contract is a good example of the type of contract most brokers use, so following its clauses point by point will enable the reader to complete a standard contract for sale of real estate that meets the requirements of law and adequately reflects the needs and wishes of the parties to the sale. This process should provide an appreciation for the issues and problems to be discussed and resolved by the parties prior to the sale.

1. The Parties (Clauses *A, N, O*)

The names of all parties to the transaction must be stated in the contract and designated as either buyer (purchaser) or seller. With married couples, it is important that each selling spouse be made a party to the contract. The title to the property will not be clear unless both spouses who are selling are named in the contract and both signatures are obtained, since a spouse has a right of descent in the other spouse's property, as discussed in Chapter 3.

2. Description of the Property (Clauses *B, C*)

The property being conveyed must be described clearly and ac-

Contract for Sale of Real Estate

A   RECEIVED of   19

hereinafter called the purchaser, the sum of ($)

DOLLARS

as earnest money and in part payment on account of the purchase price of the following described real estate,
B   situated in the County of   and State of   to wit:

C   The following items to be included in this sale:

D   the TOTAL purchase price being ($)

DOLLARS

E   payment to be made as follows:

Said deposit is received and held by the broker, subject to the following conditions:

F   1. That   , shall hold said earnest money or deposit and act as
escrow agent until transfer of title; that   days shall be given for obtaining the owner's acceptance; and, in event of the owner's non-acceptance, this deposit shall be promptly returned to the purchaser.

2. That a good and sufficient deed, showing good and merchantable title, shall be delivered to the purchaser, and it
is agreed that this transaction shall be closed and the purchaser shall pay the purchase price as provided herein and
execute all papers necessary for the completion of his purchase within   days from the date hereof. However, should the title prove defective, then the seller shall have a reasonable time after due notice of
such defect or defects, to remedy the title; after which time, if such defect or defects are not corrected so that
there is a merchantable title, then the purchaser may, at his option, withdraw said deposit and be relieved from
all obligations hereunder.

G   3. That the property shall be conveyed by   deed, and shall be free and clear of all
H   encumbrances except easements and zoning restrictions of record.
I   That full possession will be given
J   and that the following items shall be pro-rated as of transfer of title: Utilities   , Fuel   , Rents   ,
Real estate taxes from   19   to   19   .

K   4. The risk of loss or damage to said premises by fire or otherwise, until transfer of title hereunder is assumed by the Seller.

5. That in case of the failure of the Purchaser to make either of the payments, or any part thereof, or to perform
any of the covenants on his part made or entered into, this contract shall, at the option of the Seller, be terminated
and the Purchaser shall forfeit said earnest money or deposit; and the same shall be retained by the Seller as liqui-
L   dated damages, and the escrow agent is hereby authorized by the Purchaser to pay over to the Seller the earnest
money or deposit.

M   6. That time is an essential part of this agreement, and that all covenants and agreements herein contained shall extend
to and be obligatory upon the heirs, executors, administrators and assigns of the respective parties.

7. This contract is subject to an approved   mortgage of   % of the purchase price, at an interest
rate not to exceed   % and amortized over a period of not less than   years.

I hereby agree to purchase the above described property at the price and upon the terms and conditions above set
forth.

N

Witness	*Date*	*Purchaser*

Witness	*Date*	*Purchaser*

hereby accept the offer and agree to deliver the above described property at the price and upon the terms and conditions above stated.   further agree to pay the broker above named as commission for his services,   percent of the sale price. In the event said earnest money or deposit is forfeited by said purchaser, one-half thereof shall go to said broker and the remainder to   , provided, however, that the broker's portion shall not exceed the full amount of the commission specified.

O

Witness	*Date*	*Seller*

Witness	*Date*	*Seller*

P

Broker	*Co-Broker*

OFFICE

FHA

"It is expressly agreed that, notwithstanding any other provisions of this contract, the purchaser shall not be obligated to complete the purchase of the property described herein or to incur any penalty by forfeiture of earnest money deposits or otherwise unless the seller has delivered to the purchaser a written statement issued by the Federal Housing Commissioner setting forth the appraised value of the property for mortgage insurance purposes of not less than $, which statement the seller hereby agrees to deliver to the purchaser promptly after such appraised value statement is made to the seller."

"The purchaser shall, however, have the privilege and option of proceeding with the consummation of this contract without regard to the appraised valuation made by the Federal Housing Commissioner."

Purchaser	*Seller*

VA

"It is expressly agreed that, notwithstanding any other provisions of this contract, the purchaser shall not incur any penalty by forfeiture of earnest money or otherwise or be obligated to complete the purchase of the property described herein, if the contract purchase price or cost exceeds the reasonable value of the property established by the Veterans Administration. The purchaser shall, however, have the privilege and option of proceeding with the consummation of this contract without regard to the amount of the reasonable value established by the Veterans Administration."

Purchaser	*Seller*

EXTENSION

The time for the performance of the within instrument is hereby extended until ....
Witness our hands this .... day of .... 19.......

Purchaser	*Seller*

Purchaser	*Seller*

Contract for Sale of Real Estate

Buyer

Seller

Property

19

Dated

---

curately to satisfy the statute of frauds, as stated earlier in this chapter. The description must be complete enough to allow the parties and the court to easily and accurately identify the property being conveyed.

Example ——————————————————————————————

A conveyance of "Seller's two-story house on Elm Street" may not adequately describe the property. If the seller had more than one two-story house on that street, such a general description would not be sufficient to enable the court to decide which house the parties intended to buy and sell.

In some cases, the street name and number will be sufficient. However, it is always a good idea to include an additional description of the property to ensure that there will be no question as to which property is being conveyed. The contract may describe the property through the use of a formal legal description or by referring to a prior recorded deed or map.

Example ——————————————————————————————

". . . the following described real estate, situated in the County of Cumberland and State of Illinois, to wit: House and land at 35 Elm Street, being the same property conveyed to seller by John Jones by deed dated June 10, 1970, and recorded in the Cumberland County Registry of Deeds in Book 2,000, Page 100.''

A broker should make the parties aware that because fixtures are part of the real estate they will automatically be conveyed with the rest of the real estate, as explained in Chapter 1. If the parties wish to include other items of personal property in the sale, these items should be listed accurately in the contract for sale to prevent later disputes. For example, if a contract does not specify items of personal property included in the sale, and the buyer signs on the mistaken assumption that the refrigerator, washer, and dryer are included in the purchase price, problems are sure to arise. Inclusion of all items of personal property in the contract ensures that the agreement fully and accurately reflects the needs and wishes of the parties.

3. Purchase Price (Clauses *D, E*)

Purchase price and the exact method of payment must be specified in the contract.

4. Type of Deed (Clause *G*)

The contract should specify the kind of deed, discussed in depth in Chapter 8, to be granted. If the buyer is not willing to purchase unless a warranty deed is given, or if the buyer mistakenly believes that the words *good and merchantable title* mean that the seller is under an obligation to deliver a warranty deed, there will be problems with the sale. To prevent such difficulties, the contract should specify the type of deed to be delivered.

5. Merchantable or Marketable Title (Clause *F*)

Title is merchantable when it is free from reasonable doubt about any defects. Title need not be perfect to be *marketable;* it may be marketable if there is a possibility of a defect, provided the defect is unlikely to lead to litigation, or when there is an obvious but curable title defect.

It is the seller's responsibility to make sure there are no defects that would render the title unmarketable. The buyer will have a title search made of the property before the closing.

Many defects can make a title unmarketable. There may be defects in the chain of title, caused by failure of a spouse to release rights of descent, as discussed in Chapter 3. Defects in the chain of title may also be caused by an error in a prior deed's description of the property or by an improperly executed deed. Other defects may arise due to easements, tax liens, or undischarged mortgages on the property involved. The title search, covered in Chapter 10, will discover any title defects, so they can be resolved to make the title marketable.

6. Encumbrances (Clause *H*)

An *encumbrance* is a claim, lien, charge, or liability attached to and binding real property. It may consist of easements, covenants, or violations of existing zoning laws. To be marketable, title must be free not only from defects in the chain of title, but also from encumbrances, unless the contract specifically excepts existing encumbrances from title marketability. Failure to exclude existing encumbrances is grounds for *rescission,* or voiding, of the contract. Rescission as a remedy for breach is discussed later in this chapter.

Most contracts include a provision to the effect that the property is conveyed "free and clear of all encumbrances except...." Or the contract may simply state that the property is sold "subject to covenants and restrictions of record, if any." Such a provision puts the buyer on notice that he or she must search the record for such encumbrances or bear the risk that they exist.

7. Time for Performance (Clauses *F* and *M*)

The time for performance is ordinarily dependent upon the schedule of the bank or loan association financing the closing and often cannot be predicted with certainty by the parties to the transaction. Nevertheless, the contract should specify the time of day, date, and place where the deed will be delivered. If the anticipated closing date becomes inconvenient, the parties may always extend the time for performance by signing a written amendment to the agreement.

If *no* time for performance is specified in the contract, the court will allow the parties what it determines is a reasonable time for performance; what is a reasonable time will vary with the circumstances of the case.

Closing the deal a few days or so after the anticipated time for performance is not ordinarily a problem, especially in the sale of residential property. However, it can cause tremendous problems for one of the parties in some cases. In a sale of commercial property, for example, a one- or two-day delay in closing and beginning operations can cost the company large amounts of money in lost profits.

In such cases, the time for performance is essential, and the contract should make it clear that failure to meet the time for performance constitutes breach of contract. A *"time is of the essence"* clause is used in such a case.

Example ——————————————————————————————

"Such deed is to be delivered at 9:00 A.M. on the 10th day of June, 1979, at the Cumberland County Registry of Deeds, unless otherwise agreed upon in writing. It is agreed that time is of the essence of this agreement."

———————————————————————————————————

When the contract specifies that time is of the essence, and one of the parties fails to perform on the specified date, there is a breach of contract. Ordinarily, the breach will mean that the buyer need not purchase if the seller is not ready, willing, and able to sell on the date specified or that the seller need not deliver the deed, and the buyer's part payment is forfeited, if the time for performance is not met.

The broker should limit use of this clause to situations in which time really is a critical factor. In other situations, use of this clause may stand in the way of a sale that both parties wish would go through, forcing one of the parties to breach simply because the closing did not take place at the expected time. The licensee should, therefore, consider the intentions of the parties, and the effect such a clause might have on those intentions, before including the clause in a contract.

8. Risk of Loss (Clause *K*)

Sometimes, between the time of signing the contract for sale and the time of actual delivery of the deed, the property to be conveyed is destroyed or damaged because of fire or natural disaster. Who suffers the loss, the buyer or the seller? In many states, the seller bears the risk of loss to the property. In these states, when the seller is unable to deliver the premises as they were contracted—i.e. by repairing the damage loss before the time for performance—the seller cannot recover or retain any part of the purchase price tendered. In other states, the loss would fall on the buyer.

It is crucial that the parties agree who bears the risk of loss and that the contract contain provisions fixing that risk on one or the other of the parties.

Example

The parties may agree to a clause such as "the risk of loss or damage to said premises by fire or otherwise, until transfer of title hereunder, is assumed by seller."

Since each party has an insurable interest in the property after the time of signing the contract, each party may protect that interest by arranging for insurance coverage. Inclusion of a *risk of loss* clause is the best way to inform the parties as to their respective rights and liabilities and to put them on notice that additional insurance coverage may be necessary.

9. Possession (Clause *I*)

Whether the property involved in the transaction is commercial or residential, the date of possession is usually of major concern to the parties. The contract should contain a provision fixing that date, whether it be at closing or several days before or after that time.

10. Closing Adjustments (Clause *J*)

Although the parties are not legally bound to apportion the income and expenses of the property, the contract should provide for proration of such items as taxes, utilities, fuel, and rent assessment.

The parties may decide on an equitable apportionment of utility costs by examining past monthly bills, by having meters read before closing, or by making arrangements with the utility companies to change the billing names as of a certain date. Whatever arrangements for apportioning utility costs are made by the parties, they should be written into the contract.

When the property to be conveyed is an income property, the contract should contain a provision as to apportionment of rental income, even if the closing date falls on a day when rents are due. In any case, the exact method and date of apportionment should be set out in the contract.

11. Earnest Money (Clause F)

A buyer is not legally required to make a down payment on the purchase price. However, most contracts provide for payment of an earnest money deposit, usually five to ten percent of purchase price, primarily to deter the buyer from breaching the agreement. State laws establish procedures a broker must follow in handling the earnest money deposits. Generally, the deposit is put into an escrow account until the date of closing.

12. Breach of Contract (Clause L)

In the interest of clarity for the buyer and seller, a purchase of sale contract for real estate should include a clause that spells out the consequences of the buyer's failure to live up to his or her agreement, also known as *breach of contract*. Of course, the parties may wish to make the contract conditional on some other event, such as on the buyer's obtaining financing based on the hopes of obtaining a variance in the current zoning ordinance or on the buyer's being able to sell his or her own home. The contract must include whatever conditions the parties decide upon, spelled out in as much detail as possible.

Once a valid contract for the sale of real estate has been negotiated and signed by both parties, each party is bound to perform according to its terms. Should one of the parties fail to perform, the other may bring a lawsuit to enforce the contract. Generally, a party will have a choice of three remedies and, on the advice of an attorney, will decide which of those remedies would be most appropriate. In any case, the court will grant, at its discretion, whatever remedy it finds reasonable and appropriate to the facts of the case. The remedies are described briefly below.

1. Rescission. A party may seek to *rescind*, or cancel the contract when he or she has been induced to sign by fraud, duress, or undue influence.

Similarly, if the buyer and seller make a contract for a piece of property and both reasonably but mistakenly believe there will be no zoning problem with the buyer's expected use of the property, the buyer may seek rescission. Of course, a contract may always be rescinded by mutual consent of the parties.

For a contract to be rescinded, each party must restore the other to the position he or she held before the making of a contract. In the case of a contract for the sale of real estate, this often means that the seller must return all money received from the buyer as payment, and the buyer must restore possession, if held, to the seller.

2. Action for damages. Unless the contract has a liquidated damages clause, either party may bring an action for damages to restore that party to as good a position as he or she would have held if the other party had not breached the contract. The measure of damages is generally the difference between the contract price and the market value of the property at the time the deed was to have been delivered.

Example

Buyer and seller sign a $50,000 contract for the sale of a house and lot. Buyer pays $5,000 toward the purchase price. Seller breaches the contract. It is determined in court that the property was worth $56,000 on September 1, 1978, the date originally set for closing. Buyer may receive $11,000 in damages—the difference between the contract and market price plus the down payment already made.

---

3. Specific Performance. *Specific performance* provides a party with the means to enforce a contract by compelling the breaching party to do what he or she contracted to do. For example, if the buyer brings a specific performance action to court and succeeds, the seller will be forced to deliver title.

Example ————————————————————————————————

Buyer contracts with the seller to buy a piece of property with the swimming pools, golf course, and wooded grounds that the buyer needs to set up a country club. Because the property is uniquely tailored to the buyer's needs, and because there is no other property in the area that could replace it, the buyer's best remedy would be specific performance, insisting that seller go through with the sale.

Forfeiture and Liquidated Damages

Occasionally, a buyer will want to back out of a real estate contract and refuse to complete the sale. The seller in such cases is understandably upset because he or she will have taken the property off the market for the period during which it was expected that the buyer would conclude the sale. Most real estate purchase and sale contracts provide for this event; clause (L) in the sample agreement is a typical provision that requires the buyer to forfeit the earnest money deposit. The forfeiture is automatic on the buyer's nonperformance. The parties to the agreement acknowledge that this sum will constitute *liquidated damages*. They agree in advance that this sum will cover the loss the seller will experience. If the seller accepts the forfeited down payment as liquidated damages, no further suit for damages is brought.

The amount designated in the contract as liquidated damages for the buyer's breach must be reasonable. A court of law will not enforce a liquidated damages clause if it finds the amount unreasonably large in light of anticipated or actual damages resulting from the breach. If the amount of liquidated damages is unrelated to actual loss, a court may find them to be punitive in nature and, therefore, improper.

Example

A offers to purchase Blackacre for $90,000, which seller B accepts. A makes a ten percent earnest money deposit with a contract that contains the liquidated damages clause (L) in the sample contract. The next day, A's company transfers him to another part of the country, so he decides not to complete the transaction. The broker for the sale finds another buyer for B's house within a week, someone who buys at the same price. The liquidated damages clause is clearly unfair in this case; A's forfeiture of $9,000 is excessive where it can be shown that B suffered no loss. It would be unfair for B to keep the deposit.

13. Assignment and Recording

Once negotiated and signed, a valid contract confers rights on each party—the buyer has the right to delivery of the deed and the seller has the right to the purchase price. Unless a contract expressly provides otherwise, either party may sell his or her rights under the contract to a third party; such a sale or transfer is called an *assignment*.

Contracts for the sale of real estate may be recorded in the registry of deeds. Recording may protect the buyer from a possible transfer of title by the seller to a third person who purchases in good faith, with no notice of the pre-existing contract; recording is of no advantage to the seller. If either party has any intention of assigning rights to the contract, or the buyer plans to record the conveyance, it is appropriate that the purchase and sale contract specify the parties' rights to assign or record.

SUMMARY

The importance of contract law to the broker cannot be underestimated. Although the topics of fixtures, estates in land, concurrent ownership, and deeds are all important, the subject of contracts has special importance for one reason: When a buyer and seller have signed a valid contract, they have committed each other to completing a transaction that will result in the broker's earning a commission. The failure of another party to go through with his or her promise generally leads to a lawsuit and forfeit of an earnest money deposit. Since the broker's business is to bring buyers and sellers together in a binding contract, it is crucial that he or she understand the concepts of offer and acceptance, including how long offers remain open and can be accepted, how offers can be accepted by correspondence or mail, etc.

The broker also must understand the requirements of the statute of frauds—that the contract be in writing and contain certain minimal terms to be enforceable. Even a minimal form agreement is not really adequate to provide for the proration of taxes, occupancy date, time for performance, and other matters that routinely apply in a real estate transaction.

A word of caution for real estate brokers is in order at this point: Drafting contracts is generally considered lawyer's work, and brokers who get involved in drafting clauses to fit the particular transactions they have negotiated are engaged in the unauthorized practice of law. In the practice of their profession, brokers tread a line that often takes them very close to the jurisdiction of the legal profession. It is generally permissible for brokers to fill in the blanks on preprinted forms prepared by an attorney; it is not proper for brokers to create their own contract clauses.

Chapter 13 discusses the problem of the unauthorized practice of law in greater detail.

MULTIPLE CHOICE QUESTIONS

1. Which of the following elements is (are) necessary to create a contract?

   a. offer
   b. acceptance
   c. consideration
   d. all of the above

2. An exchange of promises creates which kind of contract?

   a. unilateral contract
   b. bilateral contract
   c. option contract
   d. voidable contract

3. The statute of frauds requires

   a. that contracts for the sale of real estate be in writing.
   b. that a full title search be done before the deed is transferred.
   c. that the deed to real estate be in writing.
   d. none of the above.

4. The statute of frauds protects primarily

   a. land owners who don't want to sell their land from the fraudulent claims of would-be purchasers.
   b. brokers who want their commissions.
   c. buyers.
   d. all of the above.

5. The purpose of an option contract is to:

   a. avoid violating the statute of frauds.
   b. invite bids.
   c. keep an offer open for a certain length of time.
   d. avoid the requirements of offer and acceptance.

6. Which of the terms below is not essential to form a legal contract?

    a. time for performance
    b. names of the parties
    c. subject matter of the contract
    d. price

7. A contract for the sale of property will be considered too vague unless it includes:

    a. the names of the parties.
    b. a description of the property.
    c. the purchase price.
    d. all of the above

8. A revocation of an offer becomes effective:

    a. when the offeree receives it.
    b. when the offeree should have received it, although it may have become lost.
    c. when it is postmarked.
    d. none of the above

9. The acceptance of an offer becomes effective when:

    a. it is postmarked.
    b. the offeree receives it.
    c. it is posted according to the "mailbox rule."
    d. the offeree should have received it, although it may have become lost.

10. Contracts made by a minor are:

    a. voidable.
    b. void.
    c. void for vagueness.
    d. fraudulent.

11. Which of the following is not required by the statute of frauds in a contract for the sale of real estate?

    a. notarization
    b. a written memorandum
    c. signature
    d. description of land

12. To be marketable, a title must:

    a. be conveyed by a warranty deed.
    b. have a high value.
    c. be held by a willing seller.
    d. be generally free from defects.

13. Which of the following may cause a title defect?

    a. failure to have the title searched
    b. failure of a spouse to release rights of descent to marital property
    c. failure of the owner to keep the premises in good repair
    d. failure of the buyer to inspect the property before the sale

14. A "time is of the essence" clause:

    a. means that if one of the parties fails to meet the specified time of delivery, that party will have breached the contract.
    b. indicates the unusual importance of meeting the specified time of delivery.
    c. is found mainly in contracts for the sale of commercial property.
    d. all of the above

15. Joe's Pizza Place is going out of business. Mo's Cheese Shop agrees to buy Joe's business. Their contract includes a liquidated damages clause and is conditional upon Mo's obtaining financing. By the closing date, Mo had not received financing; in fact, he had made no effort to do so. What can Joe do?

    a.   He has no remedy at law.
    b.   He can bring suit against Mo to buy the property.
    c.   He must cancel the contract and return Mo's deposit.
    d.   He may keep Mo's deposit, which Mo has forefeited.

DISCUSSION QUESTIONS

1. Imagine that you own property in Jonesville and receive the following unsolicited letter from X:

> Dear Sir:
> Will you sell me your store property, which is located on Main Street in Jonesville, running from Montgomery's Drug Store on one corner to the grocery store on the other corner, for the sum of $6,000?

You reply to X as follows:

> In reply to your letter of October 23rd, which has been forwarded to me in which you inquire about the Bradley Block in Jonesville.
>
> Because of improvements, which have been added at an expenditure of several thousand dollars, it would not be possible for me to sell it unless I were to receive $16,000 cash.
>
> The upper floors have been converted into apartments with baths and the building put into first class condition.
> Very truly yours,

You then receive the following from X.

> ACCEPT YOUR OFFER FOR BRADLEY BLOCK JONESVILLE TERMS SIXTEEN THOUSAND CASH SEND DEED TO EASTERN TRUST AND BANKING CO. BRIDGEPORT, PLEASE ACKNOWLEDGE

Four days later, you notify X that you do not wish to sell the property. Later, X brings suit for breach of contract. Was a contract created through the exchange of the above correspondence? Why or why not? Was there an offer? An acceptance? Would the writings be sufficient to satisfy the requirements of the statute of frauds?

2. You, the broker, have matched a seller and a buyer, both of whom are ready, willing, and able to contract; both are in your office for the purpose of negotiating the contract for sale. Aside from the contract clauses that require little or no negotiation—parties and legal description of the property—what issues or questions should you raise for the parties to discuss?

8

Transferring Title

This chapter deals with the various methods by which title to a piece of real estate is transferred from one person to another. The great majority of title transfers take place between living people—called an *inter vivos,* between living persons, transfer— known as the *grantor* and *grantee.* The buyer and seller sign a purchase and sale agreement that calls for the transfer of ownership at a future date, to be accomplished by the seller's giving a deed. When the transfer of real estate is a gift, the same form of deed will be used; however, there will be no need for a purchase and sale agreement.

Not all real estate is transferred during an owner's lifetime. Property owned at the time of death is transferred through the deceased's will, where there is a will, or to heirs at law as designated by the state rules of descent and distribution where there is no will.

When a person dies owning property, whether real estate or personal estate, and without either a will or heirs, there are no apparent instructions for the distribution of the estate. In these cases, the property escheats, that is, goes to the state treasurer.

Eminent domain is the power of government to take a person's private property for a reasons of public safety or welfare. Such a transfer of title is involuntary on the part of the private owner but is recognized in our society as a legitimate use of government authority.

Adverse possession is another doctrine by which a property owner can lose title to his or her land. Each state has local laws that spell out squatter's rights and enable longtime occupants and users of property to acquire legal title from the owner of record.

Tax deeds are used by municipal governments to transfer title to land they may have acquired from local property owners who have failed to pay their taxes. Unpaid real estate taxes become a priority lien on the property, and if the proper owner fails to pay these taxes, the municipality has the authority to take the property, sell it, and keep the proceeds for the taxes that were due.

Mortgages will be discussed in Chapter 9, as will the foreclosure process, another method by which title to real estate is transferred from one owner to another.

DEEDS

The transfer of real estate from one living person to another is the most common type of transaction. The document used in the inter vivos transfer of property is a deed, a document containing much information useful to real estate brokers. A deed includes:

1. the names of the current owner or owners; to convey full title to the property, the signatures of all the owners of record will have to appear on the new deed.

2. information on how title is held—solely, jointly, tenancy in common, tenancy in partnership, tenancy by the entirety.

3. a proper legal description of the land to be transferred.

4. the legal interests of the parties, including whether they have a fee simple interest, a qualified fee, a life estate, or an estate for years. In virtually all cases, the deed shows the current owners to hold a fee simple interest.

5. possible references to easements or restrictions on the property. Where the deed is for a condominium unit, it may contain references to other recorded documents, including the declaration of trust and association by-laws that will affect the owner's rights with respect to the property.

Brokers should make it a routine practice to read the deeds of the property they are listing, showing, or selling. This is an essential step in developing "product knowledge" so that an effective selling presentation can be made to buyers.

The following paragraphs of this section describe the elements of a deed, the requirements for an effective transfer of title to real estate, and the imposition of taxes on the actual transfer and compare different types of deeds.

Types of Deeds

There are several varieties of legally acceptable deeds, including full warranty deed; limited warranty deed, sometimes known as a quitclaim deed with covenants; and quitclaim deed, sometimes called a quitclaim release deed. Although each deed must meet the same standards for an effective conveyance, the differences between them lie in the guarantees or warranties the seller makes when using one form instead of another.

Full Warranty Deed

A *warranty deed* is the most commonly used form and the type of deed preferred by buyers. It carries the broadest of sellers' assurances as to the quality of the legal title conveyed, and its guarantees are assurances against any adverse claim no matter when the claim might have arisen. In other words, the sellers' assurances go back in time to claims that may have arisen against previous owners as well as claims that may have arisen during his or her own period of ownership. A sample of a typical warranty deed begins on the following page.

A seller who conveys property with a full warranty deed makes six *covenants* or promises to the buyer:

Covenant of Seisin. This warrants that the grantor in fact owns the estate or interest being conveyed i.e. that he or she has title to the property.

Covenant against Encumbrances. This is a warrant or guarantee that there are no encumbrances against the title except those stated in the deed; in other words, there are no unmentioned liens, mortgages, easements, or covenants on the property.

Covenant of Right to Convey. This covenant is basically the same as the covenant of seisin; that is, the grantor owns the estate and thus has the power to convey.

Covenant of Quiet Enjoyment. The grantor here warrants that the grantee will not be disturbed by others claiming a lawful interest in the property being purchased.

Covenant for Further Assurances. This promise requires that the grantor execute any documents that may be needed in the future to make good the title of the grantee. This covenant is not often used in this country.

Covenant of Warranty. This covenant, essentially the same as the covenant of quiet enjoyment, assures that the grantor has sound title and that he or she *will defend* the grantee's title against other lawful claims at the date of conveyance.

Limited Warranty Deed

The limited warranty deed is also known as a *quitclaim deed with covenant.* A grantor guarantees the title he or she is conveying to the grantee and the grantee's heirs, against all persons claiming an interest or title "by, through, or under" the grantor. The grantor is simply conveying whatever present interest he or she has in the real estate and is promising that he or she has done nothing to impair title *during his or her ownership of the property.*

Warranty Deed

From

Thomas E. Blake et ux

To

Charles S. Coit, et ux

Dated December 28 ....,19 84

State of Maine,

Cumberland .... ss. Registry of Deeds.

Received ... December 28 ....,19 84

at . 15 . H . , . 44 . M . , ... M., and

recorded in Book 6127 .... Page 382

Attest: .... Register.

FROM THE OFFICE OF
Cecil Burtaskett, Esq.
One Monument Place
Portland, ME

Marks Printing House, Portland, Maine
ML 10-2

WARRANTY DEED

Know all Men by these Presents,

That THOMAS E. BLAKE and EDRIE L. BLAKE, both

of South Portland , County of Cumberland , Maine,

in consideration of one dollar and other valuable consideration

paid by CHARLES S. COIT AND DIANA M. COIT

whose mailing address is 893 Schooner Lane,

South Portland , County of Cumberland , Maine,

the receipt whereof is hereby acknowledged, do hereby **give, grant, bargain, sell and convey** unto the said

CHARLES S. COIT and DIANA M. COIT as joint tenants

their heirs and assigns forever, the following described real estate:

A certain parcel of land with the buildings thereon, situated on Schooner Lane in the City of South Portland, County of Cumberland and State of Maine, bounded and described as follows:

BEGINNING at the intersection of the westerly side of Pine Street with the northerly side of Schooner Lane; thence northerly by said Pine Street 85 feet to land formerly of Josiah Sterling; thence westerly by said Sterling land at right angles with Pine Street, 8 rods, more or less, to land formerly of Joseph Marriner; thence southerly by said Marriner land to said Schooner Lane; thence easterly by said Schooner Lane to the point of beginning.

Being the same premises conveyed to the Grantors herein by Mary B. Young by Warranty Deed dated January 18, 1982 and recorded in the Cumberland County Registry of Deeds in Book 4910, Page 138.

To have and to hold the aforegranted and bargained premises with all the privileges and appurtenances thereof to the said CHARLES S. COIT and DIANA M. COIT

their heirs and assigns, to them and their use and behoof forever.

G

And we   do **covenant** with the said Grantee^S,   their   heirs and assigns, that
we are   lawfully seized in fee of the premises, that they are free of all encumbrances
                              that   we   have good right to sell and convey
the same to the said Grantee to hold as aforesaid; and that   we   and   our   heirs shall and
will **warrant and defend** the same to the said Grantee ,   their   heirs and assigns forever, against
the lawful claims and demands of all persons.

H

In Witness Whereof,   we   the said   THOMAS E. BLAKE
                                    and   EDRIE L. BLAKE
husband/wife of the said   THOMAS E. BLAKE
joining in this deed as Grantor^S, and relinquishing and conveying all rights by descent and all other rights in the
above described premises, have hereunto set   our   hand and seal this   28th   day of the
month of   December   , A.D. 19^84 .

I

Signed, Sealed and Delivered
   in presence of

....   *Thomas E. Blake*

....   *Edrie L. Blake*

....

....

State of Maine, County of   Cumberland   **ss.**   December 28   , 19 84

Then personally appeared the above named   Thomas E. Blake and Edrie L. Blake

and acknowledged the foregoing instrument to be   their   free act and deed.

Before me,

.......*Dirk Stone*...............

Dirk Stone   Notary Public
                                        ~~Attorney at Law~~

The grantor does not make any promises to the grantee concerning previous owners who may make a claim to the property, alleging to have a better title. This is a limited warranty, one that is quite inferior to the warranty deed, whereby the grantor warrants against the claims of *all* persons whatsoever.

Quitclaim Release Deed

A *quitclaim release deed* conveys title with no warranties. By using this deed, the grantor simply releases whatever right, title, or interest held at the time of the conveyance. It is conceivable that a grantor using a quitclaim release deed would have no interest in the property at all.

Example ————————————————————

Grandfather has three grandchildren who will inherit his land, worth $300,000, when he dies. One grandchild needs $100,000 today to go into business; grandfather advances the cash, and grandchild agrees to give up any inheritance. When grandfather dies without a will, the three grandchildren are heirs at law, and as a matter of record, each have a one-third interest in the land. To convey clear title to the land, a deed from each of the three grandchildren must be secured. But since one grandchild received an inheritance early, he has no interest of value in the land; therefore, he conveys his interest with a quitclaim release deed—his legal interest is conveyed, but since he is not being paid for it, he makes no guarantees. The deed is to clarify the record, that each of the owners of record has conveyed his or her interests.

————————————————————————

The grantor who uses a quitclaim release deed has said, in effect, "I transfer all interest I might have to you. I may have no interest or title at all, or someone else may have better title than I. I make no promises." Quitclaim release deeds are generally used to clear up ambiguous situations that show up in the records at registries of deeds, to enable future owners to sell title clear of any cloudy records. The consideration paid for such deeds is generally little or nothing.

Essential Components of a Deed

A valid deed must contain certain elements. These elements are:

1. the name of the grantor/seller;
2. the name of the grantee/buyer, as well as his or her current address—street and street number, town, and state;
3. the words of grant;
4. a description of the land conveyed; and
5. the signature of the grantor.

Some states do not require witnesses, although a typical deed usually leaves a space for witnesses.

Before continuing, the reader should read the warranty deed on page 181. This deed is referred to in the following discussion of the various components of a deed. The lettered paragraphs that follow refer to the letters on the deed.

A.   Names of the Parties. At the beginning of the deed, starting with the words "Know All Men by These Presents That," the names of the grantors, or sellers, appear together with their addresses. After a recitation of the consideration, the name of the grantees and their mailing address appear. Addresses are included to assist in identifying the parties to the transaction.

B.   Consideration. A recitation of consideration, generally the purchase price, is not necessary as a matter of law in some states. The practice of reciting consideration dates back to the 16th century when such recitation was required. However, a deed today is good without disclosing the actual consideration, although a nominal amount such as "one dollar and other valuable consideration" is usually on the deed.

C.   Granting Clause Operative Words. For a grantor to convey land to another, the intent to do so must be clearly expressed by certain operative words in the deed. These words are traditionally those in big, bold letters found in our sample deed following the grantee's address: "GIVE, GRANT, BARGAIN, SELL AND CONVEY." Although all these words are customarily included in the deed as proof of grantor's intent to transfer the land, not all of them are necessary. It should be noted that a deed containing no operative words of grant is void and will not be effective as a conveying instrument.

D.   Words of Inheritance. The modern trend is that the words of inheritance, "heirs and assigns forever," are not necessary to transfer a fee simple estate by deed.

E.   Legal Description. It is important that the property's legal description and boundaries be accurately provided. The description is legally adequate if, relying on it, a competent surveyor can locate the boundaries of the property. The actual metes and bounds description need not be included in the deed if the deed refers to a plan that identifies the real estate in question and has been filed at the registry of deeds. A deed description is also adequate if it refers to the land conveyed in a prior adequate deed. Note that the legal description in this deed describes the real estate both by reference to a prior deed and by reference to a plan.

F. Habendum. Immediately following the legal description of the conveyed real estate is the *habendum clause:* "...to have and to hold." The habendum clause repeats the names of the grantees and defines the type of estate they hold. Its function is to state the nature of the estate taken by the grantees: e.g. a fee simple, a life estate etc.

G. Grantor's Covenants. This section recites any of the grantor's promises or covenants. In this example, the grantor makes the following covenants:

(a) the covenant of *seisin*, saying that the grantee is "lawfully seized in fee of the premises";

(b) the covenant against *encumbrances;*

(c) the covenant of *right to convey*, stating that the grantee has "good right to sell and convey the same to the said grantee";

(d) the covenant of quiet enjoyment; and

(e) the covenant of *warranty*, declaring that the grantor "will WARRANT and DEFEND the same against the lawful claims and demands of all persons."

H. Testimonium Clause and Release of Spouse's Interest. The clause beginning with "In Witness Whereof" and concluding with "...in the year of our Lord one thousand nine hundred and..." is the *testimonium clause* and the release of the spouse's interest. The testimonium clause is not required by law, although it is customarily included. The release of the spouse's right of descent in both a warranty and a quitclaim deed, as well as the release of all other rights in the land, follows the testimonium clause. The law does not require that the deed be dated. A deed becomes effective on the day it is delivered, not on the day it is dated.

I. Execution, Delivery, and Acceptance of the Deed. To be valid, a deed must be signed by the grantor or the grantor's legal representative. Generally, the signing is acknowledged by a notary public or justice of the peace to show that the grantor is acting on his or her own free will. The official authorized to administer the oath varies according to the law of the state, generally a notary public, a justice of the peace, or an attorney. In any event, the acknowledgment by a duly authorized officer of the state is generally necessary for the recording of the deed in the local registry of deeds. Other witnesses to the deed are generally not necessary unless the grantor is physically unable to sign his or her name. The grantor may affix his or her mark, an *X* for example, to which there must be witnesses, as state law may require.

A final step in the completion of a conveyance is the *delivery and acceptance* of the deed. These concepts are very important, and although in the vast majority of cases there will be no problems, the problems that can arise may be quite complicated.

Broadly stated, a deed cannot operate as an effective conveying instrument until it is delivered. Under normal circumstances, delivery occurs when the deed is passed from the grantor or the grantor's agent to the grantee or the grantee's agent. No special method or rules must be followed except that the grantor must *intend* to deliver the deed.

Example ———————————————————————————

John signs a deed to transfer Blackacre to Fred, but he is not sure whether he wants to complete the transfer. John loses the deed; a friend of Fred's finds it and gives it to Fred. There has been no delivery because John did not *intend* to deliver the deed at the time.

In addition to delivery of the deed by the grantor, the grantee must *accept* the deed. In most instances, the acceptance can easily be inferred from the circumstances surrounding the transaction and from the actions of the parties. However, in some cases, the grantee may not want to accept the deed to a piece of property because such an acceptance would not be in his or her interest.

Example ─────────────────────────────────────

Blackacre, worth $4,000, has a tax lien of $5,000, owed to the town. Don, who owns Blackacre, tries to give Blackacre to Earl. Earl may not want to accept a deed to Blackacre even as a gift because of the tax liability. A grantee of Blackacre must intend to accept the deed to complete the conveyance of Blackacre.

───

Delivery may also be made in *escrow*. This arrangement exists when a third party holds the deed from the grantor but is not to give the deed to the grantee until some condition has been met—e.g. payment of full purchase price.

Real Estate Transfer Taxes

A real estate *transfer tax,* known as *mortgage registration* in some states, is essentially a sales tax on the sale of land. The sale may be taxed by the state and/or the municipality in which the land is located. The amount of the tax varies from jurisdiction to jurisdiction. In some states, the seller pays the tax; in others, the buyer pays it. In still others, the parties may split the tax, and in yet others, the parties may negotiate who pays the tax.

WILLS

Brokers, who are regularly involved with transfer of title to real estate, must be aware of some of the effects a property owner's death may have on title ownership. This section and the following section on intestate succession describe what happens to property interests when the owner dies.

Wills and Real Estate

One of the most valuable rights of property ownership is the right to give or devise one's property after death and the best way for a property owner to exercise this right is to draw up a will. By drawing up a will, a person may designate those to whom the property will go and how much interest each will have in the estate. Provided the will is valid, the property will be distributed according to the property owner's wishes.

One who disposes of property by will is called a *testator* or *testatrix*. A disposition of real property by will is technically called a <u>*devise*</u>, and those for whom the real property is intended are called the *devisees*. A disposition of personal property by will is called a *bequest* or *legacy*, and those for whom the personal property is intended are called *legatees*.

A will does not become operative—i.e. have any legal effect—until the testator's death. Before such time, the testator is free to revoke the will in whole or in part, replacing certain provisions or the entire will with completely different arrangement for property disposition. Nor do the devisees and legatees automatically take the property at the testator's death. Distribution of the deceased's property takes place under the direction of the probate court, in accordance with the provisions of the will.

INTESTATE SUCCESSION

When a person dies without a will, or with a will that a court later determines to be invalid, the deceased is said to have died *intestate*. In such cases, the estate of the deceased is distributed according to the state's *laws of succession* or *rules of descent and distribution*.

Rules of descent are designed to provide for distribution of the estate in the manner the deceased probably would have chosen had he or she left a will. In other words, the law provides for relatives closest to the deceased—spouse, children, etc.—to take the estate left behind. The distribution of the estate in the case of intestacy, like distribution of the estate left under a will, is handled under the direction of the probate court.

The court will appoint a personal <u>*administrator,*</u> whose job it is to notify all creditors and heirs of the death; make an inventory of the deceased's assets; pay any income, estate, and inheritance taxes due; distribute the property to the heirs; and make a final accounting to the probate court.

Each state has its own <u>*inheritance statute*</u> that governs the distribution of the estate of a person who dies intestate. These inheritance statutes follow the same general pattern, placing the interest of the surviving spouse and children as the top priority. A typical inheritance statute might provide the following.

1. To the Surviving Spouse: the first $50,000 of the deceased's estate plus one-half of the balance if the deceased also has surviving children; *or* all of the estate if there are no children.

2. To the Surviving Children: one-half of the net estate, to be divided equally if there is a surviving spouse, *or* all of the net estate, divided equally, if there is no surviving spouse.

These are sample provisions of the Uniform Probate Code, adopted as the law of several states. Additional rules for distribution of intestate property also provide for remote degrees of relation.

When the deceased leaves an estate of $100,000 in savings accounts, the money is easily divisible among the heirs. But suppose the estate also contains a ranch worth $1 million. How is the real estate divided? In that case, each heir gets his or her statutory interest in the property as a tenant in common with the other heirs. In other words, by operation of the law, the surviving spouse automatically takes a one-half interest in the ranch as a tenant in common with her two children, who each have a one-quarter interest.

It is important for a licensee to understand how the deceased's sole ownership has been split among his heirs. In order to sell the property, Laura, the surviving spouse, and two children each must sign the deed so a new owner may own the ranch with clear title.

Escheat

Most inheritance statutes provide for the situation in which the deceased dies intestate and without heirs. In this case, the entire estate of the deceased is said to go to the state by *escheat*.

Example ────────────────────────────

Sam's heirs—Laura, Jack, and Jill—all die in an accident. There are no other living relatives. The estates of all three escheat to the state.

PROBATE

The previous sections examined how a person's real and personal property may be distributed after his or her death. The person may have provided for the distribution of the property by making a will designating the people who are to receive the estate. If the deceased died without a will, the property is distributed in accordance with the laws of intestate succession.

The main purpose of the probate process is to supervise the distribution of the decedent's estate. After the deceased's assets have been collected and debts paid, the remainder of the estate will be distributed to the beneficiaries of the estate. The process is administered by the deceased's personal representative, who may be nominated in the will or, where there is no will, appointed by the probate court.

Probating the Will

The first step in the probate process is always the determination of whether or not there is, in fact, a will. To *probate a will* means to prove the existence and validity of a will or the nonexistence of one. A will takes effect when the probate court has rendered a judgment that the will is valid. If the person died intestate, the surviving spouse or next of kin will file a *petition for administration*. In the case of intestacy, the petitioner will state that, after diligent search, no will was found.

Selling Real Property in Probate

Once the will has been authenticated, or the lack of a will has been confirmed, the representative must inventory the estate and appraise the assets. Next, the debts of the estate must be paid. The decedent's personal estate is usually applied first in satisfaction of debts. However, if the personal estate is not sufficient to satisfy all claims against it, the representative may have to sell some of the estate's real property. This is where the broker may become involved in the probate process.

When the cash owned by the deceased is inadequate to pay the bills, the probate court may order the sale of real estate to raise cash to pay bills. The court-appointed administrator or executor of the estate may come to the broker to list this estate property for sale. When a buyer has been found, the administrator will go back before the probate judge and get approval of the sale from the court. The court, which is protecting the creditors of the estate, will make sure that an adequate price is agreed upon. The court's approval of the sale also benefits the buyer, because it clears the title of the real estate of any liens of estate creditors.

The probate process varies in detail from state to state; probating an estate is attorney's work. Therefore, it is not crucial that a licensee know the details of the probate process. However, a broker should understand how and why the probate process affects real estate, so he or she can work comfortably with estate representatives, probate court officials, and the buyer, who may be frustrated and bewildered, in many cases, by the administrative delays of the probate process.

Taxes and Probate

In the United States, there are three levels of government— local, state, and federal—each with the power to tax. Two of these levels, the state and federal governments, each may impose a tax on the property of the deceased and on the property inherited by the deceased's heirs. The federal government imposes an estate tax on the estate of the deceased if the estate exceeds $220,000—by 1987, $600,000. Many states impose an inheritance tax on the recipient who takes all or a portion of the deceased's estate. Both of these taxes are a lien or cloud on the title to property. Because taxes are enacted by both the legislatures of the 50 states and Congress in Washington, and tax laws are continually subject to change, it is beyond the scope of this book to do more than point out the basic principles of taxation and the impact on real estate transactions that brokers should be aware of.

A real estate broker should understand the existence of these tax liens, that they arise automatically on the death of the property owner, and that they must be discharged. Generally, they are discharged by filing a document in the registry of deeds or with the probate court papers of the deceased's estate, showing that when a lien did exist, it was discharged. Discharge of the liens is essential for the buyer to get clear title to the property.

When property passes under the review of the probate court, the estates representative will pay the federal estate tax and any inheritance tax imposed by the state. But when property is jointly owned and thus does *not* pass through the probate court, the broker should realize that there may still be a tax lien on the property and can suggest that the seller consult an attorney as part of the selling process.

Example

Cloe and Floe are unmarried sisters who bought, 50 years ago, a 40-acre farm outside a major city for $10,000. They hold title as joint tenants. Cloe died, and Floe, as the surviving joint tenant, automatically takes title in her name alone. The property is now worth $3 million as the ideal location for a major shopping complex. This property has tax liens, which must be paid in order to give good title.

The broker should advise Floe to consult an attorney regarding the possibility of tax liens to be certain that she can convey good and clear title to the property when she sells it.

ADVERSE POSSESSION

Occupants of adjacent land can lose track of just where the boundaries lie; over time, one landowner may inadvertently begin to use the land of another. As titles are transferred to new owners, the parties make assumptions about boundaries that are different from the boundaries legally established by recorded deeds and plans. The doctrine of *adverse possession* may be applicable to boundary disputes to resolve its location.

The doctrine of adverse possession is complex. Although it is used most commonly to resolve boundary disputes, it may be used in other situations as well. A broker should be familiar with the concept of adverse possession, although he or she does not need to master all its fine points. When a boundary dispute or title to land is to be decided on the basis of adverse possession, it is an attorney's work to establish the evidence and apply the doctrine to the dispute at hand. However, an active real estate broker will probably encounter a boundary dispute at some time in his or her career and should understand how that problem may be resolved.

Example

The Anderson and Bartlett families have owned Lots A and B, adjoining lakeside properties, as summer neighbors and friends since 1920. The families built camp residences on these lots with the understanding that a certain rock marked the boundary line between the two lots. Last year, the Andersons sold Lot A to Murphy, who, after having Lot A surveyed, discovered that Lot A extends several feet beyond the rock and that part of the Bartletts' house is actually on his property. Murphy now wishes to lay claim to this valuable property, which has been occupied by the Bartletts for nearly 60 years. The Bartletts stubbornly argue that they own all land on their side of the rock. Who should prevail?

One of the rights that comes with the ownership of real estate is the right of exclusive possession of the land. If someone enters and remains on another's land and acts inconsistently with the owner's right to exclusive possession, then the owner has the right to initiate legal action to eject the trespasser. If the trespasser also intends to claim the land as his own, then he is considered an adverse possessor of the land.

The owner's right to eject the trespasser, the adverse possessor, does not last forever. A landowner's rights to oust an adverse possessor from his or her land expires if an ejectment action has not been brought to the court within a certain number of years that varies from state to state and is usually between five and 30 years. If a lawsuit is not begun in time, the adverse possessor becomes the owner of the land; even the original owner cannot eject the possessor. The law gives the trespasser title to the land and extinguishes the title of the original owner.

In the illustration above, the Bartletts occupied the land legally owned by the Andersons for many years. Whether they acquired title by means of adverse possession depends on the application of the following rules to their situation.

The Rule of Adverse Possession

The rule is that, for possession to be considered adverse and one that will ripen into title, it must be actual, open, notorious, continuous, and exclusive, under a claim of right, for the required statutory period. Unless the Bartletts have conformed to each of these characteristics of possession, their occupancy of the land on their side of the rock will *not* be deemed adverse.

The Required Characteristics of Adverse Possession.

1. **Actual, Open, and Notorious**. Actual possession depends upon the type of land involved. It requires acts appropriate to the particular property under the circumstances and means the use or occupation of the land the average person would make of it if he or she were the owner. A person who raises crops on farmland *actually* possesses the farmland even though the land is not used in the winter.

Open and notorious means possession or use of land leading the owner to conclude that the possessor is claiming the property as his or her own. The owner must then take the necessary measures—bringing an action of ejectment—to recover the premises.

2. **Continuous and Exclusive. Continuous** does not mean constant. There is no requirement that the trespasser occupy the land every minute of the day. It depends on what is appropriate to the land—an adverse possessor may have made merely a seasonal use of the land, such as hunting, farming, or grazing of animals. However, the use that is appropriate to the particular land must be continued on a regular basis throughout the required period.

Exclusive means that only the adverse possessor or his or her grantee is using the property over the statutory period. Where the owner resumes occupancy of the property, exclusiveness is lost and the adverse possession is stopped.

Although the possession must continue over a certain period, it need not be carried on by the same individual. Successive periods of possession by different persons may be tacked on or added where there is voluntary transfer of actual possession by one adverse possessor to the next by conveyance or inheritance.

Example ———————————————————————————

Smith owns Lot 1. In 1950, Andrews enters adversely. In 1963, Andrews sells this interest to Benedict, who continues to hold adversely to Smith. In 1967, Benedict dies and leaves the interest to Coyne, who continues to hold the premises adversely. In 1970, Coyne acquired title by adverse possession—13 years of Andrew's possession is tacked on to four years of Benedict's possession and three years of Coyne's own occupancy.

3. Under a Claim of Right. In most state courts, the requirement of a *claim of right* simply means that the possessor must take possession of the land with the intention of holding it as his or her own to the exclusion of all others, including the true owner. This person must claim ownership of the land. A few courts require that a claim of title in good faith exist. Regardless, this requirement is extremely important, because most adverse possession claims today arise over boundary disputes. Adjoining landowners, for example, may believe that a certain fence represents the true boundary division between their properties, while the misplacement of the fence actually favors one party by several yards. If a boundary dispute arises, the state of mind of the favored party is important if the party asserts that he or she has acquired by adverse possession. To have possessed under a claim of right, he or she must have intended to claim all of the land up to the fence, regardless of whether the fence actually marks the true boundary between the properties. If, on the other hand, the possessor intends to claim only the property rightfully his or hers and has occupied some of the neighbor's land by reason of the mistaken fence placement, no claim of right exists.

The Nature of the Title Acquired

Normally, an adverse possessor acquires title to only that portion of the land actually occupied for the required period. However, sometimes adverse possessors enter into property under an invalid deed to the land. Thus, occupancy under an invalid deed is known as possession under *color of title*, and the adverse possessor will be entitled to all of the land described in the deed. An instrument will not constitute color of title unless it appears valid on its face, is recorded, and contains an adequate description of the land in question. In other words, the adverse possessor who holds land under color of title will not need to occupy all of the land described in the deed to become entitled to it.

Once title has been acquired by adverse possession, it can be conveyed, mortgaged, and divided like any other title to land. However, since it is created by operation of the law, it does not appear in the public records at the registry of deeds. If the adverse possessor wishes to make the title appear in the records, he or she may file a lawsuit to *quiet title* against the former owner.

Tax Deed

A final way of obtaining a property interest is through a tax deed. If an owner fails to pay his or her real estate taxes and the land is eventually sold at the public auction, the buyer receives a *tax deed*. The procedure varies from state to state. In some jurisdictions, the state or county holds the property for a period of years before the sale to allow the owner to pay the taxes and redeem the property. In other states, the sale is held soon after the nonpayment; and the buyer may not receive a clear deed for a period of time after the sale. He or she may lose the property if the delinquent owner or a lienholder comes forward and redeems the property. A broker must know when a tax deed is involved in a sale in order to protect the buyer from possible loss of title or from making property improvements that he might later lose.

SUMMARY

The first chapters of this text were written to describe the interests and rights in real estate that people may own and transfer.

This chapter has described how those rights are transferred by deed, the kinds of deeds, the elements of a deed, and the elements of a valid inter vivos transfer of property. The chapter has also explained how title to real estate may be transferred after the death of the owner, either by his will or by the laws of inheritance of the state where the land is located.

In both cases, whether the transfer is inter vivos or posthumous, a tax may be imposed. Where the transfer is inter vivos, there is a state transfer tax. Where the transfer is by will or inheritance or by survivorship of a joint tenancy, there may be a state inheritance tax or federal estate tax, which must be paid before clear title can be conveyed. Conveyances by deed, will, inheritance, and survivorship are the primary methods of title transfer.

Another method of acquiring title is through adverse possession, the use of someone else's land for an extended period of time in a manner that is adverse to the owner's rightful use of the land without any objection from the owner. The intricacies of the doctrine of adverse possession are applied most commonly today by courts to cases involving boundary line disputes.

Finally, this chapter discussed acquisition of a property interest by a tax deed. The purchaser of a tax deed is the owner of the fee but is subject to the prior owner's right to redeem the fee interest by paying the back taxes within a period defined by state law.

MULTIPLE CHOICE QUESTIONS ——————————————

1. Which of the following is the most commonly used deed?

    a. full warranty deed
    b. quitclaim deed
    c. release deed
    d. limited warranty deed

2. A grantor who uses a quitclaim deed with covenant promises:

    a. to pay the real estate transfer tax.
    b. to vacate the premises within a reasonable time.
    c. that he or she has nothing to impair the title since owning the property.
    d. to warrant and defend the title against all who may make a claim against the title.

3. Why is a full warranty deed preferred by buyers?

    a. It guarantees that there are absolutely no encumbrances against the title.
    b. It includes a convenant of quiet enjoyment.
    c. Its warranties apply only to the grantor and grantor's heirs.
    d. It warrants title during the ownership of the grantor and all prior owners.

4. To be effective, a deed must include:

    a. a recitation of the actual consideration.
    b. the signatures of two or more witnesses.
    c. all of the operative words "GIVE, GRANT, BARGAIN, SELL, AND CONVEY."
    d. none of the above

5. Which of the following is (are) method(s) of describing land?

    a. metes and bounds
    b. plan for the description of property
    c. rectangular system
    d. all of the above

6. A conveyance may be void if the:

    a. deed is not acknowledged.
    b. metes and bounds description does not close.
    c. deed is not witnessed.
    d. deed bears no seals.

7. A deed becomes effective when it is:

    a. delivered.
    b. signed.
    c. dated.
    d. recorded.

8. The real estate transfer tax is paid when the:

    a. deed is acknowledged.
    b. deed is signed.
    c. deed is recorded at the registry of deeds.
    d. purchase contract is signed.

9. A dies owning Blackacre jointly with his wife, Whiteacre as a one-fourth tenant in common with his brother, Greenacre as a sole owner, and a 10-year term for years, in his sole name, in Shifting Sands, a beach resort. Which of these properties does not pass via A's will?

    a. Blackacre
    b. Whiteacre
    c. Greenacre
    d. Shifting Sands

10. The distribution of the estate of a person who has died inte
    state is determined by the:

    a. deceased's will.
    b. wishes of the deceased.
    c. desires of the deceased's next to kin.
    d. state's law of intestate succession.

11. The probate process:

    a. collects decedents' assets.
    b. pays decedents' debts.
    c. distributes assets to decedents' heirs.
    d. all of the above

12. Which of the following is (are) true of taxes imposed at the time
    of death?

    a. Estate taxes are the same as inheritance taxes.
    b. A municipality can take real estate for nonpayment of
       inheritance taxes.
    c. Property owned jointly may be subject to a tax lien at
       the death of one of the owners.
    d. all of the above

13. Which of the following is (are) true?

    I. The requirements that the adverse possessor hold the own-
       er's land "openly and notoriously" is merely another way
       of stating that the adverse possessor must give the owner
       personal notice of the possession.
    II. The adverse possessor is able to tack on the time that pred-
        ecessors occupied the land where possession has been vol-
        untarily transferred from one possessor to the next.

    a. I only   c. neither I nor II
    b. II only   d. both I and II

14. The owner of land is barred from bringing the legal action of ejectment against an adverse possessor who has occupied the property for:

   a. ten years.
   b. 15 years.
   c. 20 years.
   d. a period of years varying from state to state.

15. If a property owner does not pay his/her property taxes, the municipalities remedy is to:

   a. impose a tax lien.
   b. attach the owner's bank account.
   c. get a court order instructing the taxpayer's employer to pay a percentage of his/her income to the town.
   d. any of the above.

DISCUSSION QUESTIONS

1. You will notice that many components of a modern warranty deed were once necessary but are no longer required. Which elements are these? What necessary function might they once have served? Why might they still be included in a warranty deed?

2. John Bull made out a valid will, leaving one-half of his estate to his wife. The remaining one-half was to be shared equally by his sons and daughters, provided that any grandchildren would take the deceased parent's share in the event that any of his children died. When Bull dies, he leaves his wife and two daughters. His son has died, leaving two children. His only estate asset is a country farm. Who has what interest? Whose signatures must be obtained before the broker may sell the property? What documents must each sign?

3. Is it a reasonable principle of law that a donee or grantee actually accept a deed in order for the conveyance of land to be completed? Why or why not?

9

Financing

───────── **KEY TERMS** ─────────

acceleration clause   graduated payment mortgage
amortize   installment land contract
balloon payment   mortgage
blanket mortgage   mortgagee
budget mortgage   mortgagor
defeasance clause   novation
deficiency judge-   prepayment clause
 ment   promissory note
due-on-sale clause   purchase money mortgage
equity   term mortgage
foreclosure

Although a broker's primary function is to find a buyer for a piece of property, the agent may also facilitate a sale by helping the buyer secure financing. Because many prospective homebuyers are unsophisticated about how to finance a home, they depend on the broker to know which banks have the best rates and terms and how to make the initial arrangements. The broker should be able to offer the buyer complete advice about finding a mortgage for a piece of property. A broker who understands real estate finance will have a competitive advantage—he or she can help develop creative financing for a sale that might not have been possible without this expertise.

In the typical purchase of a home, a bank will lend money to the buyer and the buyer will put up that home as security. Thus, the bank receives a *security interest* in the property. The document used most commonly to create this security interest is called a *mortgage*. The mortgage is given by the buyer to insure repayment of the money by furnishing the bank with a resource, or asset to be used in case of the buyer's failure to pay the debt. Because the buyer gives the mortgage to the bank, he or she is called the *mortgagor*; the bank that receives the mortgage is the *mortgagee*.

There are many different types of mortgage, each of which creates a different relationship between the mortgagor and mortgagee. A real estate licensee should know and understand these different types of mortgage in order to advise a buyer as to the rights and responsibilities of each. For example, a broker should understand that the mortgagor's breach of the mortgage covenants to secure insurance, to maintain the property, and to pay taxes may supply grounds for foreclosure by the mortgagee. To avoid this possibility, a purchaser must understand these covenants. If the client is to avoid any unpleasant surprises at closing, it is essential that he or she be advised as to what the mortgage document means.

Mortgages are not the only method of financing real estate. In some parts of the country, a trust deed is more commonly used to transfer title from the seller to the buyer while the buyer is making payments. Many of its terms concerning maintenance of the property and so on are similar to those provisions found in a mortgage. In addition, buyers and sellers will use an installment contract, especially where adequate financing is unavailable elsewhere. Both the trust deed and the installment contract are described later in this chapter.

Readers should be able to identify and explain the different types of mortgage and their differences and similarities. They should also understand the difference between a mortgage and a promissory note and why these two documents are used together to finance real estate. In addition, readers should take special note of the clauses that may be included in a mortgage, the different grounds for foreclosure, and the ways foreclosure may be accomplished.

Historical Development

For a conveyance to be valid, historically, possession of the estate had to pass to the buyer. Therefore, if a landowner needed money, he or she could mortgage property only by giving possession to the lender. The landowner would convey title and possession to someone who was willing to lend money. The instrument for this transaction was a mortgage, and it was given by the landowner, or mortgagor, to the money lender, or mortgagee. The mortgage was a pledge of property for the repayment of the money. However, the mortgage included a *defeasance clause*, which provided that, if the mortgagor repaid the debt by a specified day, the lender would return the property—title and possession. If payment was not made exactly on time, the possibility of regaining title and possession was terminated, or foreclosed, forever. Because the mortgagee already had title and possession, the land became his or hers in fee simple absolute.

To ease this harsh consequence of one missed payment, courts began to allow landowners to redeem their land if they paid the debt plus interest. This right to redeem, known as the *equity of redemption,* made land taken as a security interest subject to redemption at any time. Lenders became very hesitant to lend money. Therefore, the practice developed by allowing only a specified amount of time for redemption. Thus, if the mortgagor did not repay the mortgagee within the specified period of time, the mortgagor's equity of redemption was foreclosed forever.

DOCUMENTS OF REAL ESTATE FINANCE

Promissory Note

Today in mortgage transactions, two documents are involved: (1) the mortgage, which is a pledge of property to secure a loan and gives the mortgagee a security interest in that property; (2) the *promissory note*, which is a bilateral contract in which the lender agrees to lend a sum of money in return for the borrower's promise to repay that sum with interest within a specified period of time; the borrower generally is required to make additional promises as well.

The note must be in writing and must contain several elements:

    a. the promise to repay;

    b. the amount borrowed;

    c. the rate of interest;

    d. the method of repayment; and

    e. the borrower's signature.

Beside these mandatory elements, the note may contain several other items:

    f. *prepayment clause*, allowing early repayment;

    g. an *acceleration clause*, which makes the entire loan due immediately if the borrower fails to make a payment; and

    h. a reference to the mortgage that secures the note.

This list is merely illustrative of the kinds of clauses that appear in a mortgage note; because a note is a contract, it may contain any additional terms of agreement the parties may choose.

Mortgage Note

On the following page is a sample of a typical mortgage note. Each of the key provisions is identified by a letter in the margin; the paragraphs below are lettered to correspond to these provisions of the note.

    A. "For Value Received, we the undersigned jointly and severally promise to pay . . ."

These introductory phrases in the note are important for several reasons: first, they articulate the promise to pay; second, they acknowledge that the people who are signing the note have "received value." The promise to pay money is not an idle promise, but is part of a contract from which they received consideration, one of the essential elements of a contract.

The third important concept in these introductory words involves the phrase "we . . . *jointly* and *severally*

Mortgage Note

From ....

To ....

Dated .... , 19 ....

State of Maine, ...ss. Registry of Deeds.

Received .... , 19 ....

at ...... H., ... M., ... M., and

recorded in Book .... , Page ....

Attest: .... Register.

FROM THE OFFICE OF

Marks Printing House, Portland, Maine
ML 30-7

MORTGAGE NOTE

A **For Value Received**, the undersigned, jointly and severally, promise to pay to

of   , or order,

B at the office of said   , the principal sum of

DOLLARS ($), with interest to date upon

said sum or so much thereof as from time to time remains unpaid, at the rate of

C percentum (%) per annum. The said principal sum and interest shall be paid in

installments of   DOLLARS ($) each,

the first installment on the   day of   , 19   , and subsequent installments on the

D   day of each   thereafter, until the principal sum and interest are fully paid;

provided, however, that the final payment of principal and interest, if not sooner paid, shall be due and payable

on the   day of   ,   . Each such installment paid shall be first

applied to payment of interest to date thereof upon the unpaid balance of said principal sum, and any remainder

of such installment toward payment of such unpaid balance of said principal sum.

E   The undersigned reserve   the right to pay any installment before the due date thereof and to make additional payments on account of the principal balance at any time during the life of this Note provided all accrued interest is paid to the date of each such prepayment.

(Continued)

F   If default be made in the payment of any installment under this Note or in the conditions or covenants contained in the mortgage which secures this Note, and any such default is not cured within thirty (30) days from the due date of such installment, or if the maker fails to pay any taxes constituting a lien on the said premises within eight (8) months after they are laid, or if title to said premises shall pass from the mortgagor in the mortgage securing this Note either voluntarily or involuntarily, then the entire principal sum and accrued interest shall at once become due and payable without notice, at the option of the holder of this Note. Failure to exercise this option shall not constitute a waiver of the right to exercise the same in the event of any subsequent default.

        This note is secured by a mortgage of premises located at

𝔚itness

G   ....

        ....

promise...." When more than one person is signing the note, each is agreeing to be responsible *alone* and *together* with the other signers to repay the entire amount.

Example

John and Joe borrow $10,000 and jointly and severally promise to repay the lender. If Joe can't repay, John must, and vice versa. Note that, if John pays all of it to the lender, he may be able to collect from Joe later.

B. "Pay to [Lender] or order."

This provision identifies to whom the payments will be made, i.e. "to the ABC Savings Bank." The words *or order* mean that the ABC Savings Bank may sell the note to someone else. For example, ABC Bank could sell the $10,000 note to the XYZ Bank.

The sale of mortgage notes is increasingly common in real estate finance. The Government National Mortgage Association—GNMA or Ginnie Mae—and the Federal National Mortgage Association—FNMA or Fannie Mae—are major national corporations that purchase mortgages from lending institutions, thereby generating additional cash for local lenders to reinvest in local housing markets.

C. and D. "The principal sum of TEN THOUSAND DOLLARS ($10,000) at the rate of thirteen percent paid in installments of . . . ."

This section of the note specifies exactly how the loan is to be repaid and at what rate of interest. Sometimes notes provide for a variable rate of interest, one that slides up and down with the current market rates for money; the rate in the note is linked to some independent index of interest rates and may be adjusted periodically. Other notes can be written with a plan for graduated payments, the so-called *graduated payment mortgage,* or GPM. These notes are designed for homebuyers who expect to receive periodic salary increases to start repaying their mortgage at a low rate with payments to increase roughly parallel to anticipated salary increases of the borrower.

E. "The undersigned assume the right to pay any installment before the due date . . . ."

The right of the borrower to prepay the loan may be important especially in our transient society where people own their homes for an average of only seven years. Without this provision, a borrower may *not* have the right to pay off the loan ahead of time. Some mortgages contain a clause that allows the lender to charge the borrower a penalty for any prepayment.

Lenders who invest money in mortgages at a specific

interest rate or a fixed period of time expect just that rate of return. A mortgagee does not have to accept the repayment of a mortgage debt at a time earlier than was originally agreed upon. Therefore, if a mortgagor thinks he or she will want to prepay, there should be a clause that permits it.

F.   "If default be made in the payment of any installment
     . . . or in the conditions contained in the mortgage . . .
     then the principal sum . . . shall at once become due . . . ."

This clause protects the lender by allowing the lender to demand payment of the entire debt if the borrower breaks any of the stated covenants in the mortgage or promissory note.

Example

Bob and Ann Smith owe $350 a month on a $35,000 mortgage. For three years, they have faithfully paid the sum, but they are now 90 days behind in payment. If the note did not have an acceleration clause, the lender could demand only $1,050, but because the mortgage does have the clause, the lender demands payment of the balance of the $35,000 loan.

The most common breaches, for which accelerated payment is demanded, are failure to pay principal and interest when due, failure to pay taxes or insurance, failure to maintain the property, and sale of the property. The right to demand full payment upon sale insures the mortgagee that its risk will not change by having someone other than the original borrower in possession of the property while it is still subject to the mortgage. An acceleration clause, which prevents sale of the property to a new owner, makes the mortgage nonassumable.

The right of the lender to demand full payment of the outstanding balance of the loan upon sale of the property appears in the clause that states: "or if title to said premises shall pass from the mortgagor in the mortgage securing this Note either voluntarily or involuntarily, then the entire principal sum and accrued interest shall at once become due and payable. . . ." This clause is known as the *due-on-sale clause*. The property owner may not transfer the property without first paying off the loan.

There are two reasons for the due-on-sale clause.

1. The lender has evaluated the current owners as credit risks and found them worthy of the substantial loan. To allow them to sell the property to someone else about whom the lender knows nothing would increase the lender's risk. To protect itself from this situation, the lender makes the due-on-sale clause a condition of the loan.

2. The second reason for the due-on-sale clause is to protect the lender from rising interest rates. Suppose that a lender lends $50,000 to borrowers at a rate of 13 percent in 1983. If in later years the interest rate climbs to 16 percent when the borrowers want to sell, the due-on-sale clause will require them to pay off the loan at the time of sale; they will not be able to pass their low-interest-rate loan on to their buyers. The bank will be paid off, and a new loan at the then current rate may be negotiated.

G. "Witness . . . ."

It is here that the borrowers sign the note.

The Mortgage

The second document in this method of financing transactions is the *mortgage*. Any interest in land that can be sold can be mortgaged. Because the mortgage, which is the lender's collateral for the note, is actually an encumbrance on property, it is recorded in the registry of deeds to be valid against purchasers.

The minimal requirements of a mortgage may vary somewhat from state to state, but they generally include:

a. names of the mortgagor and mortgagee;
b. words of conveyance;

   c. amount of the mortgage and sometimes the term of payment;

   d. description of the mortgaged property, including the nature of the estate;

   e. date;

   f. signature of mortgagor; and

   g. acknowledgment.

Mortgage Deed

The very simple mortgage form beginning on the next page identifies the essential clauses by letters that correspond to the lettered paragraphs of the explanation.

A mortgage is a contract. When the loan is a substantial amount to an important client of the lender, the terms of the mortgage and note may be negotiated to tailor the documents to a specific transaction. However, when the loan is a routine residential transaction, negotiation is not realistic and the borrower accepts the document, with all of its conditions, offered by the lender.

The following seven paragraphs describe the essentials of the mortgage.

   A. "KNOW ALL MEN BY THESE PRESENTS...."

The first section of the mortgage deed (A) sets out the names of the parties and consideration for the mortgage. In other words, it details who is giving the mortgage, who is receiving the mortgage, and the amount of consideration for it.

   B. "Description"

Section B of the mortgage contains a description of the land subject to the mortgage. Because a mortgage is an encumbrance and is recorded in the county registry of deeds, where it becomes a public document, it is the description that tells which property is encumbered.

   C. "provided nevertheless..." if all payments are made

Mortgage Deed

(COMMON FORM)

From

To

Dated .... 19......

State of Maine.

.... ss. Registry of Deeds

Received .... 19......

at .... H., ... M., and

recorded in Book ...., Page ....

Attest: ....

.... Register.

FROM THE OFFICE OF

LORING, SHORT & HARMON, LAW STATIONERS
PORTLAND, BRUNSWICK, LEWISTON, AUGUSTA
AND BANGOR, MAINE

(100)

Know all Men by these Presents,

That

A

in consideration of

paid by

and whose mailing address is

the receipt whereof   do hereby acknowledge, do hereby **give, grant,
bargain, sell and convey,** unto the said

heirs and assigns forever,

a certain lot or parcel of land

B

To have and to hold, the aforegranted and bargained premises, with all the privileges and appurtenances thereof, to the said

B

heirs and assigns, to   and their use and behoof forever. **And**   do **covenant** with the said Grantee ,   heirs and assigns, that   lawfully seized in fee of the premises; that they are free of all incumbrances;

that   have good right to sell and convey the same to the said Grantee to hold as aforesaid; and that   and   heirs, shall and will **Warrant and Defend** the same to the said

heirs and assigns forever, against the lawful claims and demands of all persons.

Provided Nevertheless, that if the said

heirs, executors or administrators pay to the said

heirs, executors, administrators, or assigns, the sum of

(Continued)

C

from the date hereof, with interest on said sums at the rate of

per cent per annum, during said term and for such further

time as said principal sum or any part thereof shall remain unpaid,

payable   annually, then this deed, as also   certain

promissory note   bearing even date with these presents, given by the

said

to the said

to pay the sum and interest at the time aforesaid, shall both be void,

otherwise shall remain in full force.

In Witness Whereof,   the said

and

wife   of the said

joining in this deed as Grantor and relinquishing and conveying

all rights by descent and all other rights in the above described

premises, have hereunto set   hand and seal this

day of   in the year of our Lord one thousand nine

hundred and

D

Signed, Sealed and Delivered
in presence of

....

....

....

....

E

State of Maine, } **ss.** 19 .

Personally appeared the above named

and acknowledged the above instrument to be   free act and deed.

Before me,

....

Justice of the Peace.
Notary Public.
Attorney at Law.

"...then this [mortgage] deed [and] promissory note... shall both be void."

A mortgage is a form of deed. With it the borrower actually transfers title to the real estate to the lender. The mortgage provides, however, that if its conditions are met, then the conveyance of title is void; title is divested from the lender and is restored automatically in the borrower. This clause in a mortgage is known as the *defeasance* clause because the fee interest in the property is detached from the lender in favor of the borrower.

It is in this section of the mortgage that the lender (mortgagee) may impose additional conditions. Because the lender is concerned that the value of the real estate and buildings be preserved, some of the common mortgage clauses relate to maintenance and insurance of the property. The following are examples.

1. Mortgagors shall:
   a. promptly repair, restore, or rebuild any buildings or improvements now or hereafter on the premises that may become damaged or be destroyed;

    b. keep said premises in good condition and repair, without waste, and free from mechanic's or other liens, or claims for lien, not expressly subordinated to the lien hereof;

    c. pay when due any indebtedness that may be secured by a lien or charge on the premises superior to the lien hereof, and upon request exhibit satisfactory evidence of the discharge of such prior lien to trustee or to holders of the note;

    d. complete within a reasonable time any building or buildings now or at any time in process of erection upon said premises;

    e. comply with all requirements of law or municipal ordinances with respect to the premises and the use thereof; and

    f. make no material alterations in said premises except as required by law or municipal ordinance or as authorized by the holders of the note.

2. Mortgagors shall pay before any penalty attaches all general taxes and shall pay special taxes, special assessments, water charges, sewer service charges and other charges against the premises when due and shall, upon written request, furnish to trustee or to holders of the note duplicate receipts therefor. To prevent default hereunder, mortgagors shall pay in full under protest, in the manner provided by statute, any tax or assessment that mortgagors may desire to contest.

3. Mortgagors shall keep all buildings and improvements now or hereafter situated on said premises insured against loss or damage by fire, lightning, windstorm, and such other hazards or contingencies as the holders of the note may require.

4. The mortgagor shall not sell, transfer, encumber, assign, convey, or in any manner dispose of the collateral property to any other person, firm or corporation, without the express prior written consent of the lender.

The purpose of this *due-on-sale* clause is clear. Before lending a large source of money, say $50,000, to a borrower, a bank will do a credit check on that borrower. If the borrower sells the property to someone else, the lender wants to be sure that at least the creditworthiness of the new owner is as good as that of the borrower. If not, the lender will insist on payment in full of the loan.

Other mortgage clauses include an acceleration provision, a provision that the lender may collect the rent from an income property if the borrower defaults, a provision that the borrower is not personally liable, that in the case of default the lender can collect only from the property, and a clause providing that when the property is sold the lender will share in the profits, if any.

D. "In Witness Whereof. ..."

Section D of the mortgage is where the property owners sign the mortgage instrument and give up their marital interests to the lender; i.e. "...relinquishing...all rights by descent and all other rights...." The lender requires the spouses to relinquish their marital rights in the mortgage so the mortgagee's interest is the priority encumbrance on the property and is superior to the marital rights of the spouses in the property.

E. "State of _____ County of _____...."

The acknowledgment of the mortgage before a justice of the peace, a notary public, or an attorney is evidence that the signing of the document has not been coerced, i.e. that it is the free act of the borrowers. The proper acknowledgment of the document is a prerequisite to recording it in the registry. Chapter 10 describes the recording process further.

Recording of Mortgages

Because land is so important to both business and personal wealth, or governments, at the county level, administer public registries where owners record their deeds and other interests in land. Recording interests in land in the registry tells the public at large who owns what property.

When Phillip and Elizabeth sell parcels of Eagles' Nest to neighbors, etc., the buyers will record their deeds in the registry so the public will know that they are the owners of portions of Eagles' Nest. If any of them borrows money to purchase their interest, the lender will record its mortgage to show that it, too, has an interest in the land. Recording of mortgages is routine, as any lender with an investment in property would clearly want to protect its interest in that property.

Types of Mortgages

Most mortgages are paid on a monthly basis, and the principal is usually *amortized*. This means that each payment is a partial payment of the principal, together with payment of the interest on the remaining balance. The principal is the amount that was actually borrowed, and the interest is that which would be generated by the amount borrowed over the forecast period of the loan.

Term Mortgage

A form of mortgage used frequently before the Great Depression, but less common now, is the *term mortgage*. Under this arrangement, the mortgagor makes periodic payments of interest and one payment of principal, the *balloon payment*, at the end of the term. The borrower often had to refinance the principal when it came due. Because most people cannot come up with a lump sum at the end of the term, this form of mortgage payment is not often used today.

However, in the high-interest-rate years of 1981 and 1982, it regained popularity with those buyers who were trying to avoid long-term high interest rates. When the balloon note became due, they hoped to refinance the loan at a lower rate.

Fully Amortized Loan

Today, the most common type of loan is the *fully amortized loan*. This type of loan, which came to be used following the Depression, features payments that are partly principal and partly interest. Generally, the loan is for a period of 25–35 years. The early payments are mostly interest, but with each succeeding installment the amount of the payment used to reduce the principal increases. All payments are equal in amount, but as the loan matures the rate of principal and interest changes. As the principal is paid, the equity of the mortgagor increases. *Equity* is the market value minus the unpaid mortgage debt.

Partially Amortized Loan

The *partially amortized loan* combines features of the term mortgage with features of the fully amortized loan. A portion of the mortgage debt is gradually repaid, along with the interest, over the life span of the loan. The remainder of the principal is repaid as a *balloon payment* at the end of the loan. For some individuals or businesses with uneven cash flow, this type of loan may offer an advantage. The monthly or periodic payments are lower than if the loan were fully amortized, and the remainder of the principal comes due at a time later in the life of the individual or the business, when a sum of cash may be more readily available. For others, this type of loan may have the same disadvantage as the term mortgage: the staggering burden of a huge payment at the end of the term.

Example

ABC corporation borrows a sum of money to purchase a building for expansion. Because in the past ABC has been successful and well managed, the bank agrees to a partially amortized loan. ABC will have the advantage of lower monthly payments at the beginning of the loan when the company is experiencing the costs of expanding its operations. ABC expects that several years later the lump sum payment will be easy to make.

Blanket Mortgage

A mortgage covering more than one piece of property is a *blanket mortgage*. This type of security for the lender is very common on subdivided lots in a housing development.

Example

John Smith wants to buy a house and two lots adjacent to the dwelling. Because the mortgage covers all three pieces of property, Smith has a blanket mortgage. When he sells one lot, he will generally pay the lender a proportionate part of the outstanding balance on the loan and receive a document to record in the registry of deeds showing that the mortgage, as to that lot, has been discharged.

Open-End Mortgage

An open-end mortgage allows the lender to advance additional amounts of capital using the same property as security. This mortgage will retain its priority since its debt will be paid before that of other mortgages that may have been executed at a later time. For example, a farmer might keep an open-end mortgage to enable the periodic purchase of equipment, or a homeowner might use this type to make home improvements.

For it to be a true open-end mortgage, however, the lender must be legally obligated to advance more money.

Budget Mortgage and Package Mortgage

A *budget mortgage* includes one-twelfth of the annual cost of taxes and insurance in monthly payments, in addition to the payments of principal and interest. This money is placed in an escrow account, assuring both the mortgagor and mortgagee that the money will be available to pay the essential bills when they become due. If the cost of mechanical equipment, appliances, or furniture is also included in the financing, the mortgage is referred to as a *package mortgage*.

A second buyer must be careful that all of the items included in the package mortgage are left on the premises. There is often a question concerning title to certain furnishings such as washer, dryer, and kitchen appliances purchased under a package mortgage.

Junior Mortgages

A purchaser of property may borrow from more than one lender to generate enough money to buy the property. The second, third, and even fourth lenders take back mortgages that are "junior" to the mortgage of the first lender. Junior mortgages are referred to by their recorded position.

For example, a second mortgage is second in time and second in priority to the first mortgage; a third mortgage is third in time and third in priority, etc. In the case of default, the debt of the first mortgage will be satisfied before the debt on the second mortgage. Thus, the second mortgage is a greater risk to the lender, and higher interest rates are often charged.

Example

A young man wishes to buy an apartment building for $300,000, but he has only $10,000 in cash. When the bank is willing to provide him with only a $150,000 mortgage, the owners may take back a second mortgage of $100,000 to finance part of the price; his uncle lends him $40,000 and takes back a third mortgage to finance the balance of the price.

In the example above, the bank lending $150,000 will record its mortgage first and will have the first mortgage. The owners, recording second, will have a second mortgage. The order of recording is important, because if the new owner should default on his payments, the proceeds of a foreclosure sale would be used to pay the first lender in full before paying the second lender. If the proceeds are not adequate to pay both mortgagees, the second lender may not be fully repaid.

There is no limit to the number of lenders that may be involved in financing a transaction and therefore no limit to the number of mortgages recorded on a piece of property.

Purchase Money Mortgage

The term *purchase money mortgage* can be used to describe any mortgage used to purchase property, which then serves as collateral. Included is the transaction in which the seller takes a mortgage from the buyer, who will then make periodic payments to the seller. A purchase money mortgage can be used when bank financing is difficult to get, as in periods of tight money.

Example

Green wants to buy a $100,000 house from Brown, but he is having difficulty getting financing. Brown suggests that, if Green can come up with $50,000 cash, Brown will take back a purchase money mortgage.

Installment Land Contract

An *installment land contract* is a financing agreement that is similar to a mortgage but is technically an installment contract. In this agreement, the seller retains title to the property; the buyer receives possession and agrees to make installment payments toward the purchase price. The buyer will receive the title only upon the payment of the last installment. If the installments are not met, the seller has the right of immediate possession and may keep all the payments made up to that time. This arrangement may seem harsh; however, in many situations it allows a tenant to purchase the property on which he or she lives, so the installment may approximate the rent. If this arrangement is formalized and a penalty placed upon the seller for nondelivery of the title upon payment of the last installment, it is called a *title bond* or *bond for a deed.*

Deed of Trust

When a buyer finances a purchase through a bank using a note and mortgage, or with the seller using an installment sale contract, the financing transaction has only two parties, the borrower and the lender, or the buyer and seller in the case of the installment sale contract. There is a third method of financing real estate, the deed of trust, which involves three parties: the borrower, a bank or the seller as lender; and the trustee.

The reason for involving a third person, the trustee, is to have some independent person or company responsible for monitoring or enforcing the contract. The trustee, who has no personal interest or financial investment in the sale, takes title to the real estate.

The buyer borrows money from the lender and signs a promissory note similar to one used in a mortgage transaction. The buyer makes monthly payments to the trustee, who pays the balance to the lender after deducting a fee. While the loan balance is unpaid, the trustee makes sure that the property is maintained, the taxes are paid, and the buyer makes payments as agreed. When the buyer fails to live up to the agreement, the trustee is empowered to foreclose the buyer's contract. Or when the final payment on the loan is made, the trustee's responsibility is to give title to the buyer; generally, this occurs automatically upon the last payment. In several states, the deed of trust is used more commonly than the note and mortgage.

Variable Rate Mortgage

This type of mortgage allows the interest rate on the mortgage to rise and fall with the capital market. There is usually a limit on how much the rates can vary in a given period of time. The monthly payments may also remain the same despite a change in interest rate; only the proportion of principal and interest may change.

Bridge Mortgage or Swing Mortgage

This is a type of short-term financing that a homeowner can use to purchase a new home. If the owner is having trouble selling the old home, the bank may advance funds for the down payment of the new home based upon the equity in the old home. This type of financing is available only for a short term, and usually the entire amount becomes due upon the sale of the old home.

TRANSFERS OF MORTGAGE PROPERTY

When a mortgaged property is sold, there are four ways of dealing with the mortgage. The first method is to sell the property *free and clear*. The seller pays off the entire mortgage debt together with any prepayment penalty. The new owner then arranges his or her own financing.

Sale "Subject to" a Mortgage

A second method is to sell the property *subject to the mortgage*. In this case, the property is sold and the mortgage remains in effect. The new deed will recite that the property is sold subject to the mortgage lien on the property. The buyer will pay the seller for his or her *equity*. The new owner will now have the power to redeem the property by continuing to make the mortgage payments. However, the buyer will have *no personal liability* to pay the mortgage. The original owner will still be personally liable for payment of the debt because the promissory note is still valid. The new owner can lose the equity paid and, of course, the property. However, the seller will be liable if there is a deficiency after a foreclosure.

Example ——————————————————————————————

A sells a mortgaged property worth $70,000 to B, who takes it subject to the mortgage of $60,000. A is still personally liable to the bank, the mortagee; the most B can lose is the equity paid and property. When B defaults on payments, the bank forecloses and auctions off the property to recover the $59,000 still due on the mortgage. The high auction bid is $55,000, leaving the bank $4,000 short of the amount outstanding. Now the lender can request a deficiency judgment for $4,000. A, the original borrower, is responsible for this debt since the original promissory note is still in force.

Sale "Subject to the Mortgage Which the Buyer Assumes"

The third method of selling mortgaged property is to have the new owner "assume and agree to pay" the mortgage. On the promissory note, the grantee assumes personal liability to both the mortgagor and the mortgagee. The mortgagor-grantee will also remain liable to the lender on the original promissory note. Therefore, a *deficiency judgment* may be obtained against either the mortgagor or the assuming grantee.

Example ——————————————————————————————

A buys a house with a mortgage. B buys it from A and assumes and agrees to pay the mortgage. Both A and B will have personal liability to the lender to pay the mortgage debt. Upon foreclosure, if there is a deficiency where the sale price does not equal the mortgage debt, both A and B will be liable for the difference.

Novation

A fourth method of transferring real estate subject to a mortgage is to execute a *novation*. A novation occurs when the buyer is substituted for the seller on the note and mortgage to the lender. Note that a novation is a three-party agreement—the buyer, the seller, and the current lender all agree to rewrite the loan by substituting the new buyer in the place of the seller.

Example ————————————————————————

In 1978, A bought Acres Away Farm and borrowed $100,000 from Eagle Savings Bank at ten percent for 30 years. In 1981, when A sells Acres Away to B, the lender, Eagle Savings Bank, agreed that B will sign a new promissory note for the $98,000 still owed on the original $100,000 note, and A is relieved of any further liability; in other words, B is substituted for A on the same loan. This is a novation.

Foreclosure

When a buyer obtains financing from a bank, a bank secures its interest with a mortgage deed and a promissory note. If the borrower defaults on payments, how does the bank exercise its right to repayment of the debt?

Example ————————————————————————

Jane Black, who owes City Savings and Loan $40,000 on a home mortgage, has recently lost her well-paying job. To date, she has not found a new position with a comparable salary. When Jane is unable to meet her mortgage payments, City Savings consults with Jane to try to arrange a workable repayment plan. Even the new alternative is too demanding for Jane's present income; she again defaults. After realizing Jane is not in a position to make any reasonable and regular mortgage payments, City Savings institutes foreclosure procedure.

Contrary to what some people believe, banks do not automatically or eagerly begin foreclosure proceedings. They prefer to arrange longer and lower repayment schedules to accommodate the borrower's needs. If a suit becomes necessary after unsuccessful attempts to collect, the bank will seek the court's permission to hold an auction. Before the public auction, the court requires publication of the impending sale. At the auction, the property will go to the highest bidder, who usually is required to make a cash down payment and to pay the remaining sum within 30 days. Upon payment of the balance, the new owner receives a deed.

The bank's goal, of course, is to recover the amount of its outstanding debt. If the bid does not reach the amount owed, the bank itself may bid up to that amount and recover the property. If a high bid is less than the amount owed, the bank may request a deficiency judgment against the former owner.

A broker should be familiar with the local jurisdiction's foreclosure law, which in almost all states is governed by statute. There are several types of *foreclosure*.

Strict foreclosure exists in just a few states. This harsh procedure give title to the lender as soon as the court declares that the borrower's rights have terminated. In addition, the borrower will not regain his or her equity or the difference between the amount owed on the loan and the value of the house. If the sale price exceeds the amout due, the mortgagee makes the profit.

Foreclosure by sale has become accepted in nearly all states. This method, less harsh than strict foreclosure, begins when the lender files suit for foreclosure. When the court authorizes the sale, the property will be sold at public auction.

In some states, the lender may sue the borrower if the amount raised at an auction sale does not equal the amount due on the loan. Other jurisdictions give the deliquent borrower from five months to two years after the foreclosure sale to redeem the property. By this *statutory redemption procedure*, the former owner can pay the debt owed, plus expenses to regain title. In states that have statutory redemption, the successful bidder at a public sale does not receive a deed but a *certificate of sale*, which he or she may lose within the statutory redemption period. Title will issue only after the period of redemption.

Example

Rob Green owes a $20,000 mortgage debt on a house with a market value of $60,000. After Rob has missed several payments, the lender, Local Savings and Loan, files suit for foreclosure. At a public sale, Janet Black, the high bidder, purchases the home for $30,000. There are no other outstanding liens, so the court returns to Green the excess of $10,000 made on the sale. Because the jurisdiction has a one-year statutory period of redemption, Black does not receive a title, but rather a certificate of sale for the property. Within the year, Green has the right to redeem his property, defeating Black's right to title.

Only an attorney need understand the intricacies of foreclosure, but the informed broker will understand the basic procedures used in his or her state.

SUMMARY

A successful real estate licensee is a person with many skills. In addition to being a good businessperson, he or she must be able to generate properties for sale, market the properties effectively to attract buyers, and then find appropriate financing for the buyer. Financing the buyer's purchase of a house is perhaps one of the broker's most important tasks. This chapter has given the prospective licensee an introduction to the legal side of real estate finance by discussing the most common finance documents, the promissory note and the mortgage. These documents may be used when the property is financed through a bank or by an individual. Other documents of finance are the installment contract and the bond for a deed.

Whether the financing is obtained through a bank or an individual, the mortgage may be of several different forms. The loan may be fully or partially amortized; it may be secured by a blanket mortgage covering more than one parcel of land. There may be a balloon payment. And whatever form of mortgage is used, it will contain agreements by the borrower to maintain the property, keep it insured, and pay taxes. Also, he or she may agree to a penalty clause for late payments and to an acceleration clause. A mortgage, like any other contract, is a document for which the borrower and lender may negotiate different terms. Generally, a bank will use a form document, and the borrower can either accept it or shop elsewhere for financing.

This chapter explored what happens to a mortgage when property is sold—generally, old mortgages are paid at the time of sale. However, a buyer may acquire property subject to an existing mortgage. The process of foreclosure must be understood in order to list and attempt to sell a property in foreclosure proceedings. By understanding the process, the agent will be better able to market and sell the property prior to foreclosure sale.

This chapter is an introduction to the legal foundations of real estate finance. A good broker will learn and understand the different programs for financing property that are available through the Department of Housing and Urban Development, the Federal Housing Administration, state and local housing authorities, and the Veterans Administration. The many alternatives for financing real estate available to housebuyers makes the licensee's job as a mortgage broker more interesting and rewarding.

MULTIPLE CHOICE QUESTIONS ————————————————————

1. Which of the following is (are) true about a mortgage?

    a. It creates a security interest in property.
    b. It is recorded in the registry in deeds.
    c. It is usually given by the buyer to the bank.
    d. all of the above

2. Which of the following is (are) true?

    a. The promissory note creates the personal liability for the mortgagor to fulfill mortgage covenants.
    b. The promissory note is a separate instrument.
    c. The promissory note will remain in effect until the mortgage is discharged.
    d. all of the above

3. An acceleration clause in a mortgage:

    a. is illegal.
    b. makes the conveyance to the mortgagee conditional.
    c. will operate upon a breach of the mortgagee.
    d. none of the above

4. Which of the following is (are) true?

    I. An acceleration clause allows a party to repay a mortgage without penalty.
    II. The note binds the mortgagor to repay the borrowed amount. The mortgage deed is security for that promise.

    a. I only   c. both I and II
    b. II only   d. neither I nor II

5. Real estate can be financed using:

    a. note and mortgage.
    b. installment sale contract.
    c. deed of trust.
    d. all of the above

6. Mary owns a home in Westport free and clear. She wants to buy a new home in Eastport but will have no money for the down payment until her Westport home is sold. Mary consults a local banker. The banker is likely to suggest:

    a. a bridge mortgage.
    b. an installment land contract.
    c. a variable rate mortgage.
    d. a fully amortized loan.

7. Which of the following is (are) true?

    I. A purchase money mortgage can be granted only by a bank.
    II. An installment land contract should state when the buyer takes title.

    a. I only
    b. II only
    c. both I and II
    d. neither I nor II

8. Pamela Grey, who owns a small, successful printing business, wants to enlarge her operation but fears that cash flow problems may prevent her meeting enlarged mortgage payments for about five years. She consults her banker, who is likely to suggest:

    a. a second mortgage.
    b. a fully amortized loan.
    c. a partially amortized loan.
    d. a blanket mortgage.

9. Terry Blue wants to buy a small home on the edge of town. What attracts Terry to the home is the availability of three vacant lots surrounding the house. She looks for:

    a. a second mortgage
    b. a blanket mortgage.
    c. an installment land contract.
    d. an open-end mortgage.

10. Sam buys an antique house in need of restoration. He needs money at the time of purchase to acquire the house and will need additional funds over the course of the next two years to complete the renovations. He consults a broker, who is likely to suggest:

    a.   an open-end mortgage.
    b.   a budget mortgage.
    c.   a balloon payment.
    d.   a partially amortized loan.

11. Tony has a very small down payment for the house that he plans to buy. Besides, he has little self-discipline and fears that he will not faithfully save each month for the yearly taxes and home-owners' insurance. When he asks a broker for advice, the broker should tell him to obtain:

    a.   a term mortgage.
    b.   a budget mortgage.
    c.   a partially amortized loan.
    d.   an installment land contract.

12. A client fears buying during a time of very high interest rates but wants to invest his capital before he is taxed for capital gains. Interest rates are predicted to drop markedly in six months, but by then the client will be obliged to pay taxes. The broker should suggest:

    a.   a second mortgage.
    b.   a term mortgage.
    c.   a variable rate mortgage.
    d.   a budget mortgage.

13. Which of the following is (are) true?

    I. Sam buys a house from Mary *subject to* an existing mortgage. After Sam defaults on his payments, a foreclosure sale does not raise enough money to repay the lending bank. Mary will be personally liable for the deficiency.

    II. Sam buys a house from Mary and *assumes* an existing mortgage. After Sam defaults on his payments, a foreclosure sale does not raise enough money to repay the lending bank. Both Sam and Mary will be personally liable for the deficiency.

      a. I only   c. both I and II
      b. II only   d. neither I nor II

14. A novation:

    a. increases the lender's security.
    b. decreases the lender's security.
    c. substitutes one borrower for another.
    d. is the same as a sale subject to a mortgage that the borrower assumes in order to pay.

15. Which of the following is (are) true?

    I. A borrower who fails to keep his mortgaged property in good repair may face foreclosure.

    II. Lenders may charge a penalty if a loan is paid before it is due.

      a. I only   c. both I and II
      b. II only   d. neither I nor II

DISCUSSION QUESTIONS

1. Explain the difference between a fully amortizing and a partially amortizing loan.

2. Explain the different functions of the mortgage and the promissory note.

3. Explain a sale subject to an existing mortgage and a sale in which a buyer assumes and agrees to pay an existing mortgage.

10
Recording

KEY TERMS
---

abstract of title	recording statutes
certificate of title	title insurance
chain of title	title opinion
grantor—grantee index	Torrens system
	tract index

The fact that someone offers to convey a piece of land, even by warranty deed, does not in itself assure that the seller owns, or holds title to, the property in question. He or she may not now own, or may never have owned, the property. To protect purchasers of land, systems of recording deeds provide a method for determining who owns what interest in a piece of real property. Prospective buyers can determine who has title and whether that title is good by searching the records in local registries of deeds.

Real estate brokers are usually not responsible for researching titles, the mechanics of which are described briefly below. Nonetheless, brokers can obtain much information by using the recording system. Information that can be found in the registry of deeds includes:

1. the person who is listed as the present owner of the property;

2. a legal description of the property;

3. a description of easements or restrictive covenants that affect the property; and

4. mortgages on the property.

A broker who knows how to use the registry of deeds to find this information has a competitive advantage over others.

Our system of documenting land ownership was developed to protect an innocent purchaser of land from a seller who does not have valid title to the parcel of real estate being sold. In response to this need, all states have enacted statutes that permit land transactions to be recorded in volumes of public record. Purchasers can ascertain the status of land title by consulting these volumes. Although the specific provisions of the recording statutes vary from state to state, each law serves the same purpose: to protect the innocent purchaser from fraudulent conveyances of land. This chapter describes the recording system, how it works, and whom it protects.

Recording Statutes

The policy behind _recording statutes_ is that title to real estate should be disclosed in public records and that purchasers of land should be able to rely on the status of the title as it appears in these records. These statutes also establish the policy that purchasers who abide by the rules and record their deeds prevail over previous grantees who did not record their deeds.

There are three types of recording statutes in the United States.

1.   **Notice.** Under a notice statute, a subsequent bona fide purchaser prevails over the first purchaser who failed to record, regardless of who records first after the second sale of the land. The important fact is that the subsequent purchaser has no actual, constructive, or inquiry notice at the time he or she buys the property. A notice statute encourages prompt recording by the first grantee so that he or she will not lose title to one who unwittingly purchases the property at a later date.

Example ————————————————————————

Smith conveys Lot 1 to Anderson on June 1. Anderson fails to record. On June 10, Smith grants the same premises to Bartlett, a bona fide purchaser. Bartlett prevails over Anderson even if Anderson records before him, because he had no notice of the Smith-Anderson transaction at the time he purchased the property.

---

2. Race. Under a race statute, whoever records first prevails. Notice is immaterial. Such a statute provides a strong incentive for immediately recording a deed upon purchase of the land.

Example ————————————————————————————

Smith conveys Lot 1 to Anderson on June 1. Anderson fails to record. On June 10, Smith sells the same premises to Bartlett. It does not matter whether Bartlett knows of the Smith-Anderson conveyance. Whoever records first will prevail, since he will have won the "race" to the recorder's office.

---

3. Race-Notice. Under a race-notice statute, a subsequent bona fide purchaser is protected only if he or she records before the prior grantee. This means that a purchaser *with notice* of the previous conveyance will never prevail even if he or she records first. An innocent purchaser will lose the right to title if he or she fails to record before the prior purchaser. This system of recording protects the innocent purchaser only if he or she abides by the rules and records the instrument at the registry of deeds.

Example ————————————————————————————

Smith conveys Lot 1 to Anderson on June 1. Anderson fails to record. On June 10, Smith sells Lot 1 to Bartlett, a purchaser without notice of the earlier conveyance. Bartlett records. Bartlett prevails. However, if Anderson had recorded before Bartlett, Anderson would have prevailed.

Recording Systems

In studying and applying the recording statutes, one must understand key terms.

Purchasers. Recording statutes protect purchasers of real estate.

For this purpose, a *purchaser* is defined as one who has paid value for real estate. Grantees such as donees and devisees, who have not paid value for the interest, are usually unprotected by the recording acts because they have not relied on the recording system to their own detriment.

Example ────────────────────────────────────

Smith conveys Lot 1 to Anderson, who fails to record. Smith dies, leaving all of his property by will to his son, David. Unaware of the transfer to Anderson, David brings an ejectment action against Anderson, who now occupies the lot. Anderson will prevail because David was not a purchaser.

Without Notice. In addition to purchasing the property, the subsequent grantee must also receive the land *without notice* of the prior unrecorded instrument.

1. A purchaser has *actual notice* if he or she has knowledge that the property is owned by someone else.

Example ────────────────────────────────────

Ruth sells ten acres to her neighbor, Judy; Judy neglects to read the deed. Judy's sister, Alice, who knows of this sale, goes to Ruth, buys the property, and receives another deed from Ruth. Alice records the deed. Alice's ownership is *not* protected by the recording statute because she had actual notice that Judy, not Ruth, owned the land.

A subsequent grantee who actually knows of the prior conveyance has no grounds on which to complain, and hence the recording statute offers no protection.

2. The law requires that persons intending to purchase real estate examine the public records relating to the parcel of land in question to ensure that the person conveying the property in fact has title to it. This is *constructive notice*. Regardless of whether or not the records actually are examined, the law assumes that the purchaser

knows everything he or she would have learned from such an examination.

The important point here is that, if the prior grantee has recorded his or her instrument, the careful buyer who examines the records will discover that the person attempting to grant the property for the second time no longer has title. Thus, constructive notice is notice from the records. A buyer who fails to examine or search the records has no recourse.

3. *Inquiry notice,* another form of constructive notice, is sometimes required by law. In certain situations, a person is expected to make reasonable inquiries and is charged with whatever knowledge that inquiry would reveal.

Example ————————————————————————————————

Smith conveys Lot 1 to Anderson, who records the deed. Later, Smith sells the same premises to Bartlett, who fails to search the records with respect to Lot 1. Bartlett acquires no title. He had constructive notice of the deed to Anderson.

4. Under a race-notice statute, as well as under a race statute, the purchaser without notice must also *record first,* before the prior grantee. A subsequent purchaser without notice of an earlier conveyance of the same land will have priority over the previous grantee only if the deed is recorded *before* that of the previous grantee. The subsequent grantee need not worry abut this obligation to record first, however. Normally, he or she will record the deed on the same day that it is delivered by the grantor. The grantee will automatically carry out the obligation to record first by recording the deed as soon as it is received.

5. A *subsequent bona fide purchaser* is one who pays for an interest in land that has already been sold to another. This party has neither actual nor constructive notice of the previous transaction, usually because the

first purchaser failed to record the sale at the registry of deeds.

All interests in land—deeds, mortgages, leases for more than two years, easements, covenants, profits, liens, attachments, and bankruptcies—should be recorded for the purchaser's protection, as should all releases and assignments of these interests.

Mechanics of Recording

Procedures for recording deeds vary from state to state, and customs may even vary within different parts of a state. The following procedures are general practices followed in most instances.

The grantee first presents the instrument to be recorded to the proper authority. In most states, the document must be acknowledged by an authorized person such as a notary public or a justice of the peace. An acknowledgment simply means that the official confirms that the instrument is properly signed by the grantor with the grantor's knowledge of the instrument's contents. The deed is then copied and placed in an official file, usually a record book, in the registry of deeds.

Copies of the recorded instruments are usually entered in record books that are maintained in chronological order. Thus, the copy of the deed conveying a piece of property might appear in Volume 3,441, pages 85–86; the next document filed, generally the purchaser's mortgage, would appear in Volume 3,441, pages 87–88.

The recorder enters certain information about the conveyance into an index, which contains references to all recorded documents. It is referred to as the *grantor-grantee index,* since it is indexed alphabetically according to both names. In addition to the names of the parties, the grantor-grantee index usually provides these pieces of information:

- the name of the other party to the land transaction;

- the type of instrument conveyed—e.g. warranty deed, mortgage, lease;

- the municipality in which the property is located;

- the volume and page of the copy of the instrument in the official records; and

- the date on which the instrument was recorded.

Indexes are generally arranged according to time intervals; e.g. one set of indexes will refer the searcher to all instruments recorded from January 1, 1965, to January 1, 1970.

Another type of index that is used in a limited number of states is the *tract index*. A tract index will contain references to all recorded deeds, mortgages, and other instruments that concern a particular tract or parcel of land. The index will list the volume and page number of each recorded instrument. Tract indexes normally supplement grantor-grantee indexes; they do not substitute for them.

A grantor-grantee index, such as the sample shown here, provides the following types of information:

GRANTOR-GRANTEE INDEX

JANUARY 1, 1970–JANUARY 1, 1975

Surname, Given Name	Reverse Party	Location of Land	Instrument	Book	Page Grantor	Page Grantee	Date of Record
Palmer,							
Floyd E. &	Jeffreys, Brian	Falmouth	WAR	3818		176	9-22-73
Mark A.	Marcotte, Louis	Portland	MORT	3597	69		3-15-71
Susan G. &	Jeffreys, Brian	Falmouth	WAR	3818		176	9-22-73
Parsons,							
Barbara A. &	Nelson, Michael	Gorham	QC	3669	222		1-21-72
Constance D.	Sawyer, Eliz.	Scarborough	DISCH	3911		11	10-11-74
David P. &	Nelson, Michael	Gorham	QC	3669	222		1-21-72
Patterson,							
John F.	Montgomery, Wm.	S. Portland	WAR	3741		57	8-20-72
Stephan M.	Abbot, Kevin	Freeport	WAR	3626	71		7-27-71

1. that Mark A. Palmer conveyed a mortgage deed to Louis Marcotte concerning land located in Portland, recorded on March 15, 1971, a copy of which may be found on page 69 of Volume 3,597 of the official records;

2. that Brian Jeffreys transferred property located in Falmouth to Floyd D. and Susan G. Palmer by warranty deed recorded on September 22, 1973, a copy of which is located on page 176 of Volume 3,818 of the official records;

3. that Barbara A. and David F. Parsons granted a quit claim deed concerning Gorham property to Michael Nelson, recorded on January 21, 1972, a copy of which can be seen on page 222 of Volume 3,669.

The *page grantor* and *page grantee* columns indicate whether the party listed in the *surname, given name* column was the grantor or grantee of the transaction. The reverse party will always appear elsewhere in the index because the grantor-grantee index lists both parties alphabetically. The symbol & appearing after the name of a party means that the listed party "and others"—usually husband and wife—conveyed the property jointly. The joining party's name will also appear in the index.

The final step in the recording process is the return of the original deed or document to the grantee or the grantee's agent. The registry of deeds retains only a copy of the document.

TITLE EXAMINATION

Let's assume that the broker for Eagles' Nest has succeeded in finding a buyer for the principal estate of Phillip and Elizabeth. The buyer, Ralph's Construction Company (RCC), is a successful developer that has signed a purchase and sale contract for $750,000, to be paid in cash. The developer's first concern before parting with three-quarters of a million dollars is to assure that he is getting good title to the property, that Phillip and Elizabeth are the proper owners, and that there are no outstanding mortgages or other liens on the property.

Without a system of recording titles and interests in land, the developer might have to accept deed simply on the faith that the sellers have good title. History has shown that not all sellers are honest; more than faith is required in a sound business transaction.

The purchaser, therefore, hires an attorney to give an opinion on the state of the title to the property. Either the attorney or a professional title examiner will search the grantor-grantee indices for the names of owners of the subject property. The search will begin with the current owners and go back as far as 30 to 100 years, depending on the law or professional standards of the state where the land lies. This list of historical owners is called the *chain of title*.

Once the chain of title is established, the examiner checks the subject property during the period each owner held title to determine that any mortgages or other liens on the property have been discharged, that all owners of record or heirs of deceased owners have signed deeds conveying their interests, that there are no unpaid inheritance or estate taxes, and that the property is not involved in a bankruptcy case. The examiner will report any easements either benefiting or burdening the property, any notices of common driveway, etc. He or she will also report any interest that may have been sold to others, e.g. the life estate sold to Uncle Henry or the qualified fee interests to the family and neighbors. The title examiner will write up an *abstract of title*, which is an outline of the major documents of the property, and a summary of his or her findings. The attorney will review the abstract and issue a *title opinion* based on the record. The opinion will indicate either that it is a *good and merchantable title* or that there are clouds on the title in the form of undischarged mortgages, unpaid liens, unsettled interests of heirs, etc.

Example ——————————————————————————————

Mr. and Mrs. Jones sign a purchase contract for a $75,000 home in a suburban development. They are borrowing $50,000 from a local lender to help finance the transaction. The attorney for the lender searches the title and finds that the title is good but that the sellers have a $39,000 mortgage with another lender. He reports this to his client. At the time of sale, part of the $75,000 purchase money is used to pay off the existing mortgage.

The recording system gives the buyer, who is investing $750,000 of his own money, confidence that he is purchasing good title to the property and that he will not lose his investment because an unpaid tax lien or unpaid lender has a claim on the property. Full public disclosure in the public registries of deeds of interests in land promotes confidence in their use in commercial and personal transactions.

Consider also the importance of the recording system to Ralph's Construction Company when the company applies to a bank for a two-million-dollar loan to build a shopping center. The lender will also have the title searched to be certain that RCC owns Eagles' Nest, free and clear, and that RCC can give a good mortgage to the lender.

RECORDING MORTGAGES AND OTHER LIENS

The first function of recording statutes is to provide a public record of ownership interests in real estate. Because land is such a valuable economic resource, owners exercise their ownership rights to borrow money, using land as a collateral for the loan. Likewise, creditors who deal with landowners can acquire interests in the real estate belonging to someone else. Each creditor who acquires an interest or lien in real estate needs a place to record his or her lien publicly—to protect his or her interest in the real estate.

Consider the following problem of recording priority of mortgage liens.

A young couple decided to purchase a 100-unit apartment building for $350,000. Because they had only $25,000, they had to borrow from several different lenders to raise the full purchase price. The first lender was a savings bank, which lent $150,000 at 14 percent, for 30 years and insisted on a first mortgage. The second lender was a finance company, which agreed to lend $100,000 at 18 percent for 20 years, secured by a second mortgage. The seller agreed to finance $75,000 at 18 percent for five years and took back a third mortgage to secure the payment of the balance of the purchase price.

These three mortgages are recorded in the registry of deeds in the order of their priority: savings bank first, followed by the finance company loan, followed by the seller's mortgage.

There is a very important consequence attached to the order of recording of the mortgages. If the couple is unable to make the various mortgage payments, and the property is sold at foreclosure for less than is required to pay off all the mortgages, the first mortgagee is paid first. Any remaining proceeds of the sale are then used to pay the second mortgagee. After the second mortgage is paid in full, any remaining funds are used to pay the third mortgage, and so on.

How are these priorities established? Priority of payment is established first of all by the agreement of the parties. In this example, each mortgagee understood the priority of his position. Thus, the second and third mortgagees received a higher interest rate on their loans to reflect the higher risk, i.e. that they would less likely be paid in the event of default.

If the parties are not part of the same transaction, but are simply independent mortgagees whose mortgages are placed on the property at different times, then the first one recorded is the first paid in the event of foreclosures. The recording statutes, therefore, play an important role for lien creditors of the property owner.

Mortgages are examples of voluntary liens; that is, the owner of the property voluntarily signs a mortgage deed to secure an obligation, to provide the lender with something tangible to sell to get his or her money back if the owner should be otherwise unable to do so.

There are other interests or liens that an owner can voluntarily put on his or her property. Suppose a new homeowner has put

$10,000 down on a new $80,000 home and gives a mortgage to a
local lender. Now the new owners want to build a new driveway,
or add vinyl siding to the house, or install a new furnace. Since
they do not have the money to pay for the improvement, they
must finance it. One way to finance the new furnace is to sign
an agreement with a seller of furnaces, which states that while
the homeowners are making payments on the furnace the furnace is still the property of the seller until the final payment is
made. The form used for this arrangement is a Uniform Commercial Code Financing Statement, an example of which appears
on the following page.

The seller files a copy of this statement in the registry of deeds
so that anyone searching the title of this particular piece of
property will see that the furnace is subject to a security interest, that anyone purchasing the house does not also automatically get the furnace. The furnace company must be paid in full
for title to the furnace to transfer to the purchaser.

Let's now suppose that attached to this house is a small office
space for which a dentist has a ten-year lease—is an estate for
years. In other words, the dentist has the irrevocable right to
occupy and use the office for that period of time, assuming that
rent is paid and the lease is not otherwise broken. This ten-year
lease is valuable to the dentist; it is clearly a possessory interest
in the real estate. Some states have statutes that require leases
of a certain duration to be recorded in the registry of deeds to
be valid. Thus, the dentist's recording of his lease in the registry
protects his interest in the office space.

Other liens on real estate are not placed voluntarily by the
owner. State laws give contractors and other people who work
on real estate, and thereby add value to a building, the right to
record a mechanic's lien when the owner does not pay them for
their work. A carpenter who adds a dormer for $12,000 and is
not paid by the seller would consult an attorney who would file
a mechanic's lien on the real estate. Before the property can be
sold with clear title, the amount owed must be paid and the lien
discharged.

Another form of involuntary lien is an attachment. An attach-

STATE OF MAINE

UNIFORM COMMERCIAL CODE — FINANCING STATEMENT — FORM UCC-1

Approved by Secretary of State

INSTRUCTIONS

1. PLEASE TYPE this form. Fold only along perforation for mailing.
2. Remove Secured Party and Debtor copies and send other 3 copies with interleaved carbon paper to the filing officer. Enclose filing fee of $5.00
3. If the space provided for any item(s) on the form is inadequate the item(s) should be continued on additional sheets, preferably 5" x 8" or 8" x 10". Only one copy of such additional sheets need be presented to the filing officer with a set of three copies of the financing statement. Long schedules of collateral indentures, etc., may be on any size paper that is convenient for the secured party.
4. If collateral is crops or goods which are or are to become fixtures, describe the real estate and if the debtor does not have an interest of record give name of record owner.
5. When a copy of the security agreement is used as a financing statement, it is requested that it be accompanied by a completed but unsigned set of these forms, without extra fee.
6. At the time of original filing, filing officer should return third copy as an acknowledgement. At a later time, secured party may date and sign termination legend and use third copy as a Termination Statement.

This FINANCING STATEMENT is presented to a filing officer for filing pursuant to the Uniform Commercial Code:

1 Debtor(s) (Last Name First) and address(es)	2 Secured Party(ies) and address(es)	3 Maturity date (if any):
		For Filing Officer (Date, Time, Number, and Filing Office)

4 This financing statement covers the following types (or items) of property:

ASSIGNEE OF SECURED PARTY

Name

Address

Check [X] if covered: ☐ Products of Collateral are also covered

No. of additional Sheets presented:

Filed with:

Date

By... Signature(s) of Debtor(s)

By... Signature(s) of Secured Party(ies)

Approved by Secretary of State , STATE OF MAINE

Filing Officer Copy — Alphabetical

FORM U. C. C. 1

MARKS PRINTING HOUSE, PORTLAND, ME.

ment is a court-ordered lien that arises when the owner of real estate is the defendant in a lawsuit. Suppose the homeowner ran up credit charges on all credit cards and then lost his job and was unable to repay the loans. One of the credit companies that brought suit asked the court to issue a writ of attachment for $8,500 to be recorded in the registry of deeds where the homeowner's property is located. Since this is his only asset, and it now has an attachment recorded against it, the property cannot be sold without taking care of the attachment.

Taxes are another source of involuntary liens on real estate. Local, state, and federal governments have the taxing authority, and thus the power, to place liens on properties for unpaid taxes. Local authorities place tax liens on property for unpaid real estate taxes. Their liens give the municipality the power to take the legal title of the property away from the owner, to sell the real estate to raise money to pay the taxes, and to transfer the property in a tax deed title to a new owner, generally after a period of redemption during which the former owner may reclaim title.

The Internal Revenue Service and state revenue service similarly have the authority to put liens on real estate to secure the payment of outstanding taxes.

Interesting legal issues arise when a homeowner, enjoying financial success, buys an expensive home, puts in a swimming pool financed with a second mortgage, and runs credit cards to the limit. A loss of job or sudden reverse in the stock market results in unpaid mortgages, credit card holders with attachments, unpaid real estate taxes, and unpaid federal and state income taxes—all secured by a variety of lien and attachments on the real estate. It is beyond the scope of this text to unravel such issues; the spectre of such a situation is raised only to illustrate why a title search is so important to a buyer. The buyer's attorney must make certain that each of the lienholders is paid in full and that a discharge of each lien—a document referring to a specific lien and stating that it is paid—is recorded in the registry of deeds so that future buyers of the property will understand that the liens are no longer outstanding. This is the only way to be certain that title to the purchase property is free of the claims of so many potential lienholders.

TITLE INSURANCE

In Chapter 8, the concept of adverse possession was discussed. Examples explained how neighbors might acquire title to a portion of the property because they behaved over time as if the boundaries were relocated and how one party might acquire an easement by prescription through the prolonged passing over a corner of the subject property. An interest in property acquired by adverse possession would not be revealed by a search of the records.

Example ─────────────────────────────

A title search of Eagles' Nest showed that Phillip and Elizabeth jointly owned the property free and clear of all mortgages and other encumbrances, and that it had been acquired by conveyance from Victoria, Elizabeth's mother. The attorney who searched the title gave an opinion of good title, but noticed that the surveyor's plan showed an "old cart path" and tracks of an old road in a corner of the property. Is this possibly evidence of an easement not disclosed in the registry? Suppose RCC built a store over this corner, and shortly thereafter a neighbor claimed a right of passage over that corner.

The surveyor's notation of an old cart path is actual notice to the parties that there may be a claim to pass over that part of the property. Assuming that Phillip and Elizabeth are unable to explain the cart tracks, there is a risk to RCC of an adverse claim to part of the property. Given the risk, should Ralph buy, or is the risk so insignificant that he can go ahead and purchase? If he purchases the property, will a lender agree that the risk is negligible? Or will a lender perceive it as a substantial risk that seriously affects the value and utility of the property?

Here is a situation in which *title insurance* can help close a transaction. Attorneys for the title company study the possible claim, decide that the risk is negligible, and issue an insurance policy to defend RCC if a claim is ever made and also to cover his losses if the claim to an easement by prescription is sustained. The policy can also cover the lender's risk, or a separate policy can be issued to the lender.

Title insurance is important in real estate transactions for another reason. In Chapter 9, it was noted that GNMA and FNMA purchase real estate mortgages for investors. Because the investors want assurances that their investments are secure, free from risk, or that the risks are at least insured, they are requiring title insurance policies to cover risks to the title to real estate in the same amount as the mortgage. In other words, just as the lenders require insurance to protect against loss by fire, they also require insurance to protect against risk of loss resulting from a faulty title.

TORRENS SYSTEM

The conventional recording systems just described are a mechanism whereby landowners and others with interests in land can record their interests for public knowledge and reference. This system provides only for notice of interests; it does not provide for resolution of any conflicting interests that may exist. In other words, the fact that a person records a certain boundary line as his or hers does not preclude the neighbor from contesting that claim.

Some states have a recording system that specifies and guarantees as accurate title to land, the existence of easements, the exact location of boundaries, etc. The system is called the *Torrens system* of land *registration*. In the states that use it, a landowner brings a petition to a judge in a special land court to have all issues pertaining to the property adjudicated once and for all. The land court orders a title examination and a special survey of the property. Special notice of the court process is sent to anyone who could possibly have an interest in the land—neighbors, abutting landowners, holders of easements, etc.—and notice of hearing is published in appropriate local newspapers. Everyone with a possible adverse claim is given an opportunity to present that claim in a hearing before the judge of the land court. The hearing is really a trial in which evidence is offered, legal argument is presented, and a decision is made by the court as to the status of the title. The decision is final and is binding on all future owners and parties in interest.

The owner of a registered parcel of land gets a copy of the *certificate of title* from the land court. The original certificate is kept in the land court records and shows all existing and recognized encumbrances and liens on the property. Any lien, except for federal tax liens and claims in bankruptcy that is not shown on the certificate in the land court does not exist.

The Torrens system has two significant advantages over the more common recording systems of registries of deeds: (1) it provides for absolute certainty of title with the authority of the state to guarantee it; and (2) there is no need to search titles because all encumbrances are shown on the certificate of title issued by the land court. However, it is an expensive system involving legal fees, court costs, and expensive surveys for each parcel. It is an appropriate system for resolving title disputes where they exist, but it is inappropriate for most transactions, where there are no adverse claims or interests in land.

SUMMARY

Ownership of real estate is the keystone to this country's system of private property ownership and social distribution of wealth. For most Americans, the purchase of a home represents the largest investment that will be made in a lifetime. To provide stability and security to the investment, states have enacted statutes that provide for a public recording of land ownership. A purchaser of real estate will have these public records examined to determine that the seller is giving good title to the land. The buyer, or donee, will record the deed in the registry to protect ownership rights in the property. Although recording statutes vary somewhat from state to state, their objectives and results are the same—the protection of property rights by giving public notice of ownership.

MULTIPLE CHOICE QUESTIONS

1. Landowner Lawrence deeds Lot 1 to Anne on June 1. Anne fails to record. One June 10, Lawrence dies and leaves Lot 1 to Brian in his will. Who is considered to own the lot?

   a. the state
   b. Anne
   c. Brian
   d. all of Lawrence's heirs

2. Which of the following interests in real estate would be recorded in a registry of deeds?

   a. long-term leases
   b. life estates
   c. mortgages
   d. all of the above

3. A tract index is organized according to:

   a. neighborhoods.
   b. names of grantors.
   c. names of grantees.
   d. particular parcels of land.

4. A person has constructive notice of a previous conveyance:

   a. after being told of the conveyance by his or her grantor.
   b. by asking the person currently in possession of the land.
   c. when the prior transaction is recorded.
   d. any of the above

5. Which of the following statements is true?

   a. Mortgages are not governed by race, notice, or race-notice recording statutes.
   b. Only fee simple estates are required to be recorded.
   c. Mortgages, unlike deeds, need not be recorded.
   d. Deeds, mortgages, easements, and long-term leases are interests in land that should be recorded.

6. Which of the following people may acknowledge a deed?

    a. a secretary
    b. a notary public
    c. a title searcher
    d. all of the above

7. A title abstract is:

    a. the opinion of the attorney on the state of the title.
    b. the certificate of good and merchantable title.
    c. an outline of the records in the registry of deeds.
    d. none of the above

8. A grantor-grantee index is organized:

    a. alphabetically.
    b. by the name of the grantor.
    c. by the name of the grantee.
    d. all of the above

9. It is important for the _____ to have the title to a piece of property searched, since he or she bears the risk of loss should the title fail.

    a. purchaser
    b. seller
    c. real estate agent
    d. purchaser's lawyer

10. *Chain of title* refers to:

    a. the quality of the title held by the current owner.
    b. the names of the prior owners.
    c. any liens or encumbrances on the title.
    d. a method of passing title.

11. What is the function of title insurance?

   a. reimbursement to the buyer should the title prove defective
   b. protection for the title searcher in case he or she was careless in examining the records
   c. protection for the seller in case the buyer should want to rescind the contract
   d. assurance for the real estate broker that a commission will be received

12. Title examination assures the buyer of a piece of property that:

   a. the seller has good title to convey.
   b. the seller is solvent.
   c. there are no liens on the property.
   d. the seller has an estate in fee simple absolute in the property.

13. After recording, who retains the original deed?

   a. the grantor or the grantor's agent
   b. the grantee or the grantee's agent
   c. the registry of deeds
   d. the lending bank

14. After recording, who retains the original mortgage deed?

   a. the grantor
   b. the registrar of deeds
   c. the attorney for the mortgagor
   d. the mortagee.

15. Why might a state not want to establish a Torrens system of land registration?

   a. It would virtually eliminate the need for private title insurance.
   b. It might lessen the need for private title searches.
   c. The cost of starting the system would be too high.
   d. Any landowner could register any land with relative ease.

DISCUSSION QUESTIONS ――――――――――――――――――――――

1. Discuss the differences among the three types of recording statutes.

2. What is the purpose for recording real estate documents? Who is protected? Buyers? Sellers? Financing institutions? Anyone else?

3. Discuss the reasons why a buyer of real estate, or a lender whose loan is secured by real estate, should insist on a title examination.

11

The Landlord/Tenant Relationship

Chapter 8 discussed the conveying of property interests by deed, by will, and by laws of intestate succession. A deed may grant all interests outright to another in fee simple absolute or limit the buyer's right of ownership according to stipulated conditions, as in the "qualified" estates. In any case, the buyer acquires ownership in the land. Estates granting some degree of ownership in land are called *freehold estates*. Of course, not all people who enjoy the use of real estate actually own it. Many people pay rent to the owner for the temporary privilege of using a parcel of land. Even though people who rent an apartment, a house, or office space do not own the premises they rent, they do have a temporary interest in that property, a *nonfreehold* or *leasehold estate*, of which there are several different kinds. This chapter will describe the conveyance of leasehold estates, the interest conveyed, and the legal relationship of landlord and tenant.

As part of their business, real estate licensees may act as rental agents for properties owned by others. It is important, therefore, that they understand the basic features of the rental relationship between the landlord and the tenant.

After reading the first portion of this chapter, the reader should be able to identify the elements of each of the four leasehold estates and be able to describe how each estate may be created, how long it lasts, and how it is terminated. The broker must also know which lease agreements are to be in writing and the legal consequences of the landlord's or tenant's refusal to abide by the terms of the lease agreement.

Landlord-tenant law is in a state of change. The following text covers the basic features of landlord tenant law, but should not be relied upon in lieu of competent legal advice. Any agent having or anticipating problems of the kind discussed in this chapter should see an attorney.

Finally, a potential licensee should have a working knowledge of the mutual rights, duties, and liabilities of the landlord and tenant. These are discussed in the latter portion of this chapter.

LEASEHOLD ESTATES

Not all people who enjoy the use of land own it. Almost everybody today has had the experience of paying a landowner for the privilege of using property. Like the landowner, the person who rents land from another has a property interest in that land and therefore has an estate in land. The essential difference between the owner's freehold estate and the tenant's leasehold estate is simply that the freehold estate carries with it rights of ownership, while the leasehold confers only the right to temporary possession.

Although a hotel guest is granted temporary right to possession of a hotel room, the guest is usually not considered a tenant. A person is deemed to be a tenant when he or she is entitled to exclusive possession of the property.

Types of Leasehold Estates

The transfer of the right of possession is effected through a written or oral agreement, the lease. The parties to the agreement are called the *landlord, lessor,* and the *tenant,* or *lessee.* The following is a discussion of the types of leasehold estates.

Estate for Years

An estate for years is one in which the tenant has the right of possession for any fixed or computable period of time.

Examples ─────────────────────────

T's lease grants her the right to possession from January 1, 1979, to December 31, 1999. T has an estate for years (term of years).

L transfers property to A for life, then to T for five years. Although we cannot determine when T's estate will become a present interest, we do know that upon A's death T will have right to possession for five years. T has a term for years.

L leases an apartment to T for ten days. T has a term for years.

─────────────────────────

Creation. Chapter 7 discussed the statute of frauds, which requires that agreements affecting an interest in land be in writing. Leaseholds are interests in land, so the statute of frauds applies to them as well. Because the statute is written differently from state to state, its application to leases depends on the jurisdiction. In the majority of states, an estate for years can be created by oral agreement if it is less than one year in duration. If the tenancy is to be more than one year in duration, it must be in writing to be enforceable. Other states require an estate for years to be in writing no matter how long it lasts. It should also be noted that, because leases are interests in land, they may be recorded in registries of deeds to protect the interest of the tenant. Although the law varies from state to state, some jurisdictions require that leases of more than two years be recorded to be enforceable.

Termination. Generally, an estate for years ends without notice upon the natural expiration of the term. But, like the freehold estates discussed above, an estate for years may also be qualified. An estate for years may be made subject to a possibility of reverter, a power of termination, or an executory limitation. To create an estate for years that may be terminated before expiration of the term, the conditions upon which the estate may be terminated must be stipulated in the lease.

Examples ─────────────────────────

L leased a parcel of land to T for 15 years "so long as the premises are used for religious purposes." T opened a day care center two years after taking possession. The term for years automatically terminates upon the use of the premises for a nonreligious purpose. T had a determinable *term years subject to a possibility of reverter.*

L leased a building to T for ten years "on condition that the building not be used for the sale of groceries; but if the premises are used for such a purpose, the landlord shall have the right to reenter and take possession." T has a *term years subject to a condition subsequent.* L will have the power to terminate the estate. But the estate will not automatically terminate until L takes affirmative action to evict T.

L leased an apartment to T for six months, "but in the event T fails to pay rent, then to A." If T fails to pay rent, the tenancy automatically shifts to A. T's estate is called an *estate for years subject to an executory limitation.*

─────────────────────────────────────

Generally, unless the qualifying language is incorporated in the lease, an estate for years cannot be terminated before its expiration date.

Finally, an estate for years may terminate when the landlord consents to the tenant's surrender of the premises. Sometimes consent to the surrender of the premises is shown by the conduct of the parties.

Example ─────────────────────────

T is two months into a term for nine months. T abandons the premises, and L re-enters, cleans, redecorates, and seeks to lease the premises to someone else. Even though L might not have ver-

bally consented to release T from the lease, when L took possession of the premises after the abandonment, he is deemed by his
conduct to have consented to the surrender.

If the landlord chooses this alternative and is able to rent the
property for as much as he would have earned if the first tenant
had not broken the lease, he has suffered no real economic harm.
If, however, in his attempt to mitigate or diminish the damage
caused by the tenant who departed, L is unable to relet the
property at the same rent but can get only a lesser rent, L may
sue the original tenant for the difference between what he would
have received and what he actually received.

Periodic Estate

A *periodic tenancy* is an estate that continues for successive
periods unless terminated by proper notice. The base period of
the estate may be a day, a week, a month, a year, or any division
or multiple thereof. The unique characteristic of the periodic
estate is that one term will be followed by another of the same
length ad infinitum unless one of the parties to the lease terminates the estate with proper notice.

Example ————————————————————————

L transfers the right to possession of a parcel of land to T "to continue from year to year." T has a periodic estate from year to year
until proper notice is given. If notice is not given, the tenancy will
continue indefinitely.

Creation. A periodic tenancy can be created in an oral or a written lease or by operation of law. A few states require a written
lease. A periodic estate may arise in two ways. First, it arises
when the lease expressly says that the tenant's right to possession is for a specific period.

Example ————————————————————————

L transfers possession to T "to continue from month to month
with rent payable on the first of each month."

The periodic estate may arise by implication if the lease does not specify the duration of the estate, but provides for the periodic payment of rent. In this instance, the rent arrangements determine the base period of the tenancy.

Examples

T's lease stipulates that she may take possession on the first of January at a rent of $250 per month. No duration is specified, but the monthly rent agreement establishes a periodic tenancy from month to month.

T's lease reads, "Lease shall commence January 1, 1980, at an annual rental of $4,200, payable at $350 per month on the first of each month. In most jurisdictions, T has a periodic estate from year to year despite the monthly rent payment because the lease creates an annual rental fee. In a minority of states however, this lease would create a tenancy from month to month.

In many states, periodic estates may arise by implication when a tenant for years remains in possession of the premises after the expiration of the estate and continues to pay rent.

The essential difference between a periodic estate and an estate for years is that an estate for years automatically terminates without notice upon expiration of the term, while a periodic estate continues indefinitely until terminated by proper notice. Thus, when a lease is prepared by an attorney, it is important that it reflect the intentions of the landlord and the tenant.

Termination. Termination requirements vary greatly from state to state. A common law termination of year-to-year tenancy originally was achieved by notice of either landlord or tenant at least six months before the end of the term. Statutory modification has made the period vary from 30 days to six months. Most states require written notice.

If a state requires six months' notice and the lease begins on the first of January, the last possible moment at which the landlord or tenant can notify the other of an intent to terminate the estate at the end of the term is the last day of June. It is crucial that the notice period be calculated using the last day of the term upon which the estate is to be terminated. For the lease beginning January 1, a notice mailed on July 1 and received on July 2 is ineffective, and the party wishing to terminate the lease is legally bound to honor the lease for another term.

Example

In December, L transferred a "periodic estate from year to year commencing on the first of January." In late June, L decides to terminate the estate. On July 2, L sends notice expressing his intent to terminate the estate six months after receipt of the notice. The notice is ineffective in terminating the estate because T didn't receive the notice six months prior to the end of the term.

If the base period of the periodic tenancy is less than one year, the common law requires that notice be given at least one full period before the end of the term after which the estate is desired to be terminated.

Examples

L has leased an apartment for an unspecified time, but with a stipulation that rent be paid on the 13 th of each month. If L gives notice to terminate on October 20, the earliest possible date upon which the estate can be terminated is December 14.

T has a periodic estate from month to month beginning on the first of each month. T wants to terminate the estate after the April term. L must have received notice of T's intent to terminate the estate no later than March 31, 30 days prior to the end of the April term.

Note, however, that the lessor and lessee may mutually agree to vary the notice requirements of the common law. Thus, although the law may require at least six months' notice to terminate a periodic tenancy from year to year, the parties to a lease may agree to shorten or lengthen the notice period.

In addition, termination of a periodic estate occurs through surrender in two ways. First, the landlord and tenant can agree that the tenant may give up possession of the premises and that both parties will be released from their obligations under the lease. Second, surrender occurs when the landlord resumes possession of the premises after the tenant has abandoned them. Keep in mind the landlord's option, upon abandonment, to keep the premises vacant and sue the absconding tenant for the rent due for the balance of the period.

Tenancy at Will

A *tenancy at will* is a possessory interest that is terminable at the will of either the landlord or the tenant. The tenancy at will differs from the estate for years and the periodic estate in that there is no fixed base time period throughout which the estate is to continue. Instead, the estate continues only so long as neither party acts in a manner inconsistent with its continuance. Statutory developments, however, have substantially altered this unique feature of the estate at will, as will be discussed below.

Creation. A tenancy at will can be created by oral or written lease, by taking possession under an invalid lease before making periodic payments, or by taking possession with permission of the owner but with no agreement as to duration of the lease or as to rental payments.

A lease might simply stipulate the rent and other conditions of the tenancy without mentioning the duration of the lease. In this case, the presumption is that the creation of a tenancy at will was intended by the lease agreement.

Example ────────────────────────────

L executes a written lease of unspecified duration with rent payable from time to time as demanded by L. A tenancy at will is created because there is no base period established by the lease. Since rent is not payable on a systematic basis, there is no possibility of the creation of a tenancy by implication.

───────────────────────────────────────

A tenancy at will is also created in a holdover situation. A *hold-*

over occurs when a tenant under a lease for a term of years or a periodic term remains in possession of the leased premises after expiration of the estate and has the landlord's consent. A holdover tenant has only a tenancy at will until a new written lease is executed by the parties.

Termination. According to the common law, the unique characteristic of the estate at will was its ability to terminate without notice at the will of either party. Today, in most states, statutory notice requirements have altered the terminability of this estate so that it is almost a misnomer to call this possessory interest an estate at will.

Thus, a tenancy at will can usually be terminated upon a 30-day notice given by either party. In some states, only the landlord must give notice..

Moreover, the written notice given by either party in many states must name the day on which the tenancy is to terminate. If the other party does not receive actual notice at least 30 days before the specified date, the notice will be ineffective in terminating the tenancy on that or any other day. A new notice will have to be served. In special circumstances, the law often permits the lessor to terminate the tenancy on seven-day notice. This will be discussed further in the second part of this chapter.

Another unique characteristic of the estate at will is that it terminates upon the death of either party or upon the sale of the leased property to a third party.

In most states, statutory notice provisions still apply, so that the tenancy at will does not expire until the notice period has run.

Examples ———————————————————————

T has a tenancy at will with rent payable on the first of every month. T would like to quit the premises at the end of July. To effectively terminate the tenancy, T must give a written notice no later than May 31, a full 30 days prior to the rent day on which the estate is to terminate. His written notice must state that he will quit the premises and that the estate will terminate on June 30.

L sells an apartment building in which T has an estate at will. The estate in a minority of states automatically terminates when T receives notice that the building has been sold. T need not be given notice before the sale, but he must be given notice of the sale, or lease, before the estate will terminate. He must also be given reasonable time in which to leave the premises. In most states, T must be given the statutory notice period to move out.

Tenancy at Sufferance

A *tenancy at sufferance* is the interest of a tenant who acquired possession by permission of the owner but who now continues in possession without consent after the expiration of the period to which he or she was entitled. Thus, a tenant for years who remains in possession of the premises after expiration of the estate becomes a tenant at sufferance. Likewise, tenants with a periodic estate and tenants at will who remain in possession of their apartments after termination of their leases are tenants at sufferance.

Termination. The tenancy at sufferance may end either when the landlord gives the tenant permission to stay or when the landlord takes steps toward eviction. Moreover, if the landlord fails to evict the tenant or give notice to quit, his or her conduct may imply consent to the tenant's continued possession of the property, especially if the landlord accepts rent payments.

The landlord may instead choose an action for eviction or for damages. The laws of many states authorize the commencement of a summary possession action, called a *forcible entry and detainer action*—or *entry and detainer*, or *FED* for short— to regain possession from a tenant at sufference. Once the lease has expired or is terminated, the landlord may begin an FED action to regain possession quickly. Eviction proceedings are discussed at greater length later in this chapter.

Assignment and Sublease

Unless prohibited by the lease, a tenant may transfer all or part of his or her interest in the leased premises without consent of the landlord. If the tenant transfers the balance of the unexpired term, he or she is deemed to have assigned the lease to another person. The landlord and the assignee become liable to one another on the covenants of the original lease.

If, however, the tenant transfers only a part of the unexpired term, then he or she is said to have subleased the premises. The tenant becomes the landlord of the sublessee, who can neither sue nor be sued by the original landlord. Only if the sublessee expressly assumes the covenants of the master lease will he or she be liable to the landlord as a third party beneficiary.

Examples

T has a term for 10 years with no restrictive agreements in the lease. T has occupied the leased premises for one and a half years. If T executes a written assignment of the lease to A for eight and a half years, he has transferred the entire balance of the unexpired term. T has assigned his lease.

T has a periodic estate from month to month in a 50-acre lot. T may transfer all of his interest in a one-acre lot to A for as long as the periodic tenancy continues. T has partially assigned his interest in the estate.

T has a lease for five years. After three months, T transfers his interest to A for 24 months. T has executed a sublease because he transferred his interest for only a part of the unexpired term.

The most important fact to remember about *assignments* and *subleases* is that they apply only to estates for years and periodic estates. A tenancy at will cannot be assigned or subleased. Unless the rule is modified by statute, any attempt to assign or sublease a tenancy at will automatically terminates the estate.

In most states, real estate licensing laws require people whose business involves leasing apartments or business or industrial space to be licensed as real estate brokers or salespersons. These real estate license laws apply to people who are agents not only to sell property but also to lease property belonging to others. A licensed broker may include leasehold estates in his or her inventory of properties to show and advertise. The purpose of this

first section of the landlord/soliders tenant chapter is to describe
the different types of leasehold interests that a property owner
can offer and a prospective tenant can rent. The next section of
this chapter describes the lease agreement between the landlord
and tenant that articulates the duties and responsibilities of
each. It is important that the landlord's agent be able to discuss
these issues knowledgeably with the tenant.

RIGHTS, DUTIES, AND LIABILITIES OF LANDLORD AND TENANT

The landlord and tenant have certain rights, duties, and obligations to each other and to the property the tenant occupies. The
landlord owns the property and grants the use and possession
to the tenant for a limited time only. The tenant, therefore, owes
to the landlord certain duties to preserve the landlord's interest
in that property. The landlord in turn must respect the right of
temporary possession that has been granted to the tenant. Both
the landlord and tenant will have liabilities to third persons who
enter portions of the property under their control.

The laws governing the landlord-tenant relationship began in
feudal England. Today, many laws still reflect these early ori-
gins, while others embody more modern trends. Because
landlord-tenant law is a local matter and state statutes vary
widely, the well-informed broker must become familiar with the
law of his or her jurisdiction. The Uniform Residential Landlord
and Tenant Act (URLTA) has been adopted in several states and
for those states standardizes landlord tenant law. But generally,
URLTA or the various state statutes or court cases are the
sources of law defining the rights, duties, and liabilities of the
landlord and tenant.

An agent should know whether the landlord or tenant may be
liable to third parties for personal injury or property damage
that occurs on leased premises. The sample lease should be examined to discover typical reciprocal rights and duties of the
landlord and tenant.

Lease

The lease agreement has a dual nature—it is partly contract and partly conveyance. On one hand, the lease conveys a property interest much as a deed does. To create a particular estate, the lease must conform to certain requirements for creation, duration, and termination of that estate. On the other hand, a lease is like a contract in that the parties are free to bargain for many aspects of the creation, duration, and termination of the lease. The contractual nature of the lease is becoming especially important today in defining the parties' rights and duties.

A sample lease agreement that illustrates the typical components appears beginning on the following page. Some of the more critical clauses are discussed here in paragraphs keyed to the corresponding clauses in the lease.

A. Basic Information. The first paragraph of the lease contains all the information required by the statute of frauds. It identifies (a) the parties—the landlord and the tenant; (b) the subject matter, i.e. the description of the apartment and the duration of the lease; and (c) the price of the unit.

B. Occupancy. In the occupancy clause, the landlord and tenant mutually acknowledge that the apartment is to be used for a residence only, and they agree to the number of occupants. This clause is useful because it requires the tenant to comply with local zoning regulations that would prevent the tenant from overcrowding the apartment with friends or using the apartment for business purposes.

C. Assignment, Subletting. Before the landlord rented the apartment to this tenant, he or she checked the tenant's credit history and living habits by asking the tenant's former landlords. Finding the tenant to be an acceptable risk, the landlord decided to rent to this tenant. By this clause the landlord reserves the right to approve any subsequent tenant should the selected tenant want to move before the end of the lease.

D. Alterations, Damages, Loss, Damage to Personalty, Damage or Destruction to Property. Clauses 3, 4, and 9 spell out in detail the rights and responsibilities of the parties to make alterations to the premises and to repair damages to the property.

E. Access to Premises. A landlord has a substantial investment

Lease of
Residence

Landlord

Tenant

Property

Dated   19

LEASE OF RESIDENCE

A

AGREEMENT OF LEASE, made this   day of   , 19   , by and between
                                               (hereinafter called "Landlord"), and
            (hereinafter called "Tenant"),
    WITNESSETH THAT, Landlord hereby leases to Tenant and Tenant hereby hires from Landlord; the residence described below, together with the lot of land on which it stands, to wit:

for the term of   year (s), to commence on the first day of   , 19   for a total
rent reserved of   Dollars ($), which Tenant covenants and agrees
to pay in equal monthly installments of $. each, in advance on the first day of each month during said term,
at the office of Landlord or such other place as Landlord may designate, except that Tenant shall pay the first monthly
installment of rent on the execution hereof.
    The parties hereto hereby further covenant and agree as follows:

B

OCCUPANCY
    1. The said residence shall be occupied only by Tenant and members of the immediate family of Tenant, and by no
more than a total of   persons, and Tenant agrees that the said residence shall be used only as a strictly private
dwelling and for no other purpose.

C

ASSIGNMENT, SUBLETTING, ETC.
    2. Tenant shall not assign, mortgage or encumber this Lease or his rights hereunder; nor underlet the demised
premises or any part thereof or permit the said residence to be used by others without the prior written consent of the
Landlord in each instance.

ALTERATIONS
    3. Tenant shall make no alterations, decorations, additions, affixations, or improvements in or to the said residence,
except in cases of emergency, without Landlord's prior written consent to which Landlord may attach conditions. All materials installed in or affixed to the said residence by either party including without limitation all panelling, decorations,
partitions, wall-to-wall carpeting, other attached floor coverings, floors, storm windows, storm doors, screens, window
shades, curtains, draperies, electrical, gas, oil or water appliances, shall become the sole property of Landlord, and shall
remain in and be surrendered with the said residence, as part thereof, at the end of the term hereof or any extension or
renewal thereof.

D

DAMAGE
    4. Tenant shall not commit or permit any strip or waste of the demised premises or any part thereof. Any
damage to or destruction of the demised premises or any part thereof or to or of any personal property belonging to
Landlord located in or about the said residence arising from the negligence or willful act or omission of Tenant, persons

living with Tenant, or his or their employees, invitees or guests, shall be the responsibility of Tenant, who shall reimburse Landlord for all expenses in repairing or rebuilding the demised premises, or repairing or replacing such personal property.

REQUIREMENTS OF LAW; INSURANCE RATES

5. Tenant shall comply with all laws, orders, ordinances and regulations of Federal, State, County and Municipal authorities, and with any direction of any public officer or officers, pursuant to law, which shall impose any duty upon Landlord or Tenant with respect to the demised premises. Tenant shall do or keep nothing, nor allow anything to be done or kept, in the said residence which would be denominated extra hazardous as to insurance by fire insurance companies or which would increase Landlord's fire insurance rates or which would cause any of Landlord's insurance to be adversely affected.

SUBORDINATION

6. This lease is subject and subordinate to mortgages which may now exist or hereafter be executed and delivered covering the demised premises or any part thereof.

UTILITIES AND SNOW REMOVAL

7. Tenant agrees to promptly pay and hold Landlord harmless from all charges for utilities furnished to the said residence (including without limitation electricity, water, telephone service and gas). Tenant agrees to promptly pay for all fuel delivered to the said residence. Tenant agrees at his expense to keep any driveways on the demised premises and any sidewalks abutting the demised premises free of ice and snow, and to indemnify Landlord against liability for accidents arising from Tenant's failure to remove such ice and snow.

LOSS, DAMAGE TO PERSONALTY OF TENANT

8. Landlord shall not be liable for any loss of, damage to or destruction of property located in or about the said residence occasioned by any cause whatsoever, including without limitation, fire, explosion, riot, water or any theft by any person, whether or not an employee of Landlord. Furthermore, Tenant waives as against Landlord and covenants and agrees to hold Landlord harmless from all claims by Tenant or any person claiming by, through or under Tenant by way of subrogation or otherwise, arising from the destruction of, loss of or damage to any personal property located in or about the demised premises belonging to Tenant or others, whether or not caused by a condition of the premises or negligence of the Landlord in respect thereof, to the extent that such destruction, loss or damage is covered by insurance carried by Tenant, in order that no insurance carrier shall have a claim by way of subrogation against Landlord for such damage, destruction or loss.

DAMAGE TO OR DESTRUCTION OF RESIDENCE

9. If the said residence during the original term of this Lease or any extension or renewal thereof be so destroyed or damaged by fire or other unavoidable casualty not the fault of Tenant as to render the said residence as a whole unfit for occupation, then the rent hereinbefore reserved, or a fair and just proportion thereof, according to the nature and extent of the damage sustained, shall be suspended or abated until the said residence shall have been rebuilt and put in proper condition for occupancy by the Landlord; or these presents shall, at the election of either the Landlord or the Tenant, upon written notice thereof to be given within thirty (30) days after such damage or destruction, thereby be determined and ended, without prejudice to any rights of Landlord for breach of contract, arrears of rent or otherwise.

REPAIRS AND MAINTENANCE

10. During the term of this Lease or any extension or renewal thereof, Landlord shall maintain the structural and exterior portions of said residence and repair any damage thereto not caused by the negligence or willful act or omission of the Tenant, any persons living with the Tenant, or his or their employees, invitees or guests. During the term of this Lease or any extensions or renewals thereof, Tenant shall maintain (i) the interior portions and appliances of and contained in said residence (including without limitation floors, walls, paint, wallpaper, ceilings, panelling, windows, storm doors, storm windows, screens, plumbing system, electrical system and appliances, furnace, oil tank, hot water tank, stoves, washing machine, dryer and refrigerator, if any) in as good a condition as they may now be or may hereafter be put into by the Landlord and shall repair any damage to the same occasioned by any cause (other than fire or inevitable accident not the fault of Tenant) and (ii) the said lot of land, including without limitation lawns, trees and shrubs and shall repair any damage done to any of the foregoing by Tenant, persons living with Tenant, or his or their employees, invitees or guests.

ACCESS TO PREMISES

11. Landlord or Landlord's agents shall have the right to enter the said residence during reasonable hours, to examine the same, and to show the same to prospective purchasers or lessees, and to make such decorations, repairs, alterations, improvements or additions as Landlord may deem necessary or desirable.

DEFAULT

12. If (i) the said residence shall be abandoned by Tenant, (ii) Tenant shall default in the payment of any rent when due, whether or not demanded, (iii) Tenant shall default in the observance and performance of any other covenant to be performed or observed by Tenant under this Lease for ten or more days after Landlord shall give to Tenant notice of such default and a demand to cure the same, (iv) there shall be filed by or against Tenant a petition under any Chapter of the Bankruptcy Act of the United States or any other insolvency proceeding relating to the debts of Tenant shall be brought by or against Tenant, or Tenant shall make an assignment for the benefit of creditors, or shall be insolvent or unable to pay his debts as they mature, then and in any one or more of such events Landlord may, at Landlord's sole election, give to Tenant a notice that the term of this Lease has terminated, and the term hereof shall terminate upon the giving of such notice, and Tenant shall thereupon quit and surrender the demised premises to Landlord, and Landlord may, without further notice, re-enter the demised premises with or without legal process and dispossess Tenant and remove Tenant's effects. In case of termination of the term of this Lease for any such cause, Landlord shall be deemed to have waived no rights hereunder, and shall be entitled to recover damages as for breach of contract, which may include, without limitation, the amount of the total rent remaining due under this Lease for the full term as if the same had not been terminated, less any proper credits, and Landlord's reasonable attorney's fees and any other expenses of Land-

(over)

(Continued)

F lord incurred in connection with the retaking of possession of the demised premises and the removal and storage of Tenant's effects and the recovery of damages. Any demand or notice to Tenant under this or any other section of this Lease shall be deemed effective and delivered to Tenant if (i) left at the said residence in a conspicuous place or affixed to the front door of said residence, whether or not any person is in said residence at the time of delivery or thereafter, or (ii) mailed to Tenant by ordinary mail, postage prepaid, addressed to Tenant at the said residence or at an address designated by Tenant in writing to Landlord as the address to which all notices and demands hereunder shall be mailed.

END OF TERM

G 13. Upon the expiration or other termination of the term of this Lease or any extension or renewal thereof, whether by reason of Tenant's default or otherwise, Tenant shall quit and surrender the demised premises to Landlord, broom clean, in as good condition as they now are or may be put into by the Landlord or the Tenant, ordinary wear excepted, and damage by fire or other inevitable accident not the fault of Tenant or persons living with Tenant or his or their employees, guests or invitees excepted, and any other item which it is the responsibility of Landlord to maintain or repair excepted. Tenant shall remove all personal property of Tenant as directed by Landlord.

SECURITY DEPOSIT

H 14. Tenant has deposited with Landlord an amount equal to one month's rental hereunder as security for the full and faithful performance by Tenant of all the terms, covenants and conditions of this Lease, including without limitation Tenant's duty not to damage the said residence or any of Landlord's personal property located therein. If Landlord uses any of such security deposit to fulfill obligations of Tenant hereunder, Tenant will deposit sufficient monies so that said security deposit will be at all times equal in amount to one month's rent. Landlord shall be under no obligation to segregate or hold apart from Landlord's other funds the said security deposit, and no interest on the same shall accrue in favor of Tenant.

HOLDOVER

G 15. If the said residence is retained by Tenant beyond the term of this Lease or any extension or renewal thereof, and Landlord shall not within thirty (30) days before or after the expiration of such term demand possession of the said residence in writing, then this Lease shall continue in full force and effect and all the terms (including rental terms) shall apply, except the term of this Lease shall be for one month commencing on the day after the date of termination of the original term as so extended or renewed and the term of one month shall be automatically renewed for successive terms of one month thereafter until either party shall cancel this Lease and the one month term hereunder then in effect or to come into effect by giving to the other a written notice of cancellation, such written notice and cancellation to be effective at the expiration of the one month term specified therein (irrespective of the date of delivery of such notice), whether the first one month term or any successive one month term.

RENEWALS AND EXTENSIONS

16. If the term of this Lease is renewed or extended by an instrument executed by Landlord and by Tenant, all of the terms, covenants, provisions and conditions of this Lease (including without limitation provisions as to rental) shall be in full force and effect during the extended or renewal term, except that the termination of the extended or renewal term shall be as specified in such instrument.

HEADINGS

17. The headings or captions in this document shall not be taken into account in construing the meaning of the provisions hereof.

NO WAIVER

18. The waiver of a breach of any term, condition or covenant contained in this Lease shall be effective only if in writing, and shall not be considered to be a waiver of any other term, condition or covenant, or of any subsequent breach of any nature.

GENERAL

19. This Lease shall inure to and be binding upon the respective heirs, executors, administrators, successors and assigns of the parties. This Lease is made in accordance with the laws of the State of Maine. If there is more than one tenant, the word "Tenant" shall include the plural as well as the singular, and the obligations of all tenants hereunder shall be joint and several. If there is more than one Landlord hereunder, the word "Landlord" shall include the plural. The masculine gender shall include the feminine.

NO REPRESENTATIONS

20. Except as otherwise provided by law as to the implied warranty of habitability, Landlord makes no representations as to the condition of the said residence or lot of land, or as to any of the contents thereof or personal property located therein, and the Tenant accepts the same in their present condition as is.

INDEMNIFICATION

21. Tenant covenants and agrees to forever save and hold Landlord harmless from and against all claims for damage to or loss of property, and all claims for injuries to or death of persons, in or about the demised premises caused by the negligence or willful act or omission of Tenant, or his or their employees, invitees or guests, and/or resulting from Tenant's failure to observe or comply with any of Tenant's obligations undertaken in this Lease.

IN WITNESS WHEREOF, the Landlord and Tenant have respectively caused this Lease to be duly executed and delivered in their respective names and behalves all on the day and year first above written.

WITNESSED BY:

.... Landlord

By: ....

.... Tenant

.... Tenant

• • •

The term of the within Lease is hereby extended to   19   at the
monthly rate of rental hereinbefore provided.

.... Landlord

By: ....

.... Tenant

.... Tenant

---

in the real estate leased to the tenant and thus wants to supervise and protect the investment in any way possible. Without this clause, which gives the landlord the right to inspect at reasonable hours, the landlord has no right to enter the apartment leased to the tenant.

F. Default. This clause states that the landlord reserves the right to treat in any manner he deems appropriate any default by the tenant.

G. End of Term, Holdover. The purpose of clauses 13 and 15 is to define the rights of the parties should the tenant not vacate at the end of the term. These clauses are helpful in a lease because they give the parties specific rights and impose on them specific obligations. The stating of these terms prevents traumatic confusion if, for some reason, the tenant does not move at the end of the term.

H. Security Deposit. The tenant's advance of one month's rent, to be held by the landlord, is designed to give the landlord security for the tenant's performance. Some states have passed laws that permit security deposit of two months' rent or limit it to two months' rent. The landlord keeps the deposit for use towards any repairs to the property required because of damage caused by the tenant.

I. "In Witness Whereof...." It is here that the lease is signed. As pointed out above, the statute of frauds in some jurisdictions requires that all enforceable leases be signed; in other states, the statute requires signatures on a written agreement if the lease is not to be performed within one year.

Use of Premises

During the tenancy, the lessee has the right of exclusive possession of the leased premises. A landlord who enters without the tenant's consent is a trespasser. Along with the tenant's right of exclusive possession goes the obligation to use the premises in the manner for which they were intended and the implied obligation to use reasonable care to prevent damage to the landlord's property. Any damage or injury that results from a lack of reasonable care or from a use for which the premises were not intended may give the landlord cause to bring suit or retain a portion of the security deposit.

A tenant cannot freely alter leased premises without the landlord's permission. Such modification, even if beneficial to the landlord's property, may make the tenant liable for damage to the landlord's property. Any express provisions in a lease regarding the alteration of the premises will prevail, and a landlord should include any restrictions on use or alteration in the lease. A tenant is not liable for any damage caused by normal wear and tear of the premises. *Normal wear and tear* means the deterioration that occurs while using the premises as intended, without carelessness, accident, or abuse. Neither will a tenant be liable for lasting or substantial damage to areas that the tenant may use but over which the landlord has retained control, as long as the tenant is not at fault for the damage.

Example

Tenant Black is not responsible for the wearing down of a rug and the peeling of paint and wallpaper, but she is responsible for having carelessly broken a window in the hallway to the rental unit, even though the landlord has retained control of this area so other tenants may use it.

Condition of the Premises

Until recently, most states applied the rule of *caveat emptor*—let

the buyer beware—to rental property. Under this rule, the landlord had no duty to deliver premises of a particular quality and
was under no duty to repair.

Today, many states are abandoning this rule in favor of either
an implied common law or a statutory *warranty of habitability,*
whereby in an oral or written agreement to rent a dwelling unit
the landlord guarantees that the rental unit is fit for human
habitation. If the rental unit has a condition that would seriously endanger the health or safety of the tenant, it is not fit for
human habitation.

The landlord must deliver premises, therefore, that are fit for
human habitation. The landlord may also have the statutorily
imposed duty to comply with any applicable building, housing,
sanitary, or other code ordinances, regulations, or statutes.

Courts and legislatures in many states have recently imposed
upon the landlord the duty of repairing any condition that
would seriously impair the health or safety of a tenant. If this
condition was not caused by the tenant, the tenant can make a
written complaint to the landlord. If the landlord fails to repair
the condition within a reasonable time, the tenant may petition
a court for certain remedies, which include:

1. ordering the landlord to make the repairs;

2. charging the tenant only what it considers to be the fair
   rental value with the condition;

3. stopping all rental payments until the defect is cured; and

4. allowing the tenant to repair and deduct the cost from
   rent due.

In some states, a tenant may accept, in a written agreement,
specified conditions that violate habitability or other code provisions, in exchange for a reduction in rent.

Duty to Make Repairs

In the absence of a specific agreement in the lease, a landlord
has no general duty to make repairs to a dwelling unit. This absence of responsibility exists because most leases in the past

conveyed rural property to tenants who were expected to repair the buildings included in the leased property. Therefore, if the dwelling unit needed repairs during the term of the lease, the landlord has no duty to repair. Traditionally, property law regards a lease as the equivalent of a conveyance for the term of the lease. Because the tenant takes control of the premises, he or she is then subjected to the responsibilities as owner and occupier of the property, which would include the duty to make repairs in the occupied areas. Reform in this area of law is expanding the landlord's duty to repair.

However, the landlord has always had a duty to repair those areas over which he or she retains control. These areas, such as stairs and hallways, must be kept in reasonably safe repair for the occupants of the premises and all other permissive users.

Example

A rug in a hallway that several tenants use and a rug in tenant Brown's apartment are both in need of identical repair. The landlord has a duty to repair the hall rug to make the hall reasonably safe, but he or she has no duty to repair the rug in the tenant's apartment.

The tenant has a duty to repair his or her occupied areas but is limited to making those repairs necessitated by negligence or fault, not those due to wear and tear. The tenant's obligation is not generally to repair, but to refrain from *voluntary waste.*

Example

A tenant who allows grease from the stove to blacken kitchen walls commits permissive waste, and in the absence of a prior agreement, is under no duty to repair the damage. By contrast, a tenant who makes a hole in the wall to accommodate stereo equipment commits voluntary waste and is liable for the repair cost.

If the damage done by the tenant is not due to ordinary wear and tear, or if the tenant has committed voluntary waste, he or she will be liable for those repairs in an action for damages.

Liability for Injuries

Traditionally, the landlord had very limited liability for personal injury or property damage that occurred on the rented premises. Because the landlord has no general duty to repair premises that are in the possession and control of the tenant, he or she cannot be held liable for damage resulting from the condition of the premises.

Both the landlord and the tenant owe a duty of reasonable care in all circumstances to all persons lawfully in the portion of the leased premises under their possession and control.

Possession and control are determining factors when dividing responsibility between landlord and tenant. Whoever has possession and control of an area will be responsible for injuries that occur due to dangerous conditions in that area. Therefore, the tenant may be liable for injuries that occur in the rented premises, while the landlord may be liable for injuries resulting from failure to maintain such areas as stairways, hallways, and walkways. The landlord is deligated to exercise ordinary care in keeping common areas reasonably safe for their intended use.

Examples ——————————————————————————————

Landlord L rents her residential building but retains possession and control of the building's roof. Over the winter, snow repeatedly has fallen from the roof onto a sidewalk. Pedestrian P is hit by a falling chunk of snow while passing by L's building and falls, spraining his ankle. L is liable for P's injury.

A railing on a staircase in a hallway used by all tenants and similar railings on staircases in all of the apartments are broken. The landlord is responsible for injuries resulting from a fall that a sound railing on the public staircase would have prevented.

———

Since possession and control are the crucial factors, landlord L in the first example above would not be liable for P's injury if L has leased the entire premises. If the tenant's lease included possession and control of the roof, then the tenant would be responsible for P's injury.

The landlord, however, will be liable for damages due to *latent defects*. Latent, or hidden, defects are those that are not known or generally discoverable by the careful tenant. The landlord must point out to the lessee any defects that are not obvious; failure to do so makes the landlord liable for injuries that occur because of the latent defect. The landlord will be liable even if he or she had no actual knowledge of the defect but should have known about it. If the landlord does disclose the defect, and the tenant is aware of it and accepts the premises as is, the landlord is relieved of responsibility.

Example

There is a weak spot, concealed by a carpet, in the floor of an apartment. If the tenant has not been warned of the defect by the landlord, and is injured because of it, the landlord will be liable for the injury.

If a defect arises in leased premises after the tenancy has begun, the landlord is not responsible for any injuries caused by this defect. If the landlord has agreed to repair the premises, then the landlord may be liable for the personal injuries that result from failure to repair. In some states, however, the landlord would be liable only for a breach of contract, much as an independent plumber or electrician would be liable for not fulfilling the requirements of a contract. However, if a landlord undertakes repair and performs it negligently, he or she will be liable for any injuries that result from negligence.

Example

A ceiling begins to crack, and the landlord puts in a new ceiling, although he or she has no duty to repair. This ceiling later falls and injures the tenant; the landlord will be responsible.

Modern cases are eroding traditional landlord immunities. Several cases have held that the landlord must act as a reasonable person and act to prevent injury, even if the defect arises after the tenant has taken possession and is in areas controlled by the tenant.

Security Deposit

A *security deposit* is an advance payment that protects the landlord from the tenant's violation of the rental agreement. In many states, the law concerning security deposits has been formalized into statutes, which vary widely. Generally, the statutes require the landlord to return deposits to tenants within a certain time and to account for a claim to all or part of the deposit or face specified penalties for failure to comply.

If there is cause to retain all or part of the security deposit, the landlord generally must provide the tenant with a statement itemizing the reasons for retention. Cause for the retention or security deposit may be, for example, the tenant's nonpayment of rent or utility charges, damage to property, moving without notice, or breach of other conditions in a written lease.

If the landlord fails to return the security deposit or provide the written statement, he or she may lose *all* rights to withhold any portion of the security deposit. Other penalties may also be imposed.

Obligation to Pay Rent

The obligation to pay rent is an integral part of the landlord-tenant relationship. It exists even where there has been no express promise to pay. In feudal times, rent was payable at the end of the term; the custom arose because rent was usually a portion of the crop raised on the rented premises. Today, a landlord and tenant may make any agreement as to the manner and amount of payment.

The duty to pay rent was formerly independent of the landlord's duty to supply habitable premises. In other words, the tenant had to pay rent regardless of the condition of the property. Under the old law, a tenant could not withhold rent because of some defect in the premises. This policy is changing throughout the country, as reflected in changing statutes in many states. Often the duty to pay rent is dependent upon the landlord's covenant of fitness for human habitation. If a tenant files a complaint about the condition of the premises, the court may deduct from the unpaid rent the difference between the agreed rental value and the fair value of the defective premises. This reduction will be effective from the date of the complaint until the condition is repaired or remedied. The tenant would also have to be current in rent payments at the time the complaint was made.

Example

An apartment rents for $200. In the middle of the winter, no heat is provided. If the tenant is current in rental payments and gives the landlord written notice of the condition, a court will make the tenant liable only for the fair rental value of the premises—for example, $100—from the day the heat stopped. The court may also order the landlord to repair the heating system.

A tenant today will probably not be liable for rent if fire or other unavoidable casualty renders the premises unfit for human habitation. However, a lease for nonresidential property can contain provisions that will make the duty to pay rent continue even if a fire or other unavoidable casualty destroys the premises.

Any lease should make clear the manner and terms of payment. If the parties desire a provision for termination of the tenancy upon the nonpayment of rent, this can be included. Because, in most cases, the exchange of money in return for the right of possession of the premises is the core of the landlord-tenant relationship, care should be taken when drafting provisions of a lease.

Eviction

A landlord has the duty to deliver quiet enjoyment of the property to the tenant. In no way may the lessor disturb the lessee's use and enjoyment of the premises. An act such as interfering with possession or even refusing to make repairs may be deemed a breach.

Actual Eviction—Interference with Possession. If a tenant is physically ousted or prevented from occupying the property, he or she may claim *actual eviction*. The tenant's obligation to pay rent ceases, and the lease may be treated as terminated. If the landlord denies possession of a *portion* of the premises, then a *partial actual eviction* may be claimed by the tenant, and the duty to pay rent ceases entirely until possession of that portion of the premises is restored to the tenant. Rent ceases entirely in a partial actual eviction because a landlord should not be allowed to apportion the wrong.

Example ─────────────────────────────

The landlord places a lock on the door to the tenant's apartment. The tenant's right to exclusive possession has been breached, and the duty to pay rent ceases immediately. The tenant may at his or her option terminate the tenancy, and the landlord may be liable for damages. If a tenant is prevented from entering a garage, which is included with the leased premises, the tenant's entire duty to pay rent ceases. This is a partial actual eviction.

Constructive Eviction ─ Interference with Use and Enjoyment. A tenant was obligated in the past to pay rent even if the landlord interrupted the tenant's use and enjoyment of the property. This harsh rule of law has now been modified by the concept of *constructive eviction.*

Example ─────────────────────────────

The landlord, who lives next to the tenant's apartment, plays loud music all night, every night. The tenant, claiming a constructive eviction, may move out and stop paying rent.

Constructive eviction allows a tenant to terminate the lease and to stop paying rent even if the landlord did not infringe on the tenant's actual possession. To claim constructive eviction, the tenant must show that by intentional or wrongful acts the landlord has permanently deprived the tenant of the beneficial use and quiet enjoyment of the premises and that the tenant has moved out as a result.

Other examples of situations that warrant constructive evictions are lack of heat, infestation by vermin, and any other condition that makes the premises uninhabitable for the purpose for which it was leased.

To claim constructive eviction, the tenant must move out of the premises. Consequently, the doctrine meant as a remedy against the landlord's wrong is often of little use to low-income people who lack the funds to move elsewhere.

Entry and Detainer

In every state, there are statutes that govern eviction procedures. The broker, when acting as a manager of rental property, or when a sale is dependent upon the delivery of vacant premises, may be involved with the eviction procedures that are used in his or her state.

Every state has a summary proceeding called a *forcible entry and detainer* or *unlawful detainer* action. An entry and detainer action can be brought only when a tenancy is terminated, for example, by the expiration of the term or by the breach of some condition in the lease. The landlord may begin an entry and detainer action if the tenant does not move out after the tenancy has been terminated.

The entry and detainer action must be commenced by notice to the tenant, but that notice may be very short, just a few days under most statutes. The sole issue in the proceeding will be who has the right to possession. Consequently, the landlord must prove that the lease has expired or that a condition of the lease has been breached.

With prompt action, a landlord may regain possession very quickly, perhaps within a month. If the tenant does not leave voluntarily, a writ of possession will be issued and the sheriff or one of his deputies will be authorized to remove the tenant physically.

An entry and detainer action may be forbidden by statute when it is taken in retaliation for a complaint about a condition that rendered the premises unfit for human habitation or for membership in a tenants' rights organization. Today, statutes in several states create a presumption of retaliation when the tenant has complained or actively sought landlord reform.

Example ─────────────────────────────────────

Landlord has recently brought a FED action against tenant, who several months ago complained about a housing code violation. A state statute raises a presumption of retaliatory eviction, which the landlord must refute before he can prevail in the action.

──

Remedies for the Nonpayment of Rent

If a tenant is behind in rent payments, the landlord may bring an action in court to recover the amount owed. The landlord may be prevented from recovering the amount owed if the following conditions exist:

1. Notice was given to the landlord, or the person who collects the rent, of a condition that rendered the premises unfit.

2. The condition was not caused by the tenant.

3. The landlord failed to take prompt, effective steps to remedy the condition.

Rent may not be recovered if the premises have been rendered uninhabitable by fire or other casualty.

Rent Control

Rent control originally appeared in the United States as an emergency measure during World Wars I and II. Goals were (1) to encourage the channeling of resources for wartime needs rather than for housing and (2) to discourage the driving up of prices by competitive bidding for apartments. Since 1970, however, rent control has emerged in many cities as an attempt to keep costs down for the average consumer, whose spending for other goods and services is skyrocketing.

There is much disagreement over the value of rent control. Supporters argue that only the landlord's increases in property taxes, utilities, and maintenance should be passed on to the tenant. Detractors say that, at best, rent control is a mixed blessing for the tenant and cite what they see as long-term detrimental effects of the procedure:

- Landlords in rent-controlled buildings neglect routine maintenance and repairs.

- Landlords should not bear the brunt of inflation.

- Construction of new buildings lags in rent-controlled cities.

- Conversion to condominiums, often a severe hardship to tenants, is frequently the recourse of the landlord subject to rent control.

- A landlord may be forced to abandon a building rather than lose money on a rent-controlled unit. Such abandonment of tens of thousands of buildings in New York City, for example, has cost the city a vast amount in lost property taxes.

The test for the validity of rent control is whether or not the landlord receives a just and reasonable return on his or her investment. If the applicable statute or ordinance does not give the landlord a fair return as economic conditions change, it is confiscatory and thus void. In addition, since 1974, rents in federally assisted housing are set by regulations of the Department of Housing and Urban Development, which overrides local controls.

SUMMARY

A real estate broker's business is to provide a market or a clearinghouse for sellers of interests in land in which buyers can find the house, land, or apartment to fit their needs. A substantial portion of a broker's business may therefore involve listing, showing, renting, and even managing rental property for property owners. This chapter has addressed the concept of a lease, as a conveyance and a contract. It has shown the various types of tenancies that may be created to fit the needs of the landlord and tenant and has explained the rights and obligations of the landlord and tenant to each other. To a broker whose business involves apartments, a sound understanding of the principles explained in this chapter is essential, as is a good working relationship with an attorney experienced in local nuances of landlord-tenant law.

MULTIPLE CHOICE QUESTIONS ───────────────────

1. A tenancy at will terminates when the:

    a. tenant dies.
    b. landlord dies.
    c. landlord sells the building.
    d. any of the above

2. A tenancy at sufferance:

    a. must be in writing.
    b. can be terminated by 30 days notice only.
    c. can be assigned or sub-leased.
    d. none of the above

3. A lease for an estate for years must be in writing because of the:

    a. Statute of Frauds.
    b. Statute of Wills.
    c. Statute of Leases.
    d. Recording Statute.

4. Where a tenant signs a one-year lease for an apartment and agrees to pay $300 per month in rent, and then leaves after 9 months, the landlord may:

    a. sue the tenant for $900.
    b. sue the tenant for $900 less the security deposit.
    c. sue the tenant for $900 plus the security deposit.
    d. none of the above

5. A landlord who wants to quickly get rid of a tenant who is behind in his/her rent should:

    a. change the locks on the doors.
    b. shut off the heat and hot water.
    c. bring a suit for eviction.
    d. any of the above

6. Which of the following is (are) true?

    I. George, a tenant at will, lives in a state that requires 30-day notice for termination. On December 3, George gives his landlord notice that he desires to terminate his lease on December 30. The notice is effective.
    II. Jeri lives in a state governed by the common law provisions on the tenancy at will. When her landlord dies, Jeri's lease automatically terminates.

    a. I only
    b. II only
    c. both I and II
    d. neither I nor II

7. Marion is a tenant at will in a small lakeside cottage. She decides to spend the winter in Florida and rents the cottage to her friend, Fritzie, informing him that she will be back in May to repossess the cottage. Which is true?

    a. Fritzie assumes the leasehold and will be liable to Marion's landlord.
    b. Marion has assigned her lease.
    c. Fritzie has no rights under this attempted sublease.
    d. none of the above

8. Clara has a lease, which expires December 31, on a basement studio where she teaches dance. Heavy rains in the last several months have caused flooding in the basement, requiring Clara to cancel classes. On August 31, Clara moves out and stops paying rent. Which of the following is true?

    a. Clara has suffered a constructive eviction and will have to pay no further rent.
    b. Clara has suffered an actual eviction and will have to pay no further rent.
    c. Clara has breached the conditions of her lease by ceasing to pay rent.
    d. Clara will have to pay rent until December 31, but can request the city health inspector to force the landlord to repair the defect.

9. Jane contracts verbally with her landlord for an apartment from month to month with rent payable on the first of each month. She has:

    a. an implied periodic tenancy.
    b. a periodic tenancy.
    c. an estate at will.
    d. an estate for years.

10. Which of the following is (are) true?

    I. A freehold estate is one in which a person has all or some of the rights of ownership.

    II. A leasehold estate is one in which a person has only the right to temporary possession of property owned by another.

    a. I only   c. both I and II
    b. II only   d. neither I nor II

11. Tom has a written lease for Larry's apartment with rent payable on the 15th of each month. Tom has:

    a. a determinable fee.
    b. a periodic tenancy arising by implication.
    c. an invalid lease because it fails to specify the duration of the estate.
    d. an estate for years.

12. A tenancy at sufferance can arise only:

    a. by an oral lease agreement between landlord and tenant.
    b. when a person decides to use another's land without permission.
    c. when the landlord agrees to the tenant's use of the premises.
    d. when the tenant continues in possession of leased premises after the expiration of the period to which he or she was rightfully entitled.

13. If a little paint is flaking off the wall of an apartment, and there is no clause in the lease covering this situation then the tenant may:

    a. make a complaint under the implied covenant of habitability.
    b. terminate the leasehold and stop payment of rent.
    c. pay what he or she thinks to be the fair value of the premises.
    d. none of the above

14. If a tenant falls through the steps of the private entrance to her dwelling unit, and there are no provisions in the lease covering these steps, the tenant may:

    a. be able to recover for personal injury in any case.
    b. not be able to sue the landlord because the stairs were in her possession.
    c. recover for breach of contract for a failure of the landlord to keep the steps in repair.
    d. none of the above

15. A tenant paints a mural on the wall and ceiling of a dwelling in violation of an express prohibition in the lease. The landlord may:

    a. give notice of forfeiture of the tenancy.
    b. retain a portion of the security deposit.
    c. sue for damages.
    d. all of the above

DISCUSSION QUESTIONS ———————————

1. Your town is considering an ordinance applying rent control to a district near a large university. Discuss the advantages and disadvantages that the proposed measure may bring.

2. Discuss several ways in which present-day law has extended the tenant's remedies over those available at common law.

3. Your friend Lily has an estate for five years in an attractive and inexpensive apartment. Recently she has decided to move to New York City to try to break into the publishing business. She is not sure she will want to stay in New York City if she does not find an exciting job. Having four years more on her lease, Lily is not sure whether to assign or sublease. Explain to her at least two differences between assigning and subleasing.

12

Licensing, Ethics, and Regulations

KEY TERMS

Code of Ethics

misrepresentation

National Association
of Realtors®

state licensing laws

It is inevitable in any business that disagreements will arise and need to be resolved. In the real estate business, there are both public and private mechanisms for the regulation of the business and the resolution of its problems. Public mechanisms are administered by state-created real estate commissions or boards, which have the responsibilities of education, licensing, and regulation of the business.

Private regulation is provided by the trade association of real estate brokers, the National Association of Realtors® (NAR). Membership in the association is voluntary, but those who do join pledge to abide by the association's Code of Ethics. In addition to enforcing its Code of Ethics, the NAR carries on sophisticated education programs for its members and arbitrates disputes between members.

This chapter looks at both the public and private institutions and the rules they have developed for the regulation of the real estate industry.

LICENSE LAWS

State licensing laws for real estate practice have been enacted in each of the 50 states and in the District of Columbia. The objective of the laws is to protect the public from the unscrupulous or inept practices of real estate agents. The laws do so by setting standards for the minimum entry-level skills required to become a real estate agent and by exercising disciplinary powers to enforce laws of practice against licensees who are not in compliance. Whether the organization in any state is referred to as a *Commission* or a *Board,* all carry out their functions in a similar manner:

- by setting educational prerequisites for real estate licensure;

- by administering examinations to measure initial competence to enter the profession;

- by disciplining real estate brokers and salespeople who violate the laws and regulations of the business; and

- by supervising the real estate industry and its practices within the state.

Education and Licensing

In meeting its objective of protecting the public, one of the real estate board's most important functions is to issue licenses. Real estate licenses are issued only to those people who meet the standards of the licensing laws, which generally include:

- residency in the state;

- no criminal record, other than traffic violations;

- high school diploma or the equivalent;

- special education in real estate;

- passing grade on a prelicensing exam.

As the practice of real estate becomes more complex, states are increasing the prelicensing requirements for license applicants, especially in the area of prelicensing education or prelicensing internship.

The prelicensing examination used may be developed by the state real estate board or, more often, developed and administered by a national testing service. In either case, each state decides on the entry-level skills for its jurisdiction as part of its prelicensing responsibilities.

Once an individual has met all these criteria, he or she will be issued a real estate license. Like a driver's license, the real estate license is a privilege granted to the individual by the state so long as the licensee complies with its rules. A license may expire if not renewed, and it can be revoked or suspended in the event of malpractice by the licensee.

A real estate license is issued for a period of time, generally one or two years. Upon its expiration, the licensee must pay a fee and apply for renewal. In approximately 22 states, licensees must attend continuing education courses in order to renew their licenses.

License Law Violations

Real estate boards are also heavily involved in the supervision and regulation of brokerage practices. Boards are organized to receive complaints from the public and are responsible for conducting investigations. Upon receiving a complaint, a staff investigator will interview participants and witnesses to a transaction, collect documents and other evidence, and present findings to the board. If the complaint cannot be resolved administratively, the board may hold a hearing at which the complainant may present his or her case. Parties to a hearing are often represented by counsel. If a broker is found guilty in the hearing, some boards have limited powers to collect fines and suspend licenses. In other states, boards make findings and recommendations and turn the case over to the state's attorney general's staff for prosecution.

Misrepresentation

The most common source of complaints to a real estate board concerning brokers' practice is *misrepresentation*. Unhappy buyers most often feel that a selling broker has lied, deceived them, or failed to disclose some aspect of the property. Because their expectations have been disappointed, they file a complaint against the broker.

Misrepresentation is a serious charge for a broker to face. In an industry that depends upon the repeat business and references of satisfied customers for success, an individual agent's integrity and reputation for honest dealing are crucial to his or her future.

A misrepresentation occurs when a broker makes a false statement about a property when that statement concerns a *material fact,* something important to the buyers in the decision to purchase the property. In addition, the buyers must show that they relied on the broker's false statement and were harmed by the false representation.

The following buyers questions and brokers' answers illustrate the topics that are most commonly at the heart of complaints or suits for misrepresentation.

Q. "What kind of sewer system does this house have?"

A. "Concrete tank with leaching field."

In fact, the broker does not know what the system is because it cannot be seen. A fabricated answer or one based on wishful thinking can get the agent into trouble. It is surprising how many times a broker will advertise a property as being on town water and sewer systems when in fact it has its own—too often inadequate—well and septic system.

Q. "What is the annual heating bill for this property?"

A. "Not bad. About $400 per year, I'd say. There's plenty of insulation."

Again, because insulation is difficult to check, and because different families have different heating requirements—a family with two small children requires more heat than a working couple, both of whom are gone all day—accurate representation of heating bills is difficult. Securing the prior owner's utility bills and comparing them with the degree-days may be useful, but a broker puts himself at risk by making statements that cannot be verified.

Q. "Is the basement dry?"

A. "Oh, yes."

Unless the broker sees water stains, a sump pump, or damp-
ness, or asks the seller, he or she has no way of knowing if the
basement is dry. A better answer from the broker might be:
"Let's ask the seller"; or "The seller tells me that there has
never been any problem during the five years he has been here."

A broker can also run afoul of misrepresentation rules when he
or she knows of a material defect in the property but fails to
mention it to the buyer. If the broker knows that the roof leaks
every time it rains, he or she is under an obligation to advise
the buyer. The broker is under a legal obligation to deal honestly
with the buyer, it is better to risk losing a sale and to preserve a
reputation than perhaps to lose both reputation and license before a real estate board.

What can agents do to protect themselves against misrepresentation? There are several simple steps:

1. Brokers should not make statements of fact unless they
   know them to be true.

2. Brokers who do not know if a heating system is forced
   hot water, steam, or air, or if a house is wired for 220-
   amp service, should consult an expert for an opinion
   rather than assume the risk of being wrong. Brokers can
   often shift the liability to others who are trained in
   these matters.

3. Brokers can reiterate their special representations by
   following conversations with a letter, keeping file copies
   as proof that certain matters such as a leaking roof or
   rotting sills were accurately disclosed to the buyers before they committed themselves to buying the house.

One last thought about misrepresentation: In many cases, complaints about misrepresentation are the result of misunderstandings—a broker says one thing, which is interpreted differently
by the purchaser, who wants to hear something else. To protect

him or herself, a broker should see that all factual data concerning the property are put on paper and given to the buyer before the purchase and sale contract is signed. Accurate representation of the property begins when the broker takes the listing from the seller. All the data entered on the listing agreement and data sheets are part of the advertising/promotion/representation of the property. The data sheet should be given to the buyer as part of the promotion of the property so the purchaser can consider the property's features before deciding to purchase. Accuracy is essential so that buyers' expectations concerning the property are not disappointed.

Trust Accounts

The second largest source of complaints to real estate boards is mishandling of trust account funds. Trust account violations generally fall into three categories:

1. embezzlement or theft;

2. incompetent accounting practices;

3. misapplication of funds.

Every trade and profession attracts its share of untrustworthy practitioners, and real estate brokerage is no exception. Real estate boards hear complaints concerning the theft of trust account funds, a situation on which no further comment is necessary.

Incompetent accounting is also a source of trust account complaints. Consider the following case: A broker who manages residential property for a client is supposed to collect rents on the first day of the month and pay the property's bills on the fifth of the month. In fact, although the bills are paid on the fifth, rents are two weeks late. How is the broker able to pay the bills on the fifth? He is inadvertently using another client's earnest money, which he deposited in the same trust account at the end of the previous month. When the tenants skipped town and failed to pay their rent, the broker did not have enough money in his trust account to close the transaction, a portion of the needed earnest money used to pay another client's bills was mishandled. Even though the broker's mishandling of funds was "innocent," he may still be reprimanded by a real estate board.

A third situation involving a complaint on a trust account might arise as follows: a broker is holding a $10,000 earnest money deposit in his trust account. He is a little short of cash to pay his secretary this week but knows that at the closing next week he will get a six percent commission. He "borrows" enough money from his trust account to meet his payroll when he should have gone to a bank for a conventional business loan. The broker's conversion of clients' funds to his own use, even if only temporary, is a subject for complaint before a real estate board.

Other Violations

Conflict of Interest. Other violations of license law are addressed in provisions of the license law of each state. One of the areas that most of the laws focus on is conflict of interest. A real estate agent is under a legal duty to disclose to all parties in a transaction whom he or she is representing, if it is not the seller, or not the seller alone. When a broker buys property for him- or herself, he or she must notify the seller. If a prospective buyer is a relative of the broker, the seller must be informed. At all times, the broker must be careful not to place him- or herself in a position in which anyone can suspect his or her loyalty to the principal.

Payments to Nonlicensees. Licensed real estate agents are prohibited from paying a finder's fee to nonlicensed people.

Example ─────────────────────

Agent Ali offers to pay his postman, his barber, and the personnel officer at a local employer $100 for all leads that generate a commission for him. If these people are unlicensed, this practice is illegal.

─────────────────────

Prizes. Licensees are prohibited by the laws of many states from offering prizes or free gifts to people as an inducement to list, buy, or sell real estate.

Example ————————————————————————

Broker Bill was having difficulty selling house lots from a development. He decided to offer a free getaway weekend in a local motel to the first ten purchasers in the month of February. Under the law of some states, this practice is illegal.

————————————————————————————————

Disclosures. A real estate agent's job is to provide accurate information to the buyers and sellers throughout the listing, negotiation, and closing phases of a real estate transaction. License laws often specify many of the disclosures that a licensee is expected to make, including:

1. expiration dates on listing contracts;

2. copies of all contracts delivered to parties at the time of signing;

3. disclosure that the buyer's earnest money deposit is only a signed note, rather than check or cash;

4. disclosure to the buyer and seller of the closing costs of a transaction and of who is expected to pay which costs;

5. delivery to all parties of a written statement following the closing, which shows how all the money was spent.

Depending on the facts of a particular violation of these provisions, a real estate board may reprimand or fine a broker or suspend or even revoke his or her license.

Fair Dealing. In many states, the license law contains a catchall provision that states that the real estate board may suspend or revoke a license for activities that constitute "fraudulent, dishonest, or improper dealings." Consider the following case.

Example ————————————————————————

A broker takes a listing on a subdivided but undeveloped parcel of land containing three lots. The broker tells the seller that the market is slow; it may take months to sell. Because the seller is desperate for cash, the broker offers to purchase the lots. Before the transaction closes, the broker advertises and resells two lots and sells the third lot within six days after taking title himself. Has the broker demonstrated bad faith or dishonest practices and untrustworthiness? The real estate board reviewing this case found the broker guilty and permanently revoked the license.

A licensee's greatest asset for avoiding trouble with the real estate board is a thorough understanding of the license laws of the state. The law has been developed over many years of experience with cases involving brokers, buyers, and sellers and codifies behavior considered ethical and proper. While the body of real estate law with which a real estate licensee must be familiar is extensive, the license law will focus the broker's attention on the law affecting his or her professional conduct.

License laws are evolving and expanding as real estate practice grows more complex. New laws pertaining to the regulation of timesharing and homeowner's warranty contracts are found in the laws of some states. A thorough knowledge of the license law will be the licensee's greatest single guide to sound professional practices throughout his or her career.

Judicial Resolution of Cases

A buyer or seller dissatisfied with the representation offered by the real estate agent is not limited to filing a complaint with the state real estate board. Anyone can hire an attorney and file suits in the appropriate court to seek redress for any loss. Because court dockets are so full, it may take longer to resolve a case in a court of law than it would before a state real estate board. It is important to recognize that an unhappy buyer or seller can pursue both a lawsuit and a complaint simultaneously; the remedies are not mutually exclusive.

ETHICS

Before licensing laws were universal in the United States, there were professional real estate associations organized to supervise the activities of agents and to raise the level of professional conduct. The National Association of Real Estate Boards (NAREB) was formed in 1908. NAREB was changed in 1974 to *National*

Association of Realtors®. In 1914, NAREB formulated and published a Code of Ethics to govern the professional conduct of its members.

The code became a model for the licensing laws of the several states and serves to promote ethical behavior among members by establishing a public and professional standard against which the conduct of member Realtors® could be judged.

By joining the board, a licensed broker becomes a Realtor®, a trademarked name, and makes a commitment to abide by the Code, which in several instances establishes a more demanding standard of conduct than the licensing laws.

The National Association of Realtors® is composed of state associations, which in turn are made up of local, often countywide, associations or boards. Each board has the duty of enforcing the Code of Ethics within its own district. Conscientious and responsible enforcement enhances the reputation of all Realtors® by letting the public know that members adhere to ethical standards more stringent than those required by law. The duties spelled out in the code involve obligations to the public at large, to individual clients, and the fellow Realtors®. The *Code of Ethics* contains 23 articles, reprinted below.

Code of Ethics[1] of the National Association of Realtors®

Revised and Approved by the Delegate Body of the Association at its 75th Annual Convention November 15, 1982

Preamble . . .
Under all is the land. Upon its wise utilization and widely allocated ownership depend the survival and growth of free institutions and of our civilization. The Realtor® should recognize that the interests of the nation and its citizens require the highest and best use of the

---

1. Published with the consent of the National Association of Realtors®, author of and owner of all rights in the Code of Ethics of the National Association of Realtors®, ©National Association of Realtors® 1982—All Rights Reserved. The National Association of Realtors® reserves exclusively unto itself the right to comment on and interpret the CODE and particular provisions thereof. For the National Association's official interpretations of the CODE, see INTERPRETATIONS OF THE CODE OF ETHICS; National Association of Realtors®.

land and the widest distribution of land ownership. They require the creation of adequate housing, the building of functioning cities, the development of productive industries and farms, and the preservation of a healthful environment.

Such interests impose obligations beyond those of ordinary commerce. They impose grave social responsibility and a patriotic duty to which the Realtor® should dedicate himself, and for which he should be diligent in preparing himself. The Realtor®, therefore, is zealous to maintain and improve the standards of his calling and shares with his fellow Realtors® a common responsibility for its integrity and honor. The term Realtor® has come to connote competency, fairness, and high integrity resulting from adherence to a lofty ideal of moral conduct in business relations. No inducement of profit and no instruction from clients ever can justify departure from this ideal.

In the interpretation of this obligation, a Realtor® can take no safer guide than that which has been handed down through the centuries, embodied in the Golden Rule, "Whatsoever ye would that men should do to you, do ye even so to them."

Accepting this standard as his own, every Realtor® pledges himself to observe its spirit in all of his activities and to conduct his business in accordance with the tenets set forth below.

Article 1
The Realtor® should keep himself informed on matters affecting real estate in his community, the state, and nation so that he may be able to contribute responsibly to public thinking on such matters.

Article 2
In justice to those who place their interests in his care, the Realtor® should endeavor always to be informed regarding laws, proposed legislation, governmental regulations, public policies, and current market conditions in order to be in a position to advise his clients properly.

Article 3
It is the duty of the Realtor® to protect the public against fraud, misrepresentation, and unethical practices in real estate transactions. He should endeavor to eliminate in his community any practices which could be damaging to the public or bring discredit to the real estate profession. The Realtor® should assist the governmental agency charged with regulating the practices of brokers and salesmen in his state.

Article 4
The Realtor® should seek no unfair advantage over other Realtors® and should conduct his business so as to avoid controversies with other Realtors®.

Article 5
In the best interests of society, of his associates, and his own business, the Realtor® should willingly share with other Realtors® the lessons of his experience and study for the benefit of the public, and should be loyal to the Board of Realtors® of his community and active in its work.

Article 6
To prevent dissension and misunderstanding and to assure better service to the owner, the Realtor® should urge the exclusive listing of property unless contrary to the best interest of the owner.

Article 7
In accepting employment as an agent, the Realtor® pledges himself to protect and promote the interests of the client. This obligation of absolute fidelity to the client's interests is primary, but it does not relieve the Realtor® of the obligation to treat fairly all parties to the transaction.

Article 8
The Realtor® shall not accept compensation from more than one party, even if permitted by law, without the full knowledge of all parties to the transaction.

Article 9
The Realtor® shall avoid exaggeration, misrepresentation, or concealment of pertinent facts. He has an affirmative obligation to discover adverse factors that a reasonably competent and diligent investigation would disclose.

Article 10
The Realtor® shall not deny equal professional services to any person for reasons of race, creed, sex, or country of national origin. The Realtor® shall not be party to any plan or agreement to discriminate against a person or persons on the basis of race, creed, sex, or country of national origin.

Article 11
A Realtor® is expected to provide a level of competent service in keeping with the standards of practice in those fields in which the Realtor® customarily engages.

The Realtor® shall not undertake to provide specialized professional services concerning a type of property or service that is outside his field of competence unless he engages the assistance of one who is competent on such types of property or service, or unless the facts are fully disclosed to the client. Any person engaged to provide such assistance shall be so identified to the client and his contribution to the assignment should be set forth.

The Realtor® shall refer to the Standards of Practice of the National Association as to the degree of competence that a client has a right to expect the Realtor® to possess, taking into consideration the complexity of the problem, the availability of expert assistance, and the opportunities for experience available to the Realtor®.

Article 12
The Realtor® shall not undertake to provide professional services concerning a property or its value where he has a present or contemplated interest unless such interest is specifically disclosed to all affected parties.

Article 13
The Realtor® shall not acquire an interest in or buy for himself, any member of his immediate family, his firm or any member thereof, or any entity in which he has a substantial ownership interest, property listed with him, without making the true position known to the listing owner. In selling property owned by himself, or in which he has any interest, the Realtor® shall reveal the facts of his ownership or interest to the purchaser.

Article 14
In the event of a controversy between Realtors® associated with different firms, arising out of their relationship as Realtors®, the Realtors® shall submit the dispute to arbitration in accordance with the regulations of their board or boards rather than litigate the matter.

Article 15
If a Realtor® is charged with unethical practice or is asked to present evidence in any disciplinary proceeding or investigation, he shall place all pertinent facts before the proper tribunal of the member board or affiliated institute, society, or council of which he is a member.

Article 16
When acting as agent, the Realtor® shall not accept any commission, rebate, or profit on expenditures made for his principal-owner, without the principal's knowledge and consent.

Article 17

The Realtor® shall not engage in activities that constitute the unauthorized practice of law and shall recommend that legal counsel be obtained when the interest of any party to the transaction requires it.

Article 18

The Realtor® shall keep in a special account in an appropriate financial institution, separated from his own funds, monies coming into his possession in trust for other persons, such as escrows, trust funds, clients' monies, and other like items.

Article 19

The Realtor® shall be careful at all times to present a true picture in his advertising and representations to the public. He shall neither advertise without disclosing his name nor permit any person associated with him to use individual names or telephone numbers, unless such person's connection with the Realtor® is obvious in the advertisement.

Article 20

The Realtor®, for the protection of all parties, shall see that financial obligations and commitments regarding real estate transactions are in writing, expressing the exact agreement of the parties. A copy of each agreement shall be furnished to each party upon his signing such agreement.

Article 21

The Realtor® shall not engage in any practice or take any action inconsistent with the agency of another Realtor®.

Article 22

In the sale of property which is exclusively listed with a Realtor®, the Realtor® shall utilize the services of other brokers upon mutually agreed upon terms when it is in the best interests of the client.

Negotiations concerning property which is listed exclusively shall be carried on with the listing broker, not with the owner, except with the consent of the listing broker.

Article 23

The Realtor® shall not publicly disparage the business practice of a competitor nor volunteer an opinion of a competitor's transaction. If his opinion is sought and if the Realtor® deems it appropriate to respond, such opinion shall be rendered with strict professional integrity and courtesy.

Note: Where the word Realtor® is used in this Code and Preamble, it shall be deemed to include Realtor-Associate®. Pronouns shall be considered to include Realtors® and Realtor-Associates® of both genders.

The Code of Ethics was adopted in 1913. Amended at the annual Convention in 1924, 1928, 1950, 1951, 1952, 1955, 1956, 1961, 1962, 1974, and 1982.

The code has some provisions that are similar to the licensing laws. For example, commingling of brokers' and clients' funds, prohibited by Article 18 of the Code of Ethics, is usually prohibited by the law as well. But other articles of the code go beyond the law in encouraging ethical behavior. Article 1, for instance, suggests that the Realtor® should stay informed on matters affecting real estate so that he or she may contribute to public thinking. Article 5 demands that the Realtor® share the lessons of experience with his or her associates. Neither requirement is articulated in licensing laws.

The published code is supplemented by *Standards of Practice*, which are interpretations of the articles. These interpretations are meant to guide the Realtor® in making his or her conduct conform to that demanded by the code. In addition, interpretations of the National Association of Realtors® code cite cases that illustrate situations in which a broker may or may not have violated an article of the code. Consider the following example.

SUMMARY

As in any business, conflicts ranging from simple misunderstandings to charges of malfeasance or incompetence may arise in the brokerage business. This is particularly true in real estate because investments are large and rules and regulations are complex. All states have enacted legislation to establish regulatory agencies to protect the public from incompetence and unscrupulous business practices. Regulatory boards or commissions are responsible for the education, licensing, and supervision of brokers in their state. Aggrieved members of the public, or licensees, have a forum in which they can file complaints and secure public hearings on problems they face with licensed members of the profession.

In addition to these responsibilities, commissions have an affirmative duty to audit the trust accounts of real estate offices periodically. Since the broker's duty to handle other peoples' money in his or her trust account is so crucial to the public's confidence in the integrity of the brokerage profession, a commission's responsibilities in this area are particularly acute.

The real estate industry recognizes that the public's confidence in its members is essential to the industry. The association's goals of increased education, adherence to ethical standards of conduct, and the availability of a forum to solve grievances have all helped to win the public's confidence. These trade associations, from which the National Association of Realtors® and its state and local chapters evolved, have elevated the professionalism of the real estate brokerage business as a whole.

MULTIPLE CHOICE QUESTIONS ——————————

1. The purpose of state real estate license laws is to:

    a. regulate the brokerage industry.
    b. establish local boards of directors.
    c. enforce the Code of Ethics.
    d. all of the above

2. The Realtors® Code of Ethics:

    a. was adopted in 1914.
    b. is the basis for many state licensing laws.
    c. expects higher professional conduct of brokers than required by license laws.
    d. all of the above

3. Which of the following is (are) true?

    I. To be liable for a misrepresentation, the broker's buyer must have relied on erroneous information.
    II. To be held liable for a misrepresentation, the broker's erroneous statement must have been intentional.

    a. I only
    b. II only
    c. both I and II
    d. neither I nor II

4. Trust accounts are used to hold:

    a. secretaries' salaries.
    b. office expense funds.
    c. clients' money.
    d. all of the above.

5. Interest paid on monies held in broker's trust account should be paid to:

    a. whomever the money belongs.
    b. the trustee for servicing the account.
    c. the bank to cover the expenses of running the account.
    d. any of the above

6. Which of the following is (are) true?

   I. Trust account funds may earn interest.
  II. Interest earned on trust account funds must not be paid to the broker-trustee.

    a. I only
    b. II only
    c. both I and II
    d. neither I nor II

7. A broker may:

    a. open separate trust accounts for each client.
    b. commingle the funds of all clients in one account.
    c. delegate bookkeeping responsibilities to an associate.
    d. all of the above

8. One of the articles of the Realtors® Code of Ethics requires that disputes between brokers be resolved by the:

    a. superior court.
    b. state regulator agency.
    c. Realtor® grievance board.
    d. state attorney general.

9. The Realtor® Code of Ethics governs:

    a. business conduct of member Realtors®.
    b. hearing procedures for real estate commissions.
    c. prelicensing educational requirements.
    d. all of the above

10. A broker deposits a client's earnest money in his business checking account. Because the broker hasn't paid federal income taxes, Uncle Sam puts a lien on the checking account, which prevents the broker from withdrawing even the client's money. The broker could have avoided this by putting the client's money in a:

    a. trust account.
    b. savings account.
    c. different bank.
    d. none of the above

DISCUSSION QUESTIONS —————————————————————

1. Discuss the role and responsibilities of the real estate board or commission in your state. Does it have the authority to revoke licenses?

2. Why do real estate licensing laws and Realtors'® Code of Ethics prohibit a broker from commingling a broker's funds with clients' funds?

3. What contribution does the National Association of Realtors® make to professionalism of the real estate brokerage industry?

13

Federal Laws
Affecting
Real Estate

KEY TERMS
---

antitrust law	Interstate Land Sales
broker-lawyer accords	Full Disclosure Act
capital gain	price-fixing
depreciation	tax credits
fair housing	tax-free exchange
installment sale	ACRS

As an introduction to the legal aspects of real estate, this book outlines a host of rules and regulations that every real estate licensee must know. This concluding chapter explains additional legal issues a broker or salesperson may face:

- basic concepts of federal taxation of income derived from real estate;

- environmental laws;

- antitrust laws;

- sales of land in a development to people who live in another state—interstate land sales; and

- the unauthorized practice of law by real estate licensees.

A licensee should be aware of the issues that arise in each situation discussed and thus understand when it is appropriate to consult an attorney or a tax professional.

TAX LAWS

Shelter, or residential real estate, is one of life's necessities. The construction industry, which builds shelter, contributes significantly to the gross national product. The industry draws upon the timber, concrete, asphalt, insulation, appliance, and furniture industries and services such as finance and insurance. The federal government, in exercising its responsibility to provide an improved quality of life for the country's citizens, has enacted tax laws creating financial incentives to encourage home ownership. Although a real estate licensee should not assume the responsibility for giving tax advice to buyers or sellers, the licensee should understand the tax implications of residential real estate purchase, ownership, and sale. When appropriate, the knowledgeable licensee should be able to explain the tax benefits of home ownership to encourage an uncertain prospect to buy, to help make the sale for the seller, to generate commissions for the agent, and to promote social stability through home ownership.

Because tax laws undergo frequent change, it is difficult to write definitively about tax laws here. However, certain general principles of tax law have been part of our real estate tax structure for many years, and it is unlikely—though always possible—that these principles will change. Thus, this section of the book will discuss some of those fundamental concepts of taxation that real estate licensees should understand.

Federal Tax Benefits of Ownership

There are four income tax benefits of home ownership:

1. deductibility of mortgage interest and property taxes from income for purposes of computing state and federal income taxes;

2. taxation at lower capital gains rates of gains on a home owned for more than one year;

3. ability to postpone tax on the gain realized on the sale of a home if certain conditions are met;

4. a once-in-a-lifetime exclusion of $125,000 of gain for homeowners aged 55 years or older.

Concerning point 2 above; the holding period for property acquired after June 22, 1984, and before January 1, 1988, to qualify for capital gains treatment is six months rather than a year. By failing to provide a holding period for property acquired after January 1, 1988, Congress is giving itself the option of re-examining the holding period at that time. This is a living example of why the tax principles set out in this text must be reviewed by a tax professional before any decisions relating to taxation of a particular situation are made.

Deductibility of Interest and Taxes

A personal residence is one of the best tax shelters available to citizens. For the homeowner, the first tax benefit of home ownership is the ability to deduct real estate taxes and mortgage interest from gross income. Suppose, for example, that the homeowner earns $24,000 per year and owns a home with a $50,000 mortgage at 12 percent for 30 years. The monthly payments are $514, or $6,171 for the year, of which the total annual interest payment on the mortgage is $6,000. The annual real estate taxes on the property are $1,800. The homeowner can deduct both the interest and the taxes, or $7,800, for income tax purposes, to the extent that mortgage interest and real estate taxes are added to other itemized deductions above the zero bracket amount. If the homeowner's tax bracket is 30 percent, the homeowner is saving $2,340 in taxes paid to Uncle Sam.

If the hypothetical homeowner were a tenant in someone else's building, he could be paying rent sufficient to cover the landlord's expenses, or $514 plus $150 for taxes. However, rent payments are not deductible for the tenant, as mortgage interest payments and local real estate taxes are deductible for the homeowner. Thus, it is clear that the tax laws are currently a powerful financial inducement to homeownership. By permitting the homeowner to deduct annual payments of interest and real estate taxes, the federal government is reducing the homeowner's tax burden, thus encouraging home ownership.

Capital Gains versus Ordinary Income

Our federal tax laws define taxable income as ordinary income and capital gain income. When a residence is sold at a profit, the profit is characterized as *capital gain*, income. Capital gain income could be either short-term or long-term.

If the home was owned for longer than six months, as mentioned earlier, the profit is taxed at long-term capital gain rates. This means that 60 percent of the profit escapes federal income taxation. This assumes that the gain is not subject to the alternative minimum tax. If the home was owned for less than six months, the gain would have been taxed as a short-term capital gain, which is similar to the tax structure for ordinary income.

However, since most homes are owned for more than six months only 40 percent of the gain risks taxation by the Internal Revenue Service. This is a significant tax break in times of both high inflation and rising property values, particularly for a transient society in which people sell their homes, buy another, and then perhaps repeat the process when they move again.

Postponement of Tax on Gain

One of the most exciting provisions of the tax laws for homeowners is the postponement of tax on all or part of the gain resulting from the sale of a residence. Simply stated, when a homeowner sells a home at a gain and another home is purchased or constructed within 24 months of the date of the first sale, gain is taxed only as far as the adjusted sales price of the old residence exceeds the cost of the new one.

Example

Richard buys a home in 1980 for $50,000 and sells it July 1, 1985, for $80,000. If, within 24 months—before or after July 1, 1985— Richard purchases or constructs a new principal residence for $80,000 or more, then he will pay no tax on the gain at this time. If Richard does not buy or build a new home within 24 months, the federal tax must be paid. And if Richard buys or constructs a new home for $75,000—less than $80,000 but more than $50,000—he postpones tax on $25,000 but now pays a tax of $5,000.

Several words of caution must be interjected at this point. It is beyond the purpose of this introductory text to discuss all the nuances of federal tax laws as they relate to residential real estate. For example, the term *gain* has been used to mean profit on the sale of the home. For tax purposes, the calculation of gain is an intricate process. It will include consideration of the purchase price adjusted upward by any improvements made to the property during the period of ownership and then downward by selling expenses and commissions paid. This calculation should be done for the homeowner by an attorney or accountant. But the licensee should understand the principles involved.

Obviously, there will be situations in which a homeowner will be required to move more than once within a 24-month period and in which more than one home will be bought and sold. If this happens, the last home purchased within the 24-month period is the one considered for purposes of calculating both the postponable gain and the currently taxable gain.

Note that, every time the homeowner moves to a more expensive residence, it is *not* necessary that the exact dollars produced by the sale of the first home be used to purchase the new home. It is permissible to take the gain made on the sale and invest it or spend it in any way the homeowner chooses.

Example

Richard bought his first home for $50,000 with $10,000 in cash and a $40,000 mortgage. When he sold on July 1, 1980, for $80,000, he paid off the mortgage and had $40,000 in cash. He bought his new home for $90,000, using $25,000 cash for the down payment. He was left with $15,000 of surplus cash from the sale, which he spent on a lavish vacation.

Note that Richard has both cash in hand and a lingering federal income tax liability. By selling and buying homes, he has deferred or postponed the tax on the gain. While Uncle Sam has encouraged Richard through the deferral of tax to purchase a home, he has not forgotten that Richard has a potential and continuing tax liability. Hopefully, Richard saved at least enough money to pay the lingering tax liability.

Over the course of his lifetime, Richard, as the archetypical homeowner, will buy and sell homes and, due to a protracted period of inflation as well as job promotions and higher earnings, will buy a succession of increasingly expensive homes. Using this provision of the tax law, designed to help homeowners upgrade their housing and standard of living, Richard may accumulate a very substantial postponed tax liability on a substantial equity, which, as Richard approaches retirement, he may need to live on when he has stopped working. Congress has recognized this potential problem and has enacted yet another tax incentive to encourage home ownership.

$125,000 Lifetime Exemption

In 1978, Congress enacted changes in the tax code to create a $100,000 exemption from taxation for homeowners aged 55 and older. The Economic Recovery Tax Act of 1981 increased this exclusion to $125,000 for sales or exchanges occurring after July 20, 1981. Again, simply stated, this tax provision permits a homeowner a once-in-a-lifetime election to exempt from any federal income taxation up to $125,000 of gain on the sale of the principal home. There are two conditions attached to this exclusion:

1. The house must be sold after the homeowner reaches age 55.
2. The homeowner must have owned and used the property as his or her personal residence for three or more years within a five-year period ending on the date of the sale.

The basic scheme of federal tax policies designed to encourage home ownership centers on the homeowner's right to buy and sell homes, at a gain, and upgrade family housing by purchasing a more expensive home, all without paying a tax on any gains made throughout the process.

Each of these transactions should be made with the advice of a tax expert. It is not normally the work of a real estate broker to offer tax advice to homebuyers and sellers.

Federal Tax Benefits for Investors

Federal tax laws also provide substantial, and complex, benefits to investors in real estate. Since every real estate situation is unique, and the laws are complex, individual analysis of each transaction should be made only by the experts. However, the basic principles of the major tax benefits for owners of investment real estate are summarized below.

Depreciation

Depreciation laws, Accelerated Cost Recovery System *(ACRS)*, encourage investors to purchase real estate by permitting them to recover their investment in the form of reduced taxes.

The theory behind the depreciation rules is that, because a building wears out over time, the purchaser of income producing property should be permitted to recover the cost of the building during the life of the building. When a new apartment of professional building is constructed, it has a hypothetical life expectancy. Each year that the building is in existence, it wears out to some extent, or depreciates. In other words, a percentage of its useful life is gone.

To encourage investors to buy real estate, and to keep the construction industry healthy, the tax laws permit the investor to deduct from his or her income an amount that reflects the building's depreciation; land may not be depreciated.

The laws governing depreciation are in a constant state of flux. The Tax Reform Act of 1984 gives investors several choices of how much depreciation may be taken on property in a given year. Although a building may have an actual physical life expectancy of 50-60 years, investors may choose to depreciate the building over 18, 35, or 45 years. Such periods for depreciation are permitted by the tax laws even though they may be no reflection of the actual life expectancy of the building. The advantage of choosing a shorter period over which to depreciate the property is that the tax benefit accrues to the investor more rapidly than when a longer period is chosen. The choice of depreciation period depends on the other income considerations of the investor and is made with the advice of a tax expert.

Example ───────────────────────────────

Ronald builds a professional office building with an actual life expectancy of 50 years for $400,000. Under the tax laws, Ronald has some choices about how rapidly he will depreciate, or "write off" the building. Under one scenario, he can depreciate the building on a straight-line basis, over 18 years. This would mean an annual depreciation deduction of $22,222. Ronald could choose to depreciate the building over a 35-year period and deduct $11,429 per year, or depreciate it over 45 years and deduct $7,778 per year.

For the investor in a high income tax bracket, this depreciation write-off can be a strong inducement to invest in real estate. If, in the example, Ronald is in the 50 percent tax bracket, the $22,222 depreciation deduction enables him to save $11,111 annually in federal income taxes.

Tax Credits

Tax credits are another form of federal tax benefit designed to attract investors in real estate. Unlike a depreciation deduction, which is subtracted from the investor's income to calculate his or her tax, a tax credit is subtracted directly from the amount of tax the investor would otherwise pay.

Tax credits are available for "qualified" expenditures made for the rehabilitation of older properties. The credit allowed on properties certified "historic" are eligible for credits of 25 percent of the expenditure; buildings over 40 years old are eligible for a 20 percent credit; buildings over 30 years old are eligible for a 15 percent credit, at least under autumn 1984 law. Like the rules on depreciation, the rules on tax credits are complex and demand the advice of tax experts.

Installment Sale

Another provision of the tax code, available to both homeowners and investors, permits the taxpayer to spread potential tax liability over a period of time. This can be done when the real estate owner conveys the property through an *installment sale*.

Example ────────────────────────────────────

Richard has a property he bought for $50,000 and is now selling for $80,000. To avoid paying a capital gain tax in one year, he offers to sell it to the buyer on a ten-year installment plan. Each year, the buyer pays $8,000, plus interest, of which $5,000 is a return to Richard of his original investment and $3,000 is gain, upon which Richard may be liable to pay a tax each year for ten years, as he receives the money.

In this example, if the property was used for investment purposes, and thus depreciation was taken on the property, the total depreciation allowed must be recognized as gain in the year of the sale. This amount is then added to the basis of the property, which changes the ratio between the amount that is return of invested capital and the amount recognized as gain each year.

Tax-Free Exchange

A third tax device to encourage real estate investment by deferring the payment of capital gains tax is called the *tax-free exchange*. Using the example in which Richard purchased an investment of a lake lot for $50,000 and plans to sell it when the value is $80,000, Richard later decides he wants a similar investment lot on the seashore for $80,000. As permitted by the rule of the tax-free exchange, Richard and the owner of the seashore lot swap *like kind* properties, and Richard pays no tax at this time on the $30,000 gain on his property.

INTERSTATE LAND SALES FULL DISCLOSURE ACT

The *Interstate Land Sales Full Disclosure Act* was originally passed by Congress in 1968 to protect those naive people who purchase or lease land sight unseen. Its purpose is to enable buyers and lessees to make informed decisions regarding property and to deter fraudulent land sales based on misrepresentations.

The act requires land developers and promoters, including brokers, who sell or lease certain kinds of property within subdivisions to file a *Statement of Record* with the Secretary of Housing and Urban Development. This statement contains basic factual and legal information about the property, including:

1. identity of the people who have an interest in a particular lot;

2. a legal description and map of the subdivision;

3. the probable range of prices at which the lots will be offered;

4. the availability of water, sewage, and other facilities and the presence of unusual noise or safety conditions;

5. identity of any liens, easements, or encumbrances on the property; and

6. a copy of the developer's deed, articles of incorporation or partnership,and a financial statement.

Under the act, the purchaser is entitled to a *property report,* which includes the information on the developer and on the liens, easements, and encumbrances on the property. If the purchaser does not receive the report before or at the time he or she signs the contract, the purchaser may rescind the deal within two years of signing the purchase and sale agreement. In this way, a purchaser or lessee is assured of a remedy should he or she later discover that the property is burdened financially or legally.

The Interstate Land Sales Full Disclosure Act does not apply to all land sales. It does not apply to subdivisions of less than 25 lots, to industrial or commercial property on which there is a residential building, or to government property or cemetery lots.

The act applies to some land sales for which no statement of record need be filed or property report delivered to the purchaser:

- a subdivision that contains less than 100 lots;

- a subdivision that leased or sold no more than 12 lots within a year of the lease or sale of the first lot;

- a lot for a mobile home;

- a lot that meets certain local standards;

- lots that have been personally inspected by the purchaser, which are part of a subdivision of no more than 20 lots; and

- transactions that take place entirely within one state.

Developers and agents who fail to submit to the purchaser a statement of record or a property report, who make false statements, or who fraudulently misrepresent a property covered by the act may be sued by a purchaser or lessee. The court can order "specific performance" by the developer or agent, demanding that the contract be fulfilled as written. Or the court may award damages, including attorney's fees, to a successful plaintiff.

Further, the Secretary of Housing and Urban Development may also take legal action against those who have violated or are about to violate the act's provisions. The Secretary may also obtain an injunction preventing promoters and others from continuing their violations.

Many real estate brokers become involved with a development project and then are subject to the Interstate Land Sales Full Disclosure Act. It is a complex law, and to ensure that licensees are complying adequately with the act's provisions it is best to consult an attorney.

REAL ESTATE ANTITRUST LAW

The real estate industry is changing and growing, as are the laws regulating it. The *antitrust law,* originally passed to ensure the vitality of the free market and to regulate large economic enterprises, applies to real estate brokers as well. Licensees should be aware of the antitrust laws, how they apply to the industry, and the consequences of violating them.

What Is Antitrust Law?

In this free-enterprise economy, competition among a large number of sellers is thought to be good for society; concentration of economic power in the hands of a few is believed to be harmful. For example, two newspapers, which serve one town, will compete for the same readers. Competition will provide both papers with an incentive to keep quality and service higher and prices lower than if there were only one newspaper.

Antitrust laws were passed to outlaw business practices that inhibit free competition. The federal antitrust law—called the Sherman Act, passed by Congress in 1890—is directed at two basic kinds of anticompetitive arrangements. It prohibits monopolies and outlaws contracts, combinations, and conspiracies that restrain trade. In January 1980, the Supreme Court ruled that the Sherman Act applies to the real estate brokerage industry. Because real estate finance involves money obtained through interstate commerce, and because of the transient nature of modern society, the Supreme Court found that all real estate transactions affect interstate commerce. Therefore, federal courts can use the Sherman Act, which applies only to interstate transactions, in all real estate antitrust cases.

States also have their own antitrust laws, which apply in cases brought into state courts. These laws vary from state to state, but, like the Sherman Act, their general purpose is to preserve a competitive marketplace.

What Is an Antitrust Law Violation?

Antitrust law may be described best using a hypothetical situation:

Brown and Black are independent, competing real estate brokers in Greenville. One day on the golf course, Brown and Black, in a discussion between holes, agreed to raise their sales commission rates from six to eight percent. Have either of these brokers breached antitrust law?

Black and Brown have conspired or planned together to set an eight percent rate. Antitrust laws prohibit this kind of agreement because it prevents price competition. Proof of an agreement or conspiracy must exist, but the agreement itself can be written or oral.

How Do Antitrust Violations Occur?

One area of real estate industry directly affected by antitrust law is the agreement to fix commissions. Commission rates within a locality tend to be uniform. Imitative business practices don't prove a violation of antitrust law but may be evidence of one. Real estate brokers, therefore, are open to charges of *price-fixing*; that is, the agreement of competing brokers like Black, Brown, and White to charge a certain price for their services. Convictions in cases brought for price-fixing are common because an agreement to fix commissions is such a significant restraint on trade.

A second area affected by antitrust law is access to multiple-listing services. A *multiple-listing-service* or MLS, is an arrangement by which brokers pool information on properties each member of the service has for sale. It has become increasingly important for brokers to have access to MLS in order to compete effectively. If membership in the MLS is not available equally to all eligible brokers, some agents will be forced to operate at a significant economic disadvantage.

Although MLS may restrict its membership "reasonably," in many cases, courts have found restriction on MLS membership to be unreasonable and, therefore, an illegal restraint on trade. A reasonable restriction might be, for example, a rural Maryland MLS that refuses to accept brokers from downtown Baltimore.

What Is the Penalty for Antitrust Violation?

A breach of antitrust law creates a civil liability on the part of the violator toward those who have suffered economic harm. An antitrust suit may be brought against an individual broker, a real estate company, or the MLS. It may be brought by a seller, another broker, or a company. Government officials also frequently bring civil suits to enforce antitrust laws.

For practical reasons, it is usually the U.S. Department of Justice, Division of Antitrust Law, that brings suit against those suspected of price-fixing. In most cases, it requests courts to issue an injunction, requiring the offender to refrain from making rate-setting agreements in the future.

Suits against multiple-listing services that limit access to listings may be brought by a government official or by a broker or seller claiming injury from restrictive practices. In such a suit under the Sherman Act, an individual or a licensee may be awarded three times the amount of damages he or she actually incurred—the amount of which may vary widely in different situations and localities. This provision for punitive damages reflects the strong public policy against antitrust violations.

A violation of the Sherman Act may be punishable by a criminal penalty, including a jail sentence. Since the consequences are potentially so serious, criminal charges are brought only in cases in which the restraint on trade is completely inexcusable, such as an instance of blatant price-fixing. Although a broker's license is not suspended automatically following an antitrust conviction, it may be suspended by the state licensing board following a criminal conviction. Every responsible broker needs to be aware of the changes in real estate antitrust law.

FAIR HOUSING

A broker, as a seller's agent or a landlord's property manager, will meet a wide variety of buyers and tenants. People of different racial, religious, and cultural backgrounds will seek a broker's advice to find a comfortable place to live. The real estate broker must treat all individuals equally in the showing, sale, or rental of property; the broker must not discriminate in any way. Federal and state *fair housing* laws have made discriminatory practices illegal. The broker who violates fair housing laws may be liable for fine, imprisonment, and revocation of his or her license. The responsible broker, therefore, must understand federal and state fair housing laws, which will be introduced in this section.

Federal Laws

The Civil Rights Act of 1866

According to *Jones vs. Mayer* 392 U.S. 409 (1968), the Civil

Rights Act of 1866 prohibits "all racial discrimination, private as well as public, in the sale or rental of property." This act is very broad in scope and can apply even to an individual who discriminates on the basis of race in the sale of his or her private home. This act covers only *racial* discrimination and, therefore, would not cover acts of discrimination based upon sex, creed, or national origin. A violation of this stature can lead to prosecution in a federal court.

The 1968 Fair Housing Law

The 1968 Fair Housing Law prohibits discrimination based upon race, color, religion, sex, or national origin. This act is, therefore, more extensive than the Civil Rights Act of 1866, which prohibits only racial discrimination. Under the 1968 Fair Housing Law, certain transactions by private owners are not reached by this act. For example, the law does not apply to the owner-occupant of an apartment building with four of fewer units. In addition, private clubs with lodgings for members, and religious organizations with dwellings for members, may be exempt under certain circumstances involving noncommercial transactions. It is best to consult an attorney when dealing with a religious group that wishes to discriminate on the basis of religion.

However, *all* transactions that involve a broker are covered, and a private owner may still be liable for suit if he or she discriminates on the basis of race under the Civil Rights Act of 1866.

The following practices are prohibited by the 1968 Fair Housing Law if based upon race, religion, color, sex, or national origin:

1. refusing to rent, deal, or negotiate with any person;

2. discriminating in terms or conditions for buying or renting housing;

3. discriminating by advertising that housing is available only to persons of a certain category;

4. denying that housing is open for inspection, sale or rent when it really is available. Steering, which is illegal under all fair housing laws, is the practice of channeling house or apartment seekers to particular areas, whether to maintain the homogeneity of an area or to change the character of an area in order to create a speculative situ-

ation. Steering is often difficult to detect because it is so subtle that the client may be unaware that his or her choices are being limited;

5. blockbusting—persuading owners to sell or rent housing by telling them that minority groups are moving into the neighborhood. This practice often creates panic selling—large numbers of owners selling at reduced prices to escape falling property values;

6. denying or making different terms or conditions for home loans by commercial lenders such as banks, savings and loans, and insurance companies; and

7. denying to anyone the use of or participation in any real estate service or other facilities related to the selling or renting of housing.

Example ——————————————————————————

A new town is being built near a major city with large black and Jewish populations. To meet the expected high demand for female workers in the town's new industries, and to achieve religious and racial balance among the new residents, the developer instructs all brokers who handle listings to:

1. express preference for women buyers and tenants, especially working women; and

2. avoid saturation by black or Jewish residents by—
   a. claiming a property is already sold or rented;
   b. quoting a higher price or rent; and
   c. forbidding secondary financing.

———————————————————————————————————————

Are all these practices forbidden by the Federal Fair Housing Law? Yes. The act forbids advertising that discriminates on the basis of sex. Claiming a dwelling is unavailable to avoid selling or renting on the basis of race or religion is illegal. Quoting higher prices on the basis of race or religion is illegal. Forbidding secondary financing on the basis of race or religion is illegal.

State Laws

Many states and municipalities have enacted fair housing laws and ordinances. Because the statutes vary widely, sometimes offering broader coverage than the federal acts, a broker should understand local requirements.

Abiding by federal, state, and local fair housing laws is an important day-to-day concern of practicing brokers. Brokers can be guilty of discriminatory behavior even if they are only following someone else's instructions, as in the preceding example.

Discrimination also occurs when a broker simply *does not tell* a certain group or individual of an available dwelling.

UNAUTHORIZED PRACTICE OF LAW

A real estate agent must not fall into the trap of doing a lawyer's work. While a broker may know that practicing law is forbidden, he or she may not be able to distinguish easily the fine line between brokerage and law.

Examples: ———————————————————————

Broker Allen has secured a buyer for the Campbells' home. Allen assists the buyer in filling out a standardized offer-to-purchase form that is used in the locality. The buyer's offer does not exactly conform to the listing agreement, the offer is $1,500 lower than the asking price of $59,500, and the offer is contingent on the buyer's ability to obtain a mortgage, but there are no other contingencies or options that the buyer wants.

Broker Allen is working with Client Darn, who would like to purchase the Campbells' home. Darn, however, has several complicated options, which he would like to include in the offer to purchase. Because Allen thinks she understands the options, she offers to help Darn draw up the offer.

How does one decide which activities in a brokerage business are the work of a broker and which activities should be left to an attorney? Filling out factual details on standardized forms is generally permissible. Deleting or adding to statements in form contracts is permissible. However, drawing up any special documents of options may amount to the unauthorized practice of law. The second example illustrates a practice the broker should not adopt.

A helpful guideline, albeit a hazy one, is that a broker can safely use forms that are customarily employed by brokers in the area. These actions are probably acceptable if it is clear that local brokers have the authority to act in such a manner. If there is anything unusual in the transaction, or anything requiring special legal or technical competence, the broker should suggest that the client employ an attorney. Remember that a broker is an agent with special powers delegated by the principal, usually the seller. The broker's authority extends only as far as is necessary to carry out his or her assigned task.

A few other aids exist to help the broker avoid the risk of doing lawyer's work. Article 17 of the National Association of Realtors® Code of Ethics cautions against the unauthorized practice of law. Several helpful examples in the code illustrate situations in which there is a question as to whether the broker's actions have exceeded his or her authority. In addition to the Code of Ethics, the *broker-lawyer-accords*, prepared by broker-lawyer associations in some states, attempt to delineate what is broker's work and what is lawyer's work.

The accords in the various states usually have several common features, including the precaution that a broker should avoid activities not commonly performed by brokers in their locality. When unusual or legal matters arise, or when extensively changing a contract, the broker should advise the client to see a lawyer. If a client asks the broker to suggest a lawyer, the broker should recommend several attorneys without indicating a preference. When a broker is also a lawyer, the accords state that he or she should not act as a lawyer and a broker in the same transaction.

In addition to setting standards for broker performance, the accords adopt regulations for attorneys' behavior to prevent usurpation of broker responsibilities. The accords also may require the establishment of broker-lawyer committees to settle grievances, promote cordial relations, recommend legislation in the public interest, and encourage use of standardized contracts and forms in the local area.

The broker can double-check his or her activity by *always* determining whether the anticipated action is one that brokers in the area commonly perform. If the answer is yes, it is probably broker's work. If there is some doubt, the broker would be safer recommending an attorney than risking engaging in the unauthorized practice of law.

Finally, a broker must be aware that court action may be taken against those who engage in the unauthorized practice of law. When a local or a state bar association files a successful suit against one not entitled to practice law, such sanctions as injunctions, declaratory judgments, fines, and imprisonments can result. The risk of prosecution is a good reason for the broker to be sure of the difference between broker's work and lawyer's work.

SUMMARY

Laws governing the conduct of a real estate broker come from several different sources: state licensing laws, common law concepts originating in England, rules and regulations of licensing boards, state statutes and local laws governing land use and, as covered in this chapter, federal laws affecting land use and taxation. Because the real estate industry has such a significant impact on the country's economy, Congress has enacted a series of tax measures that encourage home ownership. These tax laws include deductibility from income of interest on a mortgage and real estate taxes on a home; the ability to trade from one home up to a more expensive one within 24 months and postpone tax on any gain made on the sale of the first property; taxation at favorable capital gains rates of the profits made on the sale of a home; and a once-in-a-lifetime exclusion of $125,000 of gain for homeowners aged 55 and older.

There are federal tax benefits for investors as well. Taxable income may be reduced by the amount a parcel of real estate depreciates each year, resulting in tax savings, particularly for taxpayers in higher brackets; the installment-sale provisions of the tax code permit an investor to spread the taxable gain over a period of years so as to minimize the tax impact from the sale of real estate; it also permits owners of real estate to exchange properties and defer taxation on gain.

The federal government's interest in preventing land fraud led to the Interstate Land Sales Full Disclosure Act, requiring registration of certain projects which will be marketed to out-of-state buyers. The filing of a property report with the Department of Housing and Urban Development is designed to prevent fraudulent sales to distant buyers.

Congress is concerned with the economic climate of the country for business growth and development. To protect the spirit of enterprise and ability to compete, antitrust laws have been enacted to protect an environment where innovation and competition can flourish. Although these laws are most dramatically applied to large national corporations with monopolies or near-monopolies in a certain industry, these laws also protect local brokers from anti-competitive practices in the real estate brokerage industry.

Equal access to housing consistent with a person's ability to pay for it is guaranteed in this country by federal and state fair housing laws. It is generally a violation of the fair housing laws for a licensee to be involved in any conduct which inhibits free access to housing compatible with a buyer's or renter's means. Unlawful interference in this choice may result in fines or loss of license.

Good brokers and salespersons have a multitude of talents which include evaluating property, sales and marketing skills, the depth of knowledge to understand the legal complexities which affect each parcel of land, negotiating skills to bring buyers and sellers together, an appreciation for the tax implications for both the buyer and seller of real estate of a transaction, among other skills. Many of these talents require understanding of real estate law, and often put a licensee in a position of giving advice or drafting agreements which have legal ramifications for buyers and sellers alike. One of the licensee's most important skills is the ability to know when to involve a lawyer to avoid the unauthorized practice of law.

MULTIPLE CHOICE QUESTIONS ——————————————

1. Gain on a property purchased after June 1984 may be taxed as ordinary income if the owner:

    a. sold the house within six months of the original purchase.
    b. held it for more than one year.
    c. reinvested the proceeds in a new house with 24 months.
    d. none of the above

2. Which of the following is (are) recognized as significant tax advantages of home ownership?

    a. deductibility of interest and taxes from income
    b. potential taxation of gain at preferred tax rates
    c. the right to defer taxes in some circumstances
    d. all of the above

3. For couples over age 55 federal tax laws:

    a. may exempt the gain from the sale of a primary residence from taxation.
    b. encourage home ownership by authorizing depreciation.
    c. give tenants a tax credit for rent paid.
    d. none of the above

4. The primary advantage of an installment sale is:

    a. the tax exemption on the first $125,000.
    b. that a seller will get a depreciation deduction so long as the installments continue.
    c. the opportunity to spread the taxable gain on property over several years.
    d. that it applies to the seller's primary residence.

5. To take advantage of the $125,000 lifetime tax exemption, the homeowner must:

    a. sell the house after reaching 55 years of age.
    b. elect the exemption.
    c. have lived in the home for three of the five years preceding the sale.
    d. all of the above

6. For which of the following pieces of real estate may an owner take a deduction for depreciation?

    a. the family homestead
    b. an apartment building
    c. an undeveloped building lot
    d. all of the above

7. The purpose of the Interstate Land Sales Full Disclosure Act is to:

    a. prevent fraud.
    b. ensure revenue to the U.S. Treasury based on land sales.
    c. disclose to HUD interstate development plans.
    d. enforce environmental protection statutes.

8. The statement of record filed with the secretary of HUD for an interstate land sale includes:

    a. identity of current owners.
    b. a map of the subdivision.
    c. range of prices for lots to be sold.
    d. all of the above

9. Antitrust laws:

    a. regulate noncompetitive business practices.
    b. protect a client's interest in a broker's trust account.
    c. regulate public trust companies.
    d. none of the above

10. An agreement among certain brokers in a town to exclude a new broker from participation in a multiple-listing service may be a violation of:

    a. fair housing laws.
    b. antitrust law.
    c. Interstate Land Sales Full Disclosure Act.
    d. Real Estate Settlement Procedures Act.

11. In a large metropolitan area, a broker decides that he or she can make more money by raising the sales commission from six percent to ten percent. This is a violation of:

    a. Realtors'® Code of Ethics.
    b. state laws governing price fixing.
    c. the Sherman Antitrust Act.
    d. none of the above

12. A broker found guilty of an antitrust violation may face:

    a. injunction.
    b. fine and money damages.
    c. jail sentence.
    d. all of the above

13. A local apartment owner has made a practice of discrimination against people with certain racial backgrounds. A licensee who knows this and accepts the apartment listings for rent is:

    a. only the owner's agent and therefore not guilty of discrimination.
    b. protected by law from charges of discrimination.
    c. in violation of fair housing laws.
    d. in violation of the 19th Amendment to the U.S. Constitution.

14. Failure to show certain property to prospective tenants or purchasers because of their race is called:

    a. steering.
    b. blockbusting.
    c. social segregation.
    d. fraud.

15. A real estate licensee who drafts a special lease is:

    a. a real estate counselor.
    b. lucky to have the business.
    c. doing broker's work.
    d. engaged in the unauthorized practice of law.

DISCUSSION QUESTIONS

1. Discuss whether the Interstate Land Sales Full Disclosure Act is an effective deterrent to fraud or whether state laws should be sufficient.

2. Identify the following tasks as broker's work, lawyer's work, or both:

    a. giving opinions on property value
    b. taking listings
    c. creating easements
    d. recording deeds
    e. drafting deeds
    f. negotiating sales contracts
    g. developing a power of attorney
    h. drafting clauses for leases and contracts

3. Discuss how a homeowner can take advantage of federal tax law to accumulate an estate.

Glossary

abstract of title A condensed history of the legal status of a property, drawn from the public record. Abstracts generally report consecutive grants, conveyances, wills, records, and judicial proceedings affecting title, as well as all recorded liens and encumbrances.

acceleration clause A provision that allows the lender to demand the remaining payments of a mortgage or trust deed be paid immediately.

acceptance Agreement to a proposed sale or offer to contract.

actual eviction A physical ouster from the premises that negates the tenant's obligation to pay rent.

administrator The person appointed by the probate court to manage the estate of the deceased. If the person is named in the will, he or she is referred to as the *executor*.

adverse possession The acquisition of another's property by actual, visible, hostile, notorious, exclusive, and continuous possession over a certain period of time.

affirmative covenants Agreement by which one person promises to perform an act to the benefit of another.

agent A person authorized to act for another.

amortize To include both principal and interest in loan payments.

annexation The attaching or joining of one piece of property to another; usually attaching personal property to a piece of real property.

antitrust law State and federal laws that protect an open and competitive business environment by prohibiting monopolistic business practices.

assignment Transferring to another person one's interest in a lease, bond, mortgage, or other instrument.

balloon payment A final payment on an installment contract that is substantially larger than the periodic installments and that pays the debt in full.

benefited land Property that is positively affected by a restrictive covenant or easement.

bilateral contract An agreement consisting of a promise exchanged for a promise.

blanket mortgage A mortgage secured by more than one parcel of real estate.

breach of contract Failure to perform according to the terms of a contract.

broker-lawyer accords Agreements in some states between state bar associations and state broker associations to define what is lawyers' work and what is brokers' work, to prevent the unauthorized practice of law by brokers, and to protect brokers from inappropriate infringement on brokers' work by attorneys.

budget mortgage A loan payment that includes principal, interest, taxes, and insurance.

building code A local ordinance that requires construction to meet certain specifications for health and safety.

bundle of sticks Description of the concept that ownership of a property consists of beneficial interests, or rights, associated with the real estate. The buyer of real estate actually purchases all the legal rights that attach to ownership of the property.

burdened land Property that is negatively affected by a restricted covenant or easement.

capital gain The taxable profit resulting from the sale of property other than property that is held by the taxpayer generally for sale to customers in the seller's business or trade.

certificate of occupancy A document affirming that a structure complies with local building codes, and is fit for habitation.

certificate of title A formal statement given by a title examiner stating that the title is good; based on an examination of public records.

chain of title A chronological listing of past titleholders of a particular piece of land.

claim of right An adverse possessor's claim to a fee simple title despite lack of a legal right to title.

clean air act A federal law giving states the responsibility of making air quality conform to federal standards.

coastal zone management act A federal law requiring the preservation and protection of coastal areas.

co-brokerage agreement An agreement between brokers to split a commission, where more than one broker is involved in a sale, as when the listing broker is different than the selling broker.

Code of Ethics A set of rules of conduct establishing standards of fair dealing among members of the National Association of Realtors.®

color of title A condition in which an apparently good title is in fact not valid because of a defect.

commingling Mixing the broker's personal funds with deposits made by a client.

community property A form of concurrent ownership for married persons whereby each is an equal partner owning one-half of acquisitions made during marriage.

concurrent ownership A form of ownership whereby two or more people jointly hold title.

condominium A form of ownership giving exclusive ownership of a living unit with an undivided interest in the common grounds and buildings.

conflict of interest An agent's division of loyalties between competing interests, as when a broker cannot or will not work exclusively in the interest of the seller who hired him or her.

consideration Something of value given to establish a contract.

constructive attachment A condition under which property not permanently attached to real estate may nonetheless be considered a fixture; the test is generally whether there was an intention to make the property a part of the real estate.

constructive eviction A landlord's interference with tenant's rights, which is serious enough to cause the tenant to vacate. The tenant's obligation to pay rent ceases after moving out.

contingency clause A provision placed in a contract that requires the completion of a certain act or the happening of a particular event before the contract becomes binding.

contract A legally enforceable agreement.

contractual capacity A person's ability to enter into a legally binding contract.

cooperative A form of ownership whereby a person holds a cooperative share with a proprietary lease giving use of a living unit.

counteroffer A new offer made in response to an offer received from an offeror. The counteroffer terminates the original offer, which cannot then be accepted unless repeated by the offeror.

covenant An agreement or promise between two or more persons.

curtesy A common law concept giving the husband a life estate in all real estate owned by the wife during marriage.

defeasance clause A provision in a mortgage stating that title will be returned to the borrower when the underlying debt is repaid on time.

deficiency judgment An amount the borrower must pay if the sale at foreclosure does not raise enough money to pay the balance of the loan.

delivery and acceptance Essential elements of a transfer of title by deed; the grantor must intend to give the deed to the grantee, and the grantee must intend to accept the deed.

depreciation A tax-incentive concept that permits an investor to theoretically recover the initial cost of property by deducting from income a percentage of the property's value, calculated with reference to the property's life expectancy.

devise A transfer of real property under a will.

disclosure The giving of all relevant facts to a real estate seller by a broker; the legal mandate of the agency relationship is satisfied only by complete and timely disclosure.

dominant tenement The parcel of land that benefits from an easement.

dower The interest of a surviving wife (or sometimes husband) in one-third of the lands acquired by the spouse during marriage.

dual agency A situation in which a broker represents two or more people.

due on sale A due-on-sale clause in a mortgage or on a promissory note requires that if the property subject to a mortgage is sold, then the balance owed on the note must be paid.

earnest money Money submitted by a prospective buyer with an offer to buy as evidence of the buyer's serious intention to complete the transaction.

easement A limited right to use another's land for a special purpose.

easement appurtenant An easement that attaches to and can be used with only a certain parcel of land.

easement in gross An easement that is for personal benefit and not for the benefit of one's land.

easement by implication An easement that arises by operation of law either because of strict necessity or because the parties intend such an easement.

easement by prescription An easement acquired by continuous use over a long time period.

easement by reservation An easement withheld in land granted to another person.

eminent domain The power of the government to take (condemn) private property for public use, providing just compensation is paid.

employee An individual who works for and under the direction and control of another person. This concept has serious tax implications for real estate sales associates and brokers.

encroachment An unauthorized intrusion of real or personal property on another's real property, such as an overhanging roof, tree branches or roots, or a misplaced fence or walkway.

encumbrance Any claim to an interest in property by a person other than the owner, such as an easement; also, any lien against the property, such as unpaid taxes.

escheat The process by which the state takes a person's property when the person dies intestate (having left no will) and has no legal heirs.

escrow A system of transfer of a deed whereby a third person holds the deed until all conditions of an agreement are met (i.e., payment of sale price in full), and then delivers the deed to the purchaser.

estate An interest in land consisting of a bundle of rights to the property for a particular duration.

estate for years Leasehold or less than freehold estates conveyed for a specific number of years.

estoppel A legal doctrine that holds a person responsible for the consequences of previous representations. A person who has made a promise on which another person has acted, for instance, is prevented from later asserting a right or defense against that person's responding action.

equity The value of a property after payment of all liens and obligations against the property.

exclusive agency A listing agreement wherein a seller lists with only one broker, but reserves the right to sell the property independently of the broker.

exclusive right to sell A listing agreement that assures the broker of a commission if anyone sells the property during the listing period.

executory interest The future interest following a fee simple subject to condition subsequent.

express easement An easement created in a grant by deed.

fair housing State and federal laws designed to prohibit discrimination in housing based on race, sex, creed, or national origin.

fee simple absolute The most complete form of ownership conveyed for possibly infinite duration. There are no limitations on inheritability.

fee simple determinable A fee simple that will automatically end when a specified event occurs.

fee simple on condition subsequent A fee simple that may end on the occurrence of a stated event. It does not automatically end, but must be cut off by the grantor's exercise of right.

fee simple subject to executory limitation An interest in land that is lost in favor of a third person, upon the happening of an event stated in the deed.

fiduciary One who acts solely for another's benefit in matters to which he or she is entrusted; a very high expectation of trust is placed in the agent.

fixture An article of personal property that has been annexed to real property in such a way that it is regarded as part of the land.

forcible entry and detainer action A summary court proceeding whereby the landlord can regain possession of the property.

foreclosure To terminate the owner's rights to a piece of property after he or she defaults on the mortgage loan.

freehold estates Ownership of real property that will ensure for life or forever.

future interests Interests in property that will or may become possessory upon the termination of all preceding estates.

graduated payment mortgage (GEM): A mortgage in which the monthly principal and interest payment increases for a specific number of years, then levels off for the remaining term. GEMs were developed to enable people who expect rapidly rising incomes to obtain mortgages.

grantee The person who receives from a grantor a conveyance of real property; usually a buyer.

grantor A person transferring title to, or interest in, real property.

grantor-grantee index A method of master indexing recorded deeds by cross-referencing the names of the grantor and grantee with the volume and page numbers of the record book that contains the deed.

historical preservation interest An interest acquired by a preservation organization in properties of historic interest.

housing codes Local requirements that dwellings meet minimum standards for health and safety.

inchoate dower The possibility of an interest for a wife in lands held by her husband. The inchoate interest will actualize if the husband predeceases the wife.

independent contractor An individual who is employed to perform certain tasks, but who is not highly supervised or under the direct control of the employer.

infant (minor) One who has not reached the age of legal competence (majority).

inheritance statute A statute that defines an intestate person's legal heirs, and stipulates the shares of the deceased's estate to which they are entitled.

installment land contract An agreement for the purchaser of real property under which the buyer pays installments on the principal and interest or interest only for a specified term, after which the balance becomes due in full. The seller retains legal title to the property until payment in full, while the buyer gets an equitable title and possession of the property. Also called a land contract or contract for deed.

installment sale A sale in which payments are made to the seller over a period of time under such conditions that permit the seller to save taxes.

interstate land sales full disclosure act A federal law requiring developers to register the development with the Department of Housing and Urban Development if lots are to be sold to purchasers outside the state where the land is located.

intestacy The situation in which a person dies without leaving a valid will.

inverse condemnation An owner's suit demanding that the government buy the owner's property.

joint tenancy A form of concurrent ownership whereby two or more persons own as an entity with the right of survivorship.

latent defects Hidden structural defects known to the seller but not the purchaser, and not readily discoverable by inspection. Failure by a seller or broker to disclose latent defects is a tacit misrepresentation and grounds for the buyer to rescind the contract.

leasehold estate An estate whereby one has possession but not ownership of land.

legal description A description of land sufficiently accurate so that an independent surveyor can locate and identify the land.

lessee The person to whom property is rented or leased; the tenant.

lessor The person who rents or leases property to another; the landlord.

license A revocable permission to use another's land.

life estate Ownership conveyed only for the lifetime of some person.

liquidated damages An amount of money specified by contract to be paid by one who breaches the contract.

marketable title Title that is free from reasonable doubt as to defects.

metes and bounds A method of describing land, stating its boundaries in terms of length, direction, and bounds, so that the described boundaries enclose the parcel of land described.

misrepresentation A false statement or concealment of a material fact made with the intention of inducing some action by another party.

mortgage A pledge of property as collateral for a loan.

mortgagee The individual or lending organization who gives the loan.

mortgagor The individual who borrows and pledges property as a security.

National Association of Realtors® A private and voluntary association of real estate licensees for the purposes of education, political lobbying, and self-regulation of the industry.

National Environmental Policy Act A law requiring the filing of environmental impact statements for all federal actions that significantly affect the environment.

negative covenants An agreement by which one promises not to perform an act.

net listing A listing in which the broker's commission is set as the difference between the selling price and a price set by the owner. This is illegal in most states.

Noise Control Act A law setting noise pollution standards for federal projects.

nonconforming use A use inconsistent with a zoning ordinance but allowed to continue because it predated the ordinance.

novation A substitution of a new person for a party to a contract in the case where a new person agrees to repay a loan taken out by another person.

Occupational Safety and Health Act A federal law setting health and safety standards for the workplace.

offer A proposal to make a contract.

offeree One to whom a proposal of contract is given.

offeror One who proposes a contract.

open listing A listing agreement that allows the owner to engage any number of brokers, or to sell the property independently of a broker.

option A right to buy or sell at specified terms for a set period of time.

ownership A collection of rights to occupy and use properly, which includes the right to give or sell that property to another.

partnership A form of concurrent ownership whereby business partners own equal and undivided shares; upon the death of a partner, the deceased's share vests in the other associates.

permitted use A use of property permitted under a zoning ordinance "as of right." An applicant for a permitted use must be given a permit as long as he or she meets the other regulations pertaining to the district.

periodic tenancy An estate that automatically continues for successive periods unless terminated by proper notice.

personal property All property other than real estate.

possibility of reverter The future interest following a fee simple determinable.

prepayment clause A privilege that allows the borrower to repay ahead of schedule.

present interests Ownership of land that involves present possession.

price-fixing The practice of conspiring to set fixed fee or prices, in violation of the Sherman Antitrust Act. The setting of commissions and fees by local realty associations has been declared to be price-fixing by recent court decisions, as has been the establishment of standard fees for lawyers by local bar associations.

principal A person who empowers another to act in his or her behalf.

profit An interest in land whereby one has the right to take something off another's land.

prohibited uses Uses of real estate forbidden by zoning ordinances.

promissory note A written promise to pay a debt.

property tax Tax based on real estate, collected by a local government to provide community services.

purchase-money mortgage A loan to purchase real estate, usually filling the gap between the down payment and the primary mortgage.

qualified fees Ownership that may be lost upon the happening of a certain event.

quitclaim deed A deed that acts to release any title, claim, or interest in property without claiming that the grantor actually has any such interest.

ready, willing, and able buyer One who is prepared to buy now and is financially capable of doing so.

real estate Land and that which is affixed to or growing upon the land.

record books Books located in the registry of deeds that contain photostatic copies of all recorded deeds.

recording statutes State laws providing a public recording system of land ownership; three principal types are notice, race, and race-notice statutes.

rectangular survey system A system of land description based on a grid of meridians running north and south, and perpendicular base lines running east and west.

remainder A future interest in the fee simple that will become possessory after all existent life estates.

rent control Government restrictions on the rent a landlord can charge.

rescission A remedy providing cancellation of a contract.

restrictive covenants An agreement that restricts the use of one's land in some way.

reversion The fee owner's right to future possession of property presently held and occupied by another.

right of descent The statutory right of a spouse to become an heir of the deceased and receive a minimum percentage of the decedent's estate.

right of reentry The future interest following a fee simple subject to executory limitation.

security deposit An amount paid by the tenant at the beginning of the tenancy to assure he or she will perform the convenants of the lease.

servient tenement The parcel of land over which another holds an easement.

severance The termination of a joint tenancy when one of the tenants conveys his or her interest by deed.

severance damages Compensation paid when a government takes part of one's land.

special exceptions Uses permitted as needed in a zoning district, but only by grant of the local board.

specific performance A remedy compelling the breaching party to perform the contract.

state licensing laws Statutes enacted by states to regulate the real estate brokerage business, to protect the public and promote public confidence in the industry.

Statute of Frauds A law requiring an agreement to buy or sell an interest in land to be in writing.

sublease The transfer to another of part of one's rights under a lease.

surcharge To make excessive use of an easement or profit.

tax base The total value of all taxable property in a community.

tax credit A federal tax benefit applied to expenditures made to restore or rehabilitate certain classes of older real properties. Unlike tax deductions, tax credits are abstracted from the amount of taxes owed, rather than taxable income.

tax deed A deed received for paying delinquent taxes on another's property.

tax-free exchange A provision of the federal laws that permits two owners of similar property to exchange parcels with the potential for avoiding, at the time of exchange, payment of any tax.

tenancy at will An interest created with the consent of owner and tenant, which may be terminated at the will of either party.

tenancy by the entirety A form of concurrent ownership for married persons; neither has a disposable interest while the other lives and the right of survivorship exists.

tenancy of sufferance The interest of a tenant who enters lawfully, but stays on after the expiration of the lease without the landlord's permission.

term mortgage A loan that requires payments of interest only during the life of the loan with the entire principal due at maturity.

testator A person who has died leaving a valid will.

time is of the essence A contract clause that requires performance by the set date to avoid breach.

title abstract A condensed history of the title to a piece of land, containing the names of titleholders, method of conveyance, statement of encumbrances, and other relevant information.

title insurance A type of insurance designed to protect against financial loss resulting from defects in title to a piece of property.

title opinion A statement of a title company's or title attorney's belief that a given title is either marketable or is clouded by unpaid liens, undischarged mortgages, or defects in the chain of title. Generally based on the title abstract and other information derived from the public record.

Torrens Title System An alternative system of title recording whereby an owner is issued a certificate of title to a piece of property similar to an automobile registration certificate.

tract index An alternative master indexing system that cross-references a tract of land to the volume and page numbers containing any and all recorded deeds, mortgages, or other instruments concerning that tract of land.

transfer tax A tax levied on the sale of real property; a sales tax on real estate.

trust account A bank account established for a real estate office to hold clients' fund, such as buyers' deposits pending the sale of real estate.

unilateral contract An agreement in which a promise is exchanged for performance of an act.

utility easement An interest whereby utility companies have the right to use one's land for lines or pipes.

variance A permit to an individual to use land in a way not permitted in the zoning district.

vicarious liability The legal liability of a supervising broker for the acts of sales associates.

voluntary waste Purposeful commission of an act, which damages or substantially changes the premises.

warranty deed A deed in which the grantor guarantees good clear title to the property, and agrees to defend the title against any person who challenges it.

warranty of habitability A presemption, based on common law or statute, that a landlord who rents out a dwelling unit guarantees that it is fit for human habitation. This presumption has replaced the doctrine of *caveat emptor* in many localities.

Water Pollution Control Act A federal law setting standards of cleanliness for the nation's waters.

zoning Public regulations to control land use in a district.

Answer Key

Chapter One	Chapter Two	Chapter Three	Chapter Four	Chapter Five
1. a	1. a	1. a	1. d	1. a
2. d	2. c	2. c	2. c	2. a
3. b	3. b	3. d	3. b	3. b
4. d	4. a	4. a	4. a	4. b
5. b	5. c	5. b	5. a	5. d
6. a	6. c	6. c	6. a	6. d
7. a	7. b	7. a	7. b	7. d
8. d	8. a	8. a	8. d	8. c
9. d	9. c	9. a	9. d	9. b
10. c	10. c	10. b	10. d	10. c
11. d	11. a	11. a	11. b	11. a
12. c	12. b	12. b	12. b	12. b
13. b	13. a	13. a	13. a	13. c
14. a	14. d	14. c	14. a	14. d
15. c	15. a	15. d	15. a	15. d

Chapter Six	Chapter Seven	Chapter Eight	Chapter Nine	Chapter Ten
1. b	1. d	1. a	1. d	1. b
2. c	2. b	2. c	2. d	2. d
3. a	3. a	3. d	3. c	3. d
4. d	4. a	4. d	4. b	4. d
5. d	5. c	5. d	5. d	5. d
6. a	6. a	6. b	6. a	6. b
7. d	7. d	7. a	7. b	7. c
8. a	8. a	8. c	8. c	8. d
9. c	9. c	9. a	9. b	9. a
10. a	10. a	10. d	10. a	10. b
11. a	11. a	11. d	11. b	11. a
12. d	12. d	12. c	12. c	12. a
13. c	13. b	13. b	13. c	13. b
14. d	14. d	14. d	14. c	14. d
15. a	15. d	15. a	15. c	15. c

Chapter Eleven	Chapter Twelve	Chapter Thirteen
1. d	1. a	1. a
2. d	2. d	2. d
3. a	3. a	3. a
4. b	4. c	4. c
5. c	5. a	5. d
6. b	6. c	6. b
7. c	7. d	7. a
8. a	8. c	8. d
9. c	9. a	9. a
10. c	10. a	10. b
11. b		11. d
12. d		12. d
13. d		13. c
14. d		14. a
15. d		15. d

Index